Queer beyond London

Manchester University Press

Queer beyond London

Matt Cook and Alison Oram

Manchester University Press

Published by Manchester University Press
Oxford Road, Manchester M13 9PL
www.manchesteruniversitypress.co.uk

British Library Cataloguing-in-Publication Data
A catalogue record for this book is available from the British Library

ISBN 978 1 5261 4586 4 hardback

First published 2022

Typeset
by Cheshire Typesetting Ltd, Cuddington, Cheshire
Printed in Great Britain
by Bell & Bain Ltd, Glasgow

MC:
For Jaya, Chet, Harrison and Ben

AO:
For Kiera and Alex

Contents

Maps

Images

Inside front cover: Members of the Campaign for Homosexual Equality on Plymouth Hoe for *Gay News* in 1976. (Photograph: Robert Workman, courtesy of the Robert Workman Archive, Bishopsgate Institute)

Inside back cover: Clause 28 Rally, Albert Square, Manchester, 20 February 1988 (courtesy of MEN Media)

Images

Every effort has been made to trace copyright holders and to obtain their
permission for the use of copyright material. The publisher apologizes for any
errors or omissions in the above list and would be grateful if notified of any cor-
rections that should be incorporated in future reprints or editions of this book.

Acknowledgements

Queer Beyond London ends with an epilogue on queer conviviality, drawing out a key theme of the book but relating as strongly to our experience of writing it. We've been helped by colleagues, friends and family and by community groups and historians in each of our cities – together reaffirming our sense of being part of a strong, diverse, multifaceted community of care and support. The debt is too large to enumerate in full, but we want to thank especially all those who participated in our project workshops and who agreed to be interviewed and to share their experiences. The Brighton Museum and the Keep Archive Centre, Leeds and Plymouth's Central Libraries, Manchester's People's History Museum and LGBTQ+ Centre, and London Metropolitan Archive gave us space to hold events and interviews. We were assisted by archivists and librarians in each of our cities and at Bishopsgate Institute, London; our particular thanks to Andrew Bennett and Stefan Dickers. The Arts and Humanities Research Council generously supported the 'Sexualities and Localities' project (with Standard Grant AH/M011151/1) which gave us time to research and begin writing the book. Birkbeck, University of London, was a hugely supportive base for the project, and colleagues in the Department of History, Classics and Archaeology have offered guidance and help along the way. The history team at Leeds Beckett University was a wonderful group of colleagues to work with.

We were blessed with an incredible postdoctoral researcher in Justin Bengry and administrator in Katy Pettit. Jaya Rathbone, Grace Oakley, Luca Lapola and Nancy Harrison did invaluable additional research. Jenny-Anne Bishop, Kath Browne, Alan Butler, Anna Clark, Melita Dennett, Alf de Flohic, Jill Gardiner, Ali Hanbury, Ross Horsley, Rebecca Jennings, Ray Larman, Peter Molyneux, Kate O'Donnell, Lizzie Thynne, Ben Tooke, Alison Twells, Simon Watney, Jenny White and Jude Woods generously read and commented on

Acknowledgements

individual chapters and directed us to new sources and some lovely images. Fiona Candlin, Jeffrey Weeks and Justin Bengry read the entire book and helped us to think of it as a whole. Emma Brennan, our editor at Manchester University Press (MUP), has been hugely supportive of the project from the start, and we're also very grateful to the rest of the MUP team – especially Paul Clarke, Lianne Slavin, cartographer Don Shewan and copy-editor Dan Harding.

Matt adds: Harrison joined the family the day after I printed out draft one of part one. Since then he, Jaya and Chetan have brought much joy and much needed diversions into lifts, trains, history, politics and all things Spanish. Ben has been my rock throughout; I would be undone without him.

Abbreviations

ACT UP	AIDS Coalition to Unleash Power
BAAAC28	Brighton Area Action Against Clause 28
CHE	Campaign for Homosexual Equality
FAN	Feminist Archive North (University of Leeds)
GLF	Gay Liberation Front
HLF	Heritage Lottery Fund
LGB	lesbian, gay and bisexual
LGBT	lesbian, gay, bisexual and transgender
LGBTQ	lesbian, gay, bisexual, transgender and queer
LGC	Leeds Gay Community
LIP	Lesbian Identity Project (oral history project)
MCC	Manchester City Council
MDMA	Manchester Digital Music Archive
MEN	*Manchester Evening News*
MLP	Modern Lesbian Project
MRG	Minorities Research Group
NWHLRS	North-Western Homosexual Law Reform Society
PioP	Pride in our Past (Plymouth oral history project)
QBL	Queer Beyond London
TIHWGH	This Is How We Got Here (oral history project)
TV/TS	transvestite/transsexual
WLM	Women's Liberation Movement
WYAS	West Yorkshire Archive Service
WYQS	West Yorkshire Queer Stories

Introduction

Rowena described living in Manchester as a student in the late 1990s and going out clubbing to the gay village before it had become a destination for straight people as well. Though she was on the receiving end of homophobic abuse on the streets, she loved living in Manchester at a time when it was emerging as Britain's cutting-edge queer capital, with Brighton down south enduring as the more familiar seaside 'gay Mecca'.[1] Rowena's straight student friends thought her social life was 'so much more cool than anything they did'. 'They knew that', she said, 'because all their nightclubs were rubbish.' On one weekend in 1998 Rowena moved from the bars to the clubs and ended up at Manto on Canal Street to chill out as the next day dawned. The area was still edgy, not least because rival drug gangs were operating in the clubs and through some of the bouncers. Suddenly, as she and her friends chatted, 'some guys with machine guns turned up' and shot out the whole plate glass front of the bar:

> We had to hide under the tables. And nobody was injured, amazingly. But the police, who were there within minutes because you could hear the sirens, circled the outer premises of the gay village until these guys had gone. And they wouldn't come in. They didn't want to endanger themselves and they were probably paid off by the drug people, I don't know. But they certainly didn't care about protecting the lives of gay people.[2]

Rowena's story gives an intense flavour of the pleasures and dangers of Manchester's queer bar and club life in the 1990s. Behind her testimony are intertwined local contexts which make the experience particular to this post-industrial city. These contexts include the much-touted Mancunian 'give-it-a-go' spirit and council support for lesbian and gay rights which, together with the newly vacant warehouses, allowed for the development of the village in the first place. Another thread is the heightened suspicion of the police

Map 1 England and Wales

here – the legacy of an especially repressive regime from the 1960s through to the 1990s.

Queer beyond London hinges on local dynamics like these as it traces and compares the queer dimensions of Manchester and three other English cities: Brighton, Leeds and Plymouth. It shows how the local economy, population, city government and local history and culture shaped experiences of LGBTQ

Introduction

(lesbian, gay, bisexual, transgender and queer) identity and community in these places. It shows too how people's gender, the money they had, their class, ethnicity, age and education, and much more besides, affected how they engaged with the queer fabric of their particular city. The book demonstrates, unsurprisingly, that LGBTQ lives have been lived fully and in diverse ways 'beyond London', the city that has tended to be at the centre of explorations of the country's queer past and present.[3] Unfolding the queer histories of other English cities shows us that London was not necessarily hugely significant to LGBTQ people living elsewhere. Of course, events in the capital – and not least in parliament – had a regional impact. But that impact was felt differently in different places depending on local circumstances and dynamics. The partial decriminalization of male homosexuality in 1967 is regularly taken as a key turning point, for example, and in some ways rightly so. But to many in naval Plymouth the change in the law felt like an irrelevance given that male *and* female homosexuality were forbidden in the armed forces until 2000. A culture and habit of discretion remained deeply embedded there well into the new century, directing but certainly not closing down queer possibilities in this city. That measure in 2000, meanwhile, had much more impact in Plymouth than in Brighton, Leeds and Manchester where other local events shaped LGBTQ lives more immediately and dramatically than those hitting national headlines. In Brighton, the foundation of the University of Sussex in 1961 brought in many more students who changed the tenor of queer life in this seaside town. In Leeds, the years 1975–1981 were traumatically marked by the serial murders by Peter Sutcliffe, fuelling deeply felt anger at misogyny and violence against women, and contributing to the radical lesbian feminist politics in the city. The active support for gays and lesbians by Manchester City Council (MCC) from 1984 and a horrific homophobic murder in Plymouth in 1995 shifted the relationships between LGBTQ communities and the authorities in those places.

That local events and contexts like these would matter to LGBTQ people in different cities is probably self-evident, so why did it strike us as the idea for a book? Over the last decade especially, our work has drawn us into a community of independent and university-based queer historians and to a range of LGBTQ projects which expanded our awareness of the breadth and depth of regional and local queer history. These projects, plus associated websites, podcasts, screenings, art installations and walking tours, have proliferated in Britain in the 2000s, often showcased as part of LGBT+ History Month each February (since 2005) or in the rich programming of LGBTQ community history conferences nationally and internationally.[4] We became fascinated by what such projects revealed individually but also in conjunction with one another, and by how they might tug at more London-centric queer histories. It is probably no coincidence that we decided to work together on these ideas while we were both outside the capital, Alison in Leeds and Matt in Brighton, where fellow queer historian and project team member Justin Bengry was also living. In these cities we encountered distinct queer histories which exposed gaps in more established accounts of the LGBTQ past.

A growing body of work in print also inspired us to join the conversation about English local LGBTQ history. The Brighton Ourstory Project produced a compelling oral history of lesbian and gay life in their town in the 1950s and 1960s; Robert Howes created an intricate account of political organizing in Bristol and Bath since the 1970s.[5] Paul Flynn rooted his history of gay Britain in Manchester's cutting-edge dance, music and bar scenes, arguing that they affected and reflected wider national change.[6] Helen Smith, meanwhile, compared the striking differences between male sexual networks and associated self-understandings in Yorkshire, the West Midlands and London via court cases in the mid-1950s.[7] Histories which highlighted the distinctive urban and rural queer networks across other nations – from the towns spanning the Canadian prairies to the racial and rural politics of the American South – further whetted our appetite for research on places at our fingertips.[8]

We bring additional perspectives to the table by including local trans histories and by looking across the gender divide at both men and women and their intersecting queer scenes (more commonly explored separately). We take a longer (and later) time period than most of these other studies, discuss a broader range of themes and think about different places in direct comparison. In this way, we have been able to develop understandings of how particular cities have shaped queer experiences and cultures and also how these have in turn reoriented urban life and broader feelings of local identity. We found that gay and Mancunian pride were closely intertwined, for example, and that pride felt different again in Brighton, Plymouth and Leeds.

We look at our cities from around 1965, the height of the 'swinging sixties'. These were years in which some lesbian, gay and trans people were mobilizing more visibly on their own account in Britain – as part of the North-Western Homosexual Law Reform Committee and the lesbian Minorities Research Group (MRG) from 1964, and the Beaumont Society, a TV/TS (transvestite/transsexual) social and support group, from 1966. We were interested in how this apparently new consciousness played out in different places. More pragmatically, most of the available LGBTQ oral histories take us back only as far as the 1960s (with some very notable exceptions),[9] and we wanted our book to be anchored in people's testimonies of their everyday lives. Our loose end point is 2015. This was the year we gained generous funding from the UK's Arts and Humanities Research Council to pursue this research and these comparisons; 2016 was the year we began delving in earnest into the rich source materials in each city. Some of that material had been gathered together only in the previous five or six years – in projects ranging from Pride in our Past in Plymouth (2011) to Brighton Trans*formed (2014).

These years at the end of our period saw queer regional life becoming more visible through these projects and in other ways too. Regional pride events were proliferating (119 at the last count) and museums and heritage organizations across the country were engaging more actively with the queer past,[10] partly because of the requirements of the Equality Act of 2010. LGBTQ people living beyond London were also increasingly represented on film and TV and in the media. Brightonians were prominent in *Sugar Rush* (2005–2006), *My Transexual Summer* (2011) and successive seasons of *Gogglebox* (from 2013). *Last Tango in Halifax* (2014), *God's Own Country* (2017) and *Gentleman Jack* (2019) (about Anne Lister of Shibden Hall) provided queer takes on West Yorkshire. The pathbreaking drama *Queer as Folk* (1999) had earlier introduced Manchester's Canal Street to national and international audiences. Our period, we decided, should come more or less to the present day of our project; we wanted to explore the reasons behind – and the significance of – this regional queer flourish.

Changes at a national level certainly affected our cities – whether those were in laws that had an impact on LGBTQ people or cultural shifts which fluctuated between tolerance and homophobia. Lesbians and gay men were gaining a voice in mainstream media from the 1960s on national TV programmes such as *This Week* (1964 and 1965), aired in the context of debates about decriminalizing sex between men.[11] Soon after the Sexual Offences Act of 1967, countercultural and new left politics helped to generate the Gay Liberation Front (GLF) and the longer-lasting Women's Liberation Movement (WLM), both of which inspired a flowering in the 1970s of lesbian and gay political and social organizations and publications. Public opinion, while decrying the 'flaunting' of queer sexuality, also gradually moved to a greater measure of tolerance. However, the AIDS crisis from 1981 devastated the gay male community and was used as a rationale for right-wing political hostility. Gay men and lesbians were seen as vectors of disease and as a threat to familial and (in some eyes) national stability. A few left-wing local authorities actively supported their lesbian and gay citizens (Manchester included), but there was further challenge from the state in the shape of Clause 28, which, once enacted as Section 28 in 1988, prohibited the teaching or 'promotion' of homosexuality as a 'pretended family relationship'. This stimulated a surge in national activism, uniting lesbians and gay men even as wider public support dropped back. The profile of lesbians and gays (though not at this stage of bisexual and trans people) grew as a result, in TV soap operas such as *Eastenders* and *Brookside* and magazine programmes, especially *Out on Tuesday* (1989–1994). Under the New Labour government from 1997, moves towards equal citizenship really gained ground, with a string of legal reforms including the equalization of the age of consent in 2000 and Civil Partnerships in 2004.[12] The 2000s saw a less contested visibility and growing acceptance. Gay and lesbian bars were more often glass-fronted than underground; LGBTQ lives were more often folded into mainstream media in a move from the cultural margins. The oscillation between liberal reform and moral anxiety over the last half century had culminated in a loose cultural consensus in favour of equality and tolerance. This can be seen to a degree in all our cities, though not in the same ways within and between them. And just as these local contexts tempered the impact of supposedly sweeping national social, cultural and political change, so it was with international events and shifts. The Stonewall uprising in New York, the onset of AIDS, declarations on human rights or the international circulation of queer film, art and popular culture certainly had tangible effects in Brighton, Leeds, Manchester and Plymouth, but not evenly or ubiquitously.

In their testimonies queer Brightonians, Plymouthians, Mancunians and people from Leeds tend to emphasize different moments and different histories. The progress suggested by a broader story of legislative change has not necessarily been experienced as such by the people we discuss in this book; several hanker after the tighter forms of community or the fun they remember having in bars where you weren't on show through plate glass to a passing public. Such past experience and nostalgia unevenly affects everyday lives in the present. Time is not experienced in the straightforward way suggested by chronological historical narratives: fond and fearful memories sometimes direct or arrest our steps in the here and now. By taking local and everyday experiences seriously and ahead of national and international histories, we show how the former does not automatically or evenly flow from the latter.

The need felt by community groups and individuals in Brighton, Leeds, Manchester and Plymouth to explore the queer pasts of their cities is testament to the ways in which such local histories have come to matter personally, communally and politically in the present. They highlight the myriad local factors which shape sexual identities and communities. This is what we explore in this book, in Part I, 'Queer Cities', by looking squarely at each city in turn, and in Part II, 'Queer Comparisons', by discussing them in conjunction with one another. These two halves of the book are in conversation but will feel distinct, marked out by our different voices – speaking of the cities in different ways and using different approaches. We think this adds to our understanding of the queer complexity of each place and creates a sum greater than its parts. In his four chapters, Matt sketches out the distinctive social, cultural, economic and population contours and contexts of each city and shows how these relate to waxing and waning LGBTQ networks and scenes. He accounts for the difference that the seaside, radical feminist politics, post-industrial urban regeneration and the military made to queer lives in these places. In Alison's part, the first chapter ('Circling Around') teases out the particular attractions of the four cities that drew LGBTQ people to live there, while the next chapter ('Urban Accommodation') compares local cultures of home and domestic life. Finally, in 'Making Histories, Memories and Communities', her focus shifts to how local LGBTQ people and groups have looked at the past, showing how queer histories matter differently to a contemporary sense of place and belonging in Brighton, Leeds, Manchester and Plymouth.

We could have chosen pretty much anywhere in the country to explore how distinctive queer dynamics emerged from local contexts and circumstances, so what led us to these places? First, we focused in on England: we wanted to look within a single national and legal context and explore the variations within that. Legal reform in 1967, partially decriminalizing sex between men over twenty-one in private, applied only to England and Wales; Scotland and Northern Ireland did not decriminalize until 1980 and 1981 respectively. Different religious profiles and conflicts, and varying cultures, histories and nationalist aspirations, made for very different experiences of LGBTQ life in other parts of the UK.[13] Once we settled on England, and aside from our personal links, we chose Brighton, Leeds, Manchester and Plymouth because of their contrasting queer reputations and their wealth of local and community history resources, which we knew would be key to the book. A regional sense of belonging and identity was associated with each place. Though mass culture since the war has been seen to ride roughshod over such variations, the difference in culture and outlook between the 'home counties' to the immediate south of London, the 'west country' of Devon and Cornwall, and Yorkshire and Lancashire in the north were deep rooted and tangible – in ways which shaped queer lives in these areas and so also our chosen cities. They are also different sizes. Plymouth and Brighton (which with its sister town of Hove became a city in 2001) each had a total population of around 250,000 during our period. Leeds was almost three times as large with *c.*715,000 people, while the city of Manchester had a population that varied considerably around the 500,000 mark but was situated within the wider conurbation of Greater Manchester with *c.*2.7 million residents.

We selected Brighton and Manchester precisely because they were (and are) well-known queer hubs exerting a regional, national and even international draw. Brighton's queer renown extends back until at least the 1930s, and is closely related to the town's status as a seaside resort. Manchester amassed its reputation differently and in part through its post-industrial transformation and a longstanding radical tradition which extended from workers' and women's rights in the nineteenth and first half of the twentieth century into homosexual politics in the 1960s and beyond. We wanted to look more fully at the contours of these pre-eminent queer regional centres beyond London and at what made them so different from each other.

Plymouth and Leeds were less obvious case studies. Leeds gave us another northern focus, a Yorkshire foil to the north-western metropolis and a city with a particularly strong lesbian feminist history dating from the 1970s. Leeds was also part of the well-networked urban region of West Yorkshire, including the towns and cities of Bradford, Huddersfield and Wakefield. We wanted to know how this kind of hinterland, which is different from those of our other cities, affected local queer cultures here. Plymouth is more remote, distant from London and homogenous in terms of class, occupation and ethnicity. It was buttressed economically and culturally by the docks and the navy. We were keen to explore what particular queer dynamics this set in train and what it was like to live queerly in this context.

The stories we tell about these places cast London in the shade; the capital is an absent presence in the book. People do refer to it in interviews and occasionally compare it to their home cities. It is somewhere they react against, escape from or to, or visit for a night out, a weekend or for work. But London looks different from the perspectives of regional city dwellers and not least in often being at the margins of their consciousness. And so, although we do flag London's symbolic and practical significance at various points, we deliberately don't dwell on it, focusing instead on places whose queer stories have been less fulsomely told.[14] The book's title is thus a little wry: London features there because of its presumed queer centrality; our focus, though, is decisively on the 'beyond'. And that 'beyond' is not only geographical – it alludes also to what is extra to, over and above, and different from the queerness of the capital.

This brings us to the other term on our cover. We use 'queer' there even though the book is about a period when 'homosexual', 'gay', 'lesbian', 'bisexual' and 'trans' (and later LGBT – lesbian, gay, bisexual and transgender – and most recently LGBTQ) were in more common use. In the 1950s and 1960s, 'homosexual', with its medical and middle-class connotations, was being used more; 'queer' continued to circulate pejoratively – a slight that still burns for some older gay men especially. In the 1970s, 'lesbian' and 'gay' were often the terms men and women chose to describe themselves and in ways that felt more positive and politicized. GLF campaigners in Leeds in the early 1970s produced a leaflet which insisted 'we are not sick, we are not queer, we are gay – and gay is good'.[15] These identities were commonly (though certainly not always) seen as fixed and intrinsic, giving them particular significance socially, culturally and in people's everyday lives. They were nevertheless understood differently in different places. 'Gay' in Plymouth had a different cadence to being gay in Brighton; being gay in either place in the 1970s had a different complexion than in the 2000s, by which time the term had become more descriptive than overtly political. In Leeds, meanwhile, there was a local understanding of a difference between 'gay girls', 'dykes' and 'lesbians' in the 1970s and 1980s.

From the late 1980s, 'queer' was reclaimed by activists and by queer theorists amid burgeoning homophobia on both sides of the Atlantic. Queer in these contexts was radically edged and often radically questioning of apparently more settled identity categories.[16] These ideas are important to the way we think about sex, desire, relationships and identities in the book, reminding us to be alert to the ways in which the boundary between queer and 'normal' was often in flux – in the early hours in down-at-heel clubs in Plymouth's Union Street or in the African-Caribbean shebeens in Leeds' Chapeltown, for example. This is all part of the story we tell and underpins our decision to move between terms depending on the place and time we're discussing. In the chapters that follow we are more likely to use 'lesbian and gay' when discussing the 1970s and 1980s and LGBT for the 2000s, as this is how people tended to refer to themselves and their community groups. 'Queer' was used by some in the 1960s, and then again in a more radical way from the 1990s, though earlier and more often by people in Brighton than in Plymouth; the various terms had a subtly different cadence and use in each of our four cities.

Almost all of the contributors to the LGBTQ community history projects we draw on used specific terms such as gay, lesbian or trans to describe themselves, and many people critique the use of 'queer' in everyday life, seeing it as a form of erasure of those hard-won identities. We very much respect those positions and in general we use 'queer' in this book in an embracing sense, and also to refer to sexual and gender difference which might not be captured by a specific identity category like gay or lesbian. For the earlier part of our period, when we refer to a venue as 'queer' it is usually because it had a more diverse or less readily identifiable clientele than those we call 'gay' or 'lesbian'. Later, in Manchester in the 2000s, there was a tangible difference in the flavour of the 'gay scene' around Canal Street and the 'queer' alternative in other parts of the centre. More broadly, we see 'queer' signalling our commitment to greater inclusivity – of queer people of colour, bisexual or poly identifications and of non-binary people. We also use 'trans' as an umbrella term to refer to various experiences and identities associated with gender crossing and gender confirmation, again with an acknowledgement that its meanings and associations have changed over our period.[17]

Finally, we are careful with the term 'community', which is sometimes too casually used to refer to a city's queer population as a whole.[18] Behind the mask of 'LGBTQ community' lie myriad subgroups and networks involving people who had additional and cross-cutting affiliations relating, for example, to ethnicity, religion, workplace, sport, a hobby and families of birth or choice. The interplay of these various temporary or more sustained feelings of connection and belonging – as well as of alienation and exclusion – affected the way people understood and experienced their desires and relationships. As we'll see, these don't add up to any cosy or singular notion of LGBTQ community, although in and between our cities people did certainly 'come together' in various more or less convivial ways.[19]

Drilling down into local queer histories, as we do here, suggests the scope to fill silences. But this book carries with it an acknowledgement of the ephemeral nature of the queer past; writing queer history can feel like grasping at retreating shadows. There are many more stories we cannot tell – through pressures of space and time and because most voices are absent, unrecorded or lost. The invitation, then, is to imagine further passions, tensions and experiences of fleeting or more sustained community arising from the contexts we describe and which wove through daily lives in Brighton, Leeds, Manchester and Plymouth. The possibilities we open out in this book extend beyond its pages as well as beyond London. The queer historical imagination has some work to do, fired we hope by the chapters to follow but more by the extraordinary testimonies on which they are based.

Part I

Queer Cities
by Matt Cook

1

Britain's queer playground: swings and roundabouts in Brighton

Image 1 Brighton seafront, *c.*1973

In 1964 sales rep Peter Cosgrove picked up window cleaner Alan Bull and his coalman brother, Lawrence, and took them back to his central Regency Square flat in Brighton where they 'whipped [him] at his own request' and committed 'acts of gross indecency' together. Peter was 'from a good family', his father told the court during the ensuing trial; his fall from grace had been hastened by this town: 'it would be a good idea if [my] son could live somewhere [else]', he said.[1] Father and son both saw Brighton as a place of queer temptation and opportunity – facets ingrained by this time in the town's reputation and, for Peter, part of its draw. Aileen and Ted felt similarly – they described a sense of relief and release at moving here in the 1960s. 'I suppose I felt a bit euphoric', said Southampton émigré Ted: 'I didn't have to conform, I could be myself, […] and I just dived in and never looked back.' Aileen, from Glasgow, remembered that she could go out socially on a Sunday wearing a pair of 'slacks' (trousers) and that 'nobody turned around calling you a cow'.[2]

This reputation endured in the years that followed, but the texture of queer life also changed as the town became more studenty, countercultural and self-consciously arty from the 1960s, as women's and gay liberation movements waxed and waned in the 1970s and 1980s, and as AIDS took its particularly heavy toll here. The homophobic punch of Section 28 of the Local Government Act (1988), which banned the 'promotion' of homosexuality by local authorities, came as a jolt to activism in this town of historic queer ease. This yielded a more strident and visible scene and community in the 1990s which was determined to act on its own behalf. In the 2000s this was woven into the ways in which the new city of Brighton and Hove (from 2001) presented itself. The earlier conservatism and homophobia of the local authorities and press gave way to a civic pride in the city's LGBT credentials. In 2009, the council boasted a trans population double the national average;[3] five years later it claimed that between 11 and 14 per cent of the population were lesbian or gay, against a rough national average of 2 per cent. The city had a civil partnership rate five times that of the rest of the country, with a good number of ceremonies taking place in the iconic Royal Pavilion which was, from 2005, bathed in pink light for LGBT Pride celebrations each year.[4] Detractors came from new quarters – from people who missed the grassroots sense of community of earlier years and pointed to persistent exclusions and enduring problems obscured by the sheen of Pride.

This chapter charts these phases of queer life in Brighton in three chronological sections – on the 1960s and 1970s, the 1980s and 1990s, and the 2000s. The story I tell feels familiar in many ways because after London, Brighton has been the town most evoked in representations of queer life in Britain. It seemed the obvious place for the 'Little Kinsey' ethnographer to visit as part of his exploration of 'homosexual groups' in 1949; for a TV film-maker to document 'coming out' in 1976; and for producers to find a participant for *My Transsexual Summer* (2011).[5] There has barely been an issue of *Gay News* (1972–1983), *Gay Times* (from 1984), *Pink Paper* (1987–2009) or *Diva* (from 1994) without some story about the town, and it has anyway always been writ large in their listings and ad sections with the promise of gay and lesbian seaside fun – including at the boutique hotel where rooms were replete with hooks to suspend a sling for sex (sling provided for an extra fee). Brighton seemed to offer an enhanced flavour of queer life and culture, but if this seaside LGBT 'haven' has been a lodestone in Britain, it is not so much because it is indicative or typical but rather because the particular dance of local and wider contexts have made it exceptional.

Sequins, slacks and counterculture: queer Brighton in the 1960s and 1970s

Gay abandon in the 1960s

In 1961, 163,159 people lived in Brighton and around 73,000 in Hove, the adjoining seafront town to the west. This was a high point after more than a century and a half of growth which saw the small fishing village became a favourite royal and society watering hole in the late eighteenth century and then a popular seaside resort once the railway arrived in 1841.[6] The border between Brighton and Hove is unclear to many visitors (it is in fact marked by the Peace Statue on the seafront), though they might notice the shift from the eclectic and closely packed streets of central Brighton to the more spacious grid of avenues that characterize Hove, the less raucous and queerly notorious of the twin towns. Unsurprisingly for a seaside resort, Brighton's economy in the 1960s (and after) was heavily reliant on hotels, cafes, shops and sole traders rather than on the big employers that dominated Manchester and Plymouth. Only 21 per cent of the population worked in manufacturing in 1961 – 15 per cent below the national average and 26 per cent lower than Manchester; the proportion who were self-employed was meanwhile 4 per cent higher here than nationally. There was less collective workplace or union identity in Brighton than in those other cities, and though poverty was endemic more people were in professional, managerial and skilled roles.[7] Around one in twenty Brightonians commuted to jobs in London (60 miles to the north), often for office-based work which expanded postwar and opened out possibilities for women in particular to have 'lifestyles independent of family'.[8] All this fostered a spirit of individualism which was heightened from the 1960s by flourishing student and arts scenes. The new University of Sussex on the edge of town at Falmer was launched in 1961 and Brighton's College of Arts and Craft expanded and opened new central buildings in the mid-decade.[9] The Brighton Festival was inaugurated in 1967, rapidly becoming the biggest arts festival in England.

Brighton became a draw for people who wanted to express themselves differently. Bohemian beatniks were spotted sleeping rough on the beach in the early 1960s.[10] Leather-jacketed rockers and working-class mods with their sharp suits came to national attention in their running battles on Brighton seafront in 1964.[11] Middle-class dope smoking hippies were meanwhile remembered on the new university campus, though the reek of joints was common on the beach too.[12] Despite the significant differences between these groups they were each part of a growing democratization and informality in 'styles of [everyday] life' in Britain.[13] Brighton, with its longstanding seaside notoriety for pleasure seeking and escape and its more recent reputation for students and the arts, seemed especially accommodating of this broader social and cultural shift.[14] It is no surprise that its queer reputation was growing too.

In fact, the town already had a well-established central cluster of queer pubs by the 1960s. The Spotted Dog, the Greyhound, the 'terribly small', 'tatty' Pigott's bar at the St James Hotel[15] and the Regency Club were all popular with working-class men and to a lesser extent women. Pigot's was a survivor from the interwar years and, like the others, still had a piano for regular sing-alongs. The Regency was, according to Brighton-born James, 'a third lesbian, a third gay men, a third straight'. It was 'one of the friendliest clubs I'd ever known, certainly not an exploiting club'.[16] The Curtain Club in the basement of the Queens Hotel opposite the West Pier was the first club 'with anything that could be described as a dance floor', though Aileen didn't feel welcome there; she 'never felt such resentment regarding any females coming in' as she did there.[17]

On the seafront between the piers were the 'sleazy' Lorelei and Wanderin' coffee shops (open all hours) as well as the 'rough' Belvedere and Fortune of War pubs (the latter known for its butch lesbian crowd).[18] Chatfields had a similar feel and was popular with a crossover crowd of male and female sex workers, queer men and sailors who would travel from Portsmouth for a weekend of fun out of view of the military police. Kent-born accountant Grant remembers that 'anybody who had a flat or a house with a floor space, would probably go down to Chatfields and chat up a sailor and take him home for the weekend'.[19] These various places were cheek-by-jowl with 'classier' queer venues: the cocktail bar at the 'very very select' Argyle Hotel and the 'lovely, old' St Albans Club, also known locally as 'the wrinkle room' because of the age of its well-heeled actorly clientele.[20] At the Golden Fleece in nearby Market Street (see Map 2) the two bars developed distinct atmospheres: Bert was 'the soul of discretion' in one; Dennis, in the other, was 'one of those flamboyant queans'. His bar 'was hilarious and riotous' but he could be 'indiscreet' and might 'compromise you in public', James said.[21] (Quean was in popular use in the sixteenth century, meaning 'hussy' or 'harlot'; in queer parlance in the first two-thirds of the twentieth century it overlapped in meaning and use with 'queen'.)

This scene could be cliquey and exclusive. The theatre crowd were 'a mason's lot', remembered Harry, and Grant recalled that 'lots of queers would say, "oh, I wouldn't go into that place, it's frightfully rough and tumble. Oh they're awfully common in there".' His own queer set might go out during the week to avoid the 'rougher' 'queer blokes' from midland and northern cities who came at the weekends.[22] Drag queen Betty Lou's outdoor extravaganzas in the 1960s 'on the cliff near Newhaven' (to the east of Brighton) were invite-only affairs in part because of the dangers of arrest but also perhaps to ensure that the 'right' queens attended. John, originally from Lancashire and then in his twenties, said he was not surprised when he got there

> to find Betty Lou in full flight [...] There was some sort of music rigged up and everybody was dancing [...] because dancing between people of the same sex was not allowed in the clubs at this time. [... It was] old fashioned dancing [before disco]. Which was very sexy of course. And this went on the whole night-long.[23]

If, for most, discretion remained crucial, many testified to a particular 'out there' self-confidence in the town. This was exhibited by barman Dennis at the Golden Fleece and by the man the Little Kinsey ethnographer described in a Brighton queer bar 'draping himself over the staircase, smiling around the room, speaking loudly and exhibiting exaggerated gestures and mannerisms'.[24] On a Saturday night before the last train to Portsmouth at 1.30 am 'the cottage [a public toilet used for sex] at the station used to be infamous': 'the queans in drag used to descend like a plague of locusts [...] so pissed they were falling arse-over-tit to find a sailor'.[25] Michael found 'the quick-witted Brighton queans [...] very alarming' when he arrived from Luton in 1960 as a twenty-two year old, and Grant remembered that 'colour-wise [in Brighton] it was a bit grotesque [...] pink velvet trousers with a green shirt'; 'terribly Hawaiian shirts with all sorts of tulle at the neck'.[26] Filk'n Casuals – a saucy fusion of the proprietors' names, Phil and Ken – fed this distinctive style, stocking those bright shirts and their own innovations in tailored underwear (including in leather). There were echoes here of the new fashions emerging from Kings Road and Carnaby Street in London but also – in its campiness – of the earlier Sussex Arts Balls which ran in the late 1940s and 1950s and were notoriously sequin-strewn and flamboyant.[27]

Public non-conformity seems to have felt more possible here than in our other cities in the 1960s, though Vicky, from Romford in Essex, didn't feel safe walking on the streets in trousers even in Brighton.[28] These weren't sentiments voiced by many others, however. A barber in St James's Street catered openly to butch women and Laurie would commute to her office in London in 'a collar, tie, everything masculine on top, with a skirt'.[29] Aileen 'could not believe the freedom women had', including being able to wear her slacks.[30] One journalist reported that in summer male couples could be seen on the beach 'openly gazing into each others' eyes'.[31] Grant recalled that 'there was nothing in the rest of the country to compare. [...] Lots of very famous and infamous people could have been photographed [there] I can assure you', he said.[32] This was Brighton's particular appeal: the scope to be relatively relaxed and open. Kenric, the London-based lesbian group, organized weekend trips to Brighton from the capital; they would camp in the surrounding South Downs countryside before going out on the town. Vera drove down 'nearly every weekend' in the 1950s and 1960s, taking a picnic to 'sit up on the South Downs' with her girlfriend or 'to the hill past St Dunstan's' by Roedean Girls school on Brighton's eastern edge. The school was the scene of 'pashes' between girls and a queer reference point in other ways too: 'We used to say "Nancy Spain [the butch journalist and TV personality of the 1950s and early 1960s] went to Roedean".' You felt a connection, you see, because you knew she was gay' (Spain wryly fictionalized the school as Radcliff Hall in her 1949 comedy murder mystery *Poison for Teacher*).[33] In Brighton itself Vera, her girlfriend and her girlfriend's daughter 'used to go down to the funfair, take the kid on the games and things like that [...] Just a normal weekend in Brighton [...] there was nothing gay about it.'[34] Brighton's queer reputation paradoxically allowed them to feel 'normal' here (see Image 31).

John had so many queer friends visiting from London that he turned his home into a bed and breakfast (Le Chateau Gaye) in the late 1960s, though New Zealander Arthur, a frequent Brighton visitor, recalled that 'in nearly all the hotels [two] men could walk in and get a double bed'.[35] Other visitors didn't feel the need of one because of the lively outdoor sex scene associated with the beach at Telscombe to the east (screened by cliffs) and the many cottages in the town. There were infamous toilets at the station, by the Clock Tower half-way from there to the seafront and in Black Lion Street in the midst of the cluster of queer bars. These could each be visited in turn within fifteen minutes. The one in Black Lion Street was closed in 1965 because of the number of gross indecency cases, many involving men visiting Brighton from elsewhere for more

Image 2 Women's walking group, 1996

than the beach and pavilion.[36] Backward glances were common here and as a young actor, newly moved to Brighton in the early 1960s, David remembers picking up 'normal' 'men on the loose' and taking them to the run-down North Laine area just south of the station. 'There used to be all these houses that were abandoned and neglected and you used to take men there, into these houses, and have sex in those empty rooms', he said.[37] Brighton felt sexy and liberating for men like David; no wonder he, like many others we've encountered so far, visited from elsewhere and ended up staying.

As in other places, though, men ran significant risks when they had sex or picked up in public – as the threesome of Peter Cosgrove and the Bull brothers we met at the outset found to their cost: they were fined between £10 and £25 as well as being placed on probation; they were lucky to avoid jail, the judge told them.[38] Queer men were meanwhile picked out for robbery and attack on the seafront on the assumption that they would be less likely to complain to the police than other men.[39] One of the Bull brothers had a previous conviction for 'demanding money with menaces' – perhaps one of the so-called 'queer-rolling' cases which the local police chief saw proliferating in the mid-1960s as Brighton's queer notoriety grew.[40] Sandie remembered a butch friend of hers being chased and 'beaten black and blue' by a gang of 'lads'; 'that was just prejudice', she said, 'nothing else'.[41]

People's flats and houses – easily reachable from each other and the centre in this compact town – could sometimes feel safer and provided space to be more relaxed and flamboyant.[42] Phil and Ken (aka Rose and Esme Filk'n) held tea parties on Sunday afternoons in their 'beautiful flat' in Hove – replete with chandeliers and great velvet drapes.[43] 'Aunt Rose used to sit at a high chair and pour tea out of silver pots', said Bob, who was born just along the coast in Worthing.[44] Harry, a nurse from Cheshire who came to Brighton in 1958, recalled that 'there'd sometimes be as many as forty people. You knew everybody.'[45] The proximity to London and its theatreland made Brighton an obvious choice for actors to settle or take a break, and Dublin-born writer Patrick remembers 'expensive queans [...] throwing cocktail parties with art dealers and old actresses'; 'there was an awful lot that went on behind heavily brocaded curtains', he said – including, perhaps, the antics of an early 'leather clique; the motorbike crowd' who would also hold parties in each others' homes.[46] Many of these gatherings were exclusive affairs but some were less so: 'you'd be at a club and someone would say "party at so and so" and you didn't need to know who the people were, you'd simply grab a bottle and gatecrash', said Janice, one of the minority of Ourstory's interviewees born locally.[47]

Barbara, from Lancashire, remembers domestic gatherings of the MRG, a support network for lesbians founded in 1963. It was perhaps a 'gentler' way to get together than the MRG meetings in London pubs Barbara had attended before (though her trips there are a reminder of how accessible the capital's queer resources were to Brightonians).[48] Barbara hosted frequently herself: 'our house seemed to be where they could always come at any time. [...] We used to periodically put on these dos, oh, they were lovely', she said. Her neighbour would offer to help: 'The wife [next door ...] she'd say "oh flow in to me for coffee, you can't cope with all that lot". [...] She was always there, she knew. And never never openly discussed. But it was so obvious.'[49] This kind of unspoken acceptance is echoed in other Brighton testimonies. Sandie, originally from Birmingham, lived in a bedsit in a house on Grand Parade owned by a gay man who 'tried to get gay people if he could', though she lived amiably there alongside a 'straight girl and an old lady'.[50] George remembers a straight neighbour telling him that she 'heard [his] little squabbles [with his boyfriend] from time to time': she knew and she didn't mind.[51] These were reassuring gestures; nosy neighbours could land queer men in court or out on the street.

1960s to 1970s: counterculture and politics

Bill Butler, the queer American beatnik poet, moved to Brighton and opened Unicorn Books in 1967 in run-down Gloucester Road. Patrick, who discovered the psychedelically painted store as a teenager and worked there for a while, remembers it 'being a bit upmarket' in its stock – unlike a 'dirty bookshop' on nearby North Road which stocked 'lurid gay books' amid the straight. Soon after Unicorn opened the police raided nevertheless and prosecuted Butler for selling 'obscene publications' – including J. G. Ballard's *Why I Want to Fuck Ronald Reagan* (published by Butler in 1968), the countercultural *Oz* magazine and the hippie *International Times* which celebrated a 'new attitude' of permissiveness and carried queer contact ads.[52] American-based poets Allen Ginsberg and Thom Gunn were among those who helped Butler meet the fine and costs, signalling the importance of queer, countercultural and artistic networks extending well beyond Brighton. In tune with the broader push against censorship, the National Council for Civil Liberties also stepped in to help.[53] Alternative bookshops like Unicorn became significant queer hubs in Leeds, Manchester and Plymouth too; Brighton, though, was the first to have one.

The International Males Advertiser was launched from Preston Street near the seafront in 1968, a year after Unicorn opened. It became, after six issues, *Spartacus Monthly*, offering photos, fiction, features, information and pen pals explicitly 'for homosexuals, about homosexuals, by homosexuals'.[54] Unlike contemporary publications such as *Film and Filming* and the physique titles from the USA, *Spartacus* addressed homosexual men directly – buoyed perhaps by the Brighton base.[55] The office window got progressively more suggestive; Edward remembered walking past and seeing 'leather jock straps and things like that which I hadn't seen on display before'.[56] There was an enduring queer confidence and palpable cosmopolitanism in Brighton in the later 1960s and 1970s as the university and arts festival became more established. The proximity to 'swinging' London and also to the expanding Gatwick Airport (directly between Brighton and the capital) also fed this sense in and of the town. Not only did people continue to visit from elsewhere for seaside fun and the growing arts scene, but Brightonians, and especially those without children, were exploring other places and bringing back new experiences. Raymond Dargan was reported to be back waiting tables in a Brighton guest house in October 1969 following an (unspecified) brush he and a male friend had with police in Torremolenos, one of Spain's new resort destinations. On their release they

Image 3 Unicorn Books, *c*.1969

had gone directly to Morocco, a favourite destination of occasional Brighton visitor Joe Orton, his circle and many cosmopolitan queer men in the 1960s.[57] Brighton hairdresser Bernard Derwent was, it turned out in court in 1967, very well travelled: he had visited Bermuda and among his previous convictions was one for gross indecency in Australia in 1958 (for which he had been deported back to the UK).[58] We don't see the same comings and goings in our other cities this early on and it added to the sense of queer possibility here.

These were some of the ways in which Brighton 'started to liven up' in the late 1960s. By 1968 the town was '"gayer" than Hampstead' according to one woman who moved here from London (apparently partly for this reason),[59] and one journalist wrote that in 'no other European city is homosexuality so open and apparently so tolerated'.[60] 'Everything [...] loosened up: things had got gay and we had got flower power', said Dennis, who moved to Brighton permanently in 1972 to work as a chef.[61] Preston Circus, about a mile back from the seafront, was a 'hotbed of hippiedom' in the early 1970s (see Map 2). Unicorn Books was nearby until 1973 (when Butler left Brighton for Wales) and Infinity Foods and the Brighton Buddhist Centre opened in the neighbouring North Laine area in 1972 and 1974 respectively; they were to have an enduring significance for queer people in the town. After the closure of the Women's Centre at the old maternity hospital in Buckingham Road in 1976, a squatted church hall on North Road became the new hub, serving as a rehearsal and meeting space for Theatre Against Sexism, the band Devil's Dykes and the theatre company/band Siren.[62] The dole in the 1970s and early 1980s was 'incredibly freeing' for many who were part of this network: 'though it was a hard financial life, it allowed for creativity', said Jude of Siren.[63] The hippie Open Café (renamed Greens Vegetarian in the late 1970s) was five minutes up the hill in Clifton. It was the base for a weekly trans meet-up in the mid-1970s and for Brighton Lavender Line (from 1974), the forerunner to the local Gay Switchboard.[64]

There was, in short, a range of places which linked hippie, feminist, left-wing and queer people and causes here.[65] This helped make Brighton 'possibly one of the easiest places [in the country] to come to terms with an alternative from mainstream identity', said Jim, who joined the university men's group when he arrived to study.[66] It was here, rather than at the Sussex University Gay Society, that he began to discuss his sense of sexual difference, coming out first as bi and then as gay – a stepped transition followed by other interviewees talking about their university experience (on which see Chapter 5).[67] The general feeling of ease and possibility in Brighton perhaps blunted the political urgency felt elsewhere. Jim remembers Gaysoc being 'rather sleepy' until the late 1970s.[68] There were, though, some piecemeal early moves. In 1965 a student protested to the *Brighton Gazette* about its 'reactionary' opinion piece on the closure of the Black Lion Street toilets; he called for 'a militant campaign to change the law regarding homosexuals'.[69] A year later a group of Sussex students joined others from Oxford to lobby MPs in support of the Sexual Offences Act which finally passed

Image 4 Brighton Gay Switchboard flier, *c.*1982

into law in 1967.[70] A GLF group formed in 1971 with around fifty members and soon after organized what the *Evening Argus* described as a mixed 'pop music discotheque with psychedelic lighting' at the Co-op Hall near Preston Circus. 'The overall feeling', it reported, 'was one of relaxed enjoyment, natural pleasure in dancing, and lots of laughter.' The disco was a political move – providing an upbeat and community-oriented alternative to what organizer Simon Watney described as 'the extremely sordid atmosphere gay people usually have to put up with'.[71] Plans to make the event into a regular Friday-nighter were blocked by the council;[72] if Brighton had a strong bohemian and countercultural pulse it was mainly Conservatives who were elected to the council until the mid-1980s and to parliament until 1997.[73] This was, after all, a town of small businesses and without the kind of strong working-class community and history that energized the left and a wider radical politics in Manchester and Leeds.[74]

Though the Co-op Hall disco was a one-off, the GLF went on to organize a Pride event in 1973 and to protest with the Women's Liberation Front three years later outside British Home Stores on Churchill Square after Tony Whitehead lost his job for appearing on TV kissing his boyfriend at Brighton Station.[75] The Campaign for Homosexual Equality (CHE) was active in Brighton too. In

Image 5 Demonstration outside British Home Stores, February 1976

1977 they protested against the appearance of actor John Inman at the Brighton Dome (the old royal stables adjacent to the Pavilion and scene of ABBA's 1974 Eurovision Song Contest triumph). Inman offended the group because of his stereotypically camp portrayal of Mr Humphries in the 1970s TV sitcom *Are You Being Served*. A CHE group from Streatham, south London, meanwhile, travelled to Brighton to see the show, making for an uncomfortable encounter with the Brighton CHE cohort at the doors.[76] Two years later, in 1979, CHE held its national annual conference in the same venue, drawing the ire of councillors and church leaders. A leaflet warned against the dangers of paedophiles coming to Brighton to attend the conference. Soon after, CHE, Gaysoc and the Women's Liberation Front picketed *The Argus* for its homophobic reporting of an attack by skinheads on a CHE/Gaysoc screening of the American documentary *Word Is Out*.[77]

In these various ways queer Brightonians were finding their political voice, often in alliance with other groups. Lesbian separatism in the late 1970s and early 1980s didn't have the purchase in Brighton that it did in Leeds, for example. Though there were those who were 'very very separatist, revolutionary feminists',[78] historian Sue Bruley describes a more 'Bohemian' feminist network here, with 'an emphasis on creativity and women's health'.[79] Jude remembers the crossovers and collaborations rather than splits,[80] and others recall anarchist and 'crustie' squats and housing associations which brought men, women, gay and straight together.[81] 'I was living with people who were taking tons of drugs, visiting us, who were homeless, sofa surfing [...] People who lived in squats – not necessarily queer. We were always in quite close proximity', remembers Belle.[82]

Though there was a conviviality in all this, Melita noted that apparently accommodating groups in the town frequently failed to take sexual and gender politics on board. She was involved in hunt sabotage and animal rights in the early 1980s, for example, but dropped out because she was 'sick of the misogyny, the casual homophobia that a lot of these people displayed'.[83] It was in this new decade that such attitudes were felt more keenly by lesbians and gays in Brighton, and by the end of the 1980s they were mobilizing more radically in response.

Recession and reaction in the 1980s and early 1990s

Economic recession hit Brighton hard; unemployment stood at 10 per cent in 1981 compared to 3.2 per cent a decade earlier.[84] Though North Laine had been saved from demolition by a vigorous local campaign in 1977, it remained run down and dilapidated, as did the stucco Regency squares along the sea-front. Melita remembers the town being 'really scuzzy, really down-at-heel', but there was also nostalgic for these years – rents were cheap, counterculture and the arts were thriving, and the gay scene was growing and diversifying.[85] A cluster of new bars opened on or around St James' Street just to the east of the centre – the Bulldog, Aquarium and Secrets were all male-dominated, the Queen's Arms more mixed (see Map 2). The Longbranch was a women's venue run by 'this ginormously butch woman' from an upstairs room on Grand Parade. 'Every night there'd be a fight [but] it was just one of those places where everybody went.'[86] Round the corner Brighton Polytechnic hosted the annual Taking Liberties Women's Festival in the 1980s and 1990s and also a weekly gay club night, Tack, in a basement bar. It 'was quite silly, very studenty, trying to be arty … [It] was an anybody-was-welcome kind of venue', said Alf.[87] In other parts of the centre the Cricketers, Jugglers and Black Horse each had a growing gay and lesbian clientele in the 1980s.[88] Across an evening there would be movement between these and other places: 'regular punters would come on later [to The Street bar] from Rikkis in St George's Place or the 42 Club in the Kings Rd, or from the Longbranch in Grand Parade or The Caves' (another women's bar in Silwood Street).[89] Such pub crawls were hardly particular to Brighton but this account in the London *Evening Standard* underscores how close these mixed, single sex, arty and studenty venues were to each other. Whereas in Leeds women describe sharing minibuses and taxis to venue-hop, Brighton's scene could be navigated on foot.

This scene and the gay friendliness it signalled drew many gay men and lesbians to the town in this decade when homophobia was burgeoning more broadly.[90] But Brighton was no panacea. With the CHE conference of 1979 pending and the local branch of the National Union of Teachers pledging support for gay and lesbian members, *The Argus* asked Brighton's homosexuals to 'Go Gay Quietly'; the *Brighton Gazette* meanwhile warned that 'Family Life Is at Stake'.[91] The local National Front pledged to fight such 'evil'[92] – evil which apparently manifested in the horrific 1983 case of a six-year-old boy abducted by three men from a Brighton street, sexually abused at Telscombe and abandoned at Newhaven. The case fed growing contemporary fears about the dangerous paedophile stranger and linked him to the idea of a queer menace in the town.[93] Police and press attention was trained on gay men and Brighton was depicted as just the kind of place to foster such horrific crimes.[94] The national *Daily Express* identified it as 'The Town Without Innocence' awash with 'drug addicts, gamblers, homosexuals and racketeers'.[95] Its journalist found The

Street bar 'painted the colour of tar, which is also how it smelt'. There was some 'half-hearted dancing' here while at the Manhattan (on Gloucester Rd), men 'stared vacantly into their lager' or 'inspected' a display of 'lurid volumes' in the hall.[96] In the three years that followed the 1983 abduction, three so-called homosexual panic cases, in which unwanted sexual advances were cited as a defence against assault and murder charges, reached court.[97] Age differences between (younger) attacker and (older) victims were highlighted in *The Argus*, with headlines by the mid-1980s often taking the attacker's perspective: 'Sailor in Death Trial Saw Red' read one; 'My Bloody Knife Fight' another.[98] Here were stories of predatory homosexuals outraging 'normal' men with whom the reader was invited to identify. By contrast, an earlier headline in the same paper from 1971 had distanced the reader from the attacker: '"Queer bashers" sent to jail', it read straightforwardly.[99]

Reports of attacks on lesbian and gay people were on the rise. 'People would come here for queer bashing. It was rife in the 80s. People would regularly come down from Crawley and Haywards Heath. Just for sport', said Melita.[100] Assaults often took place in the street or cruising grounds and in some cases attackers went to gay venues to pick up their victims.[101] It was no surprise, then, that punters arriving at The Street and The Caves were inspected through a spy hole before being admitted. It was no surprise either that in the 1980s (as opposed to the 1990s) Jill remembers that there were 'no banners or rainbow flags or obvious gay signs outside gay venues […] everywhere I knew was very discreet'.[102] Landlords, meanwhile, complained that the police were increasingly 'heavy-handed' in their response to supposed licensing infringements, leading to the closure of the longstanding Curtain Club and the New Heart and Hand (also on the seafront) in 1981 and 1983 respectively.[103] Freddie Bateman described how his gay bookstore, Scene 22, was raided repeatedly by the police in the 1980s; they were, meanwhile, little help when the windows were smashed by passing homophobes.

The local press and Conservative councillors added their voices to the 'new moralism' accompanying 'the Thatcherite experiment' of the 1980s and voiced little sympathy.[104] Reports suggested that there was a sorry proliferation of 'gay shows' in Brighton, that the appearance of the local gay switchboard number in a community centre newsletter might corrupt the young and that the town's school children were in danger of being indoctrinated with 'gay sex lessons'.[105] Councillor Brewer announced he was 'fighting' for Brighton's 'mums and dads' to prevent a tide of political correctness washing over the town from London.[106] Fighting his corner after suggesting gays were 'no longer welcome' in Brighton,

Councillor Blackman wrote in the *Brighton and Hove Leader* that he believed in 'live and let live' but that the town 'is and always has been vulnerable [...] to lunatic fringes spewing their squalid excesses'; he resented 'public exhibitions of filth', he said.[107] Such views didn't go unchallenged. Brighton Council was swift to report the *Daily Express* to the Press Council for 'distortion' of the town's image after the 1983 abduction, while Councillor Fitch called out the 'unfair' treatment of gays in this case which ultimately went unresolved.[108] The flurry of letters to editors after each subsequent scandal or report represented a mix of views.[109] As elsewhere, though, it tended to be the most reactionary and outspoken who were given prominence on the letters pages in these years.

It was in this febrile atmosphere that the *Sunday Mirror* revealed in its 'AIDS Seaside Shocker' that four men had died in Brighton by 1985.[110] A year later *The Sun* branded it the 'town of terror' where eleven men were now dead and 1,000 infected.[111] Brighton was identified as an 'AIDS hotspot' and a place where the virus was threatening to spread to 'normal' men and women. *The Sun* said it was 'full of [bisexuals]' who 'creep out for a quickie and then return to their wives'. It was this fearful potential that braced the piece rather than any empathy for the gay couple with AIDS diagnoses who *The Sun* journalist visited in their 'chintzy' house on the seafront (the domestic detail used to demean the men as frivolous and effeminate). In fact the male–female transmission feared by *The Sun* was and remained particularly low in Brighton: the vast majority of infections resulted from sex between men (83 per cent in 1991) with most of the remainder contracting the virus through intravenous drug use (13 per cent).[112]

HIV and AIDS had an impact on queer life in all four cities and across the country. We can see this in rising fear and anxiety and in the shifting dynamic of relationships, friendship groups and sex lives.[113] There was in each place an upsurge in voluntary and community action and more interaction for many gay men with council social and housing services as well as with hospitals and doctors. In Brighton, however, these effects were especially tangible because of the size of the town and the scale of its gay population; of our four cities the rates per capita were highest here, followed by Manchester, Leeds and then Plymouth.[114] One woman remembers noticing AIDS in Brighton in 1986: on the beach she saw a 'desperately weak' young man being 'tenderly fed ice cream' by a friend; another man sitting just in front of the couple had 'a rose-like rash' across his back.[115] In the years that followed, said another, 'it absolutely decimated Brighton. [...] It was shocking how many people we lost. There was a real fear that if you said "oh, you know, have you seen so-and-so recently" they would be dead. People would literally be dead within four or six weeks of diagnosis.'[116]

There was a 'phenomenal' mobilization of care and support in this context.[117] In 1986, the Sussex AIDS helpline was set up in the same office as Gay Switchboard (by now in Ditchling Road), and by 1988 it had raised enough money locally to open its own dedicated premises on Cavendish Street in the town centre. From here it developed its buddying service; Barbara, who had hosted gatherings for the MRG in the 1960s, was an early volunteer, supporting several men in the town through to their deaths.[118] The mix of volunteers was a reminder that gay men had allies and sustained support from many different quarters in the town despite the fear and antagonism that dominated headlines. Such adverse reaction nevertheless shaped everyday life practically and emotionally. The helpline used a post office box rather than its actual address because of the risk of attack, and the woman who chaired the group reported that a number of her friends had 'stopped contacting her' out of 'fear' and 'ignorance'.[119] Ken was beaten up four times in the latter half of the 1980s in the town. Once, he said, 'I was followed home by a group of men who were singing to the tune of Rod Stewart's "Sailing", "you are dying, you are dying, you are dying, and we don't care".'[120]

Initially the political and activist response to the crisis was relatively muted here. Though there was a strong political current running through lesbian and gay life, it was less cohesive and concerted than in Manchester which had a broader and longer-standing radical tradition, a well-established gay centre and press, and a proactive council championing gay and lesbian rights. There may in Brighton also have been a particular sense of paralysis in the initial stages of the crisis and an urgent drive to care and support rather than to protest. The advent of Clause 28 in 1988 changed this. In that year there was, said Melita, an 'extraordinary' coming together of community in the town in the wake of a 'packed' anti-Clause meeting at the Brighthelm church community centre on North Rd (built on the site of the burned-out church hall which had served as a women's and gay centre in the 1970s; see Map 2).[121] Allie remembers a heady mix of people, politics, excitement and desire:

> There were all sorts there – men with those fat moustaches, and blokes who looked like teachers from school, and smiley, willowy boys who might have been students. The women overwhelmed me. I kept finding myself staring – locking my eyes onto their faces, their hair – wondering if my girlfriend was watching me watch them. I was a little bit in love with all of them – even the old ones.[122]

'There was a real galvanization that night', said Melita; 'everybody just split off, fired up with energy. [...] There was a group to do a newsletter, do publicity. A group was going to do events, do fundraising. All these different things.'[123] As in Manchester and Leeds, it was women who initiated this meeting. Under the banner of Brighton Area Action Against Clause 28 (BAAAC28), there was nevertheless a rapid coming together of men and women, of 'battle hardened protestors' with others who hadn't been politicized before. 'Bisexuals suddenly started coming out; people started wearing "Stop the Clause" badges at work. [...] It just made people very stroppy and very feisty.'[124] Over the coming three years there were proliferating protests in Brighton in which Clause 28 and AIDS were front and centre, including several against the council, a joint BAAAC28/ACT UP (AIDS Coalition to Unleash Power) zap of Princess Diana's address to the Family Congress in 1990 and protests at the Labour Party conference in 1991 (see Image 24). There was in this a switch from reactive protest to proactive activism.[125] The newsletter born of that first meeting at the Brighthelm Centre meanwhile connected a range of issues – with pieces on bisexuality, AIDS, racism and gay bashing as well as anti-Clause 28 activism elsewhere. AIDS and Clause 28 transformed feelings of community and solidarity nationally but this was especially the case in Brighton where people were facing the loss of friends and lovers as well as that celebrated sense of queer ease in the town.

A BAAAC28 survey of 1991 revealed ongoing verbal and physical abuse in Britain's gay capital.[126] Of 126 gays and lesbians interviewed (trans and bi people were still notably absent), 20 per cent had been physically attacked and 50 per cent verbally abused in the preceding year; 58 per cent felt attacks and abuse had increased and only 3 per cent reported these to the police. This is hardly surprising given the increase in arrests of gay men nationally and the revelation that the Brighton force had kept questionnaires and data from over 600 interviews with gay men conducted after the murder of barman Peter Halls in 1990. They included the names, addresses and workplaces of gay men in the town, together with information about sexual preferences and marital status. Such information in the hands of the police was troubling – as it was in Plymouth and Manchester where similar 'gay lists' had been compiled.[127] After further BAAAC28 protests and the prosecution of Halls' killer in 1992, police finally destroyed the data in front of gay and media observers.[128]

With this renewed activist and community momentum came a determination to have Brighton's lesbian and gay life rendered directly by those involved in it. In the immediate aftermath of the Clause 28 meetings, Brighton Ourstory formed and began to record voices which might otherwise have been lost or silenced. The resulting testimonies about the 1950s and 1960s spoke of the deep

Image 6 Pride programme, 1992

roots of queer community in the town. They were performed at 'really well-attended' readings in the early 1990s and appeared in the book *Daring Hearts* in 1992 (published by local community publisher QueenSpark books).[129] Ourstory recaptured queer dimensions of Brighton 'from below', taking some control of a narrative twisted out of shape by the local and national press in the mid to late 1980s especially. Brighton Gay Pride from 1991 was another attempt to seize the initiative. The first ones were 'raggle-taggle events of 300 people' involving battles with the council over the route 'and people shouting and spitting at us in the street'.[130] They were nevertheless remembered nostalgically. Judith, returning to Brighton after a fifteen-year absence, marched in the 1991 Pride: 'I showed up knowing no one yet everyone', she said. 'I paraded along Church Rd with the raucous crowd and so happy was I to finally be myself – out in my hometown – that I grinned and grinned at the bystanders hoping above all to see one of my old teachers smiling back.'[131]

Pride, Ourstory and BAAAC28 worked in different ways to counter other demeaning versions of queer life here. The level of antagonism, the scale of loss and an ebbing convivial culture meant that when gay and lesbian Brightonians did finally push back, they did so forcefully and relatively coherently. This was described in the testimonies of Melita, Allie, Jill, Judith and others gathered for later queer community history projects in Brighton in the 2010s.[132] These testimonies helped consolidate a powerful sense of Brighton being transformed in the late 1980s and 1990s by a fervent lesbian and gay politics and the emergence of a more vociferous and visible community in the town.

Concerted community and civic pride in the 1990s and 2000s

Queer tribes in the 1990s

Radical community magazine *Queer Tribe* (1989–1991), another spin off of BAAAC28, mapped a newly energized scene at the start of the 1990s. It showed eight bars, two cafes, ten club nights and four hotels.[133] This was roughly equivalent to what was on offer at the same juncture in Manchester, a city three times the size and with a vast urban hinterland. Brighton's scene was about to grow further. Revenge on Old Steine opened in 1991 as Brighton's first large-scale dedicated gay club. Club nights Shame and Wild Fruit at the Zap under the arches on the seafront provided what *Gay Times* described as 'the prototype of gay clubbing for the 1990s'.[134] Clubbers came from the capital and boarded special buses home in the early hours. Later in the decade London clubs Popstars and Crash ran one-off nights in the town, capitalizing on Brighton's resurgent cool queer reputation. Sean said that at these nights ecstasy was 'breaking down barriers between men and women' – as AIDS and Clause 28 action was doing in other ways.[135]

New bars on and around St James' Street also offered something new. A video from the early 1990s suggests that Zanzibar (from 1991) was much more mixed that the more established venues nearby.[136] Legends (from 1994) was the first bar without thick glass or grills; 'the honesty and bravado was a revelation', remembered Alf.[137] Having opened as a gay bar in 1993, the Marlborough turned lesbian from 1994 before becoming a focal point for trans and non-binary Brightonians in the 2000s. In Hove, meanwhile, The Only Alternative Left (or TOAL as it was known; see Map 2) became the town's 'mecca for lesbians' in the 1990s until Candy Bar opened on St James' Street in 2000; Marion remembers events, poetry readings, parties and an ethos of welcome at TOAL – including at the guesthouse in the upper storeys.[138]

There was now an embedded support network for the growing numbers affected by HIV and AIDS in the town. Father Marcus Riggs secured a stipendiary residence on Camelford Street just off St James' Street and gave it over to Open Doors, an AIDS support charity which ran until 2008. A candle was placed in the window each time a service user died; it was, in the first half of the 1990s, almost constantly alight. Our House (later Brighton Body Positive) began operating in 1991 from people's homes before moving for its weekly meetings to a Social Services Day Centre just off Grand Parade (and to which service users were asked to bring their own cups).[139] The group moved to its own premises (with cups they could use) in 1993. The Sussex Beacon opened on the edge of the South Downs as a dedicated AIDS hospice and respite centre in 1992. These places, alongside doctor's surgeries, the Royal Sussex and Hove General hospitals (the latter with a dedicated six-bed AIDS ward from 1990)[140] and Woodvale Crematorium on Lewes Road became further coordinates on the queer map of Brighton in these years. Visits to pubs and clubs, to cruising grounds or to the homes of friends or pick-ups might now be punctuated by trips to these other places for treatment, support or remembrance. A quarter of the gay men surveyed by Project Zorro in 1996 had used or volunteered for one of these AIDS and HIV charities.

More 'traditional' queer sites felt different now too. Cruisers on Duke's Mound on the seafront to the east of the St James' Street scene were often joined by volunteers distributing condoms. The bars, pubs and clubs held regular fundraisers and glasses were raised to customers lost. Most people (gay or straight) knew or knew of someone who was ill or had died. Many had lost partners, friends or colleagues. Ken once went to three funerals in one day.[141]

What this meant for Brighton and Brightonians is difficult to gauge; grief, loss, anxiety and uncertainty play out in multiple and unpredictable ways.[142] We can, though, see ways in which the community that mobilized in the late 1980s was consolidated in the 1990s. We can see too that there was a particularly strong push 'from below'. This was also hugely important in Manchester where AIDS had delivered a near equivalent punch. There, however, the city and health authorities were more proactive in working with community groups, by virtue in part of the solidly Labour council pushing an equalities agenda from 1984. Though there was a local Labour administration in Brighton from 1986, it was less secure and more cautious in developing such an equalities strategy than were our cities in the north. The local health authority meanwhile remained astonishingly disengaged from the gay community, especially given that rates of infection were twelve times higher here than nationally.[143] While the Department of Health recommended that half of the overall prevention budget should be spent on core groups (here unquestionably gay men), in Brighton spending was significantly less than this – estimated at around £200,000 per annum out of a total prevention budget of £1.1 million.[144] There was no dedicated HIV clinic and, until 1995, no specialist HIV physician employed by the health authority.[145] Local activist Arthur Law told the *Guardian* that 'the lack of communication with the community [on the part of the local health authority] was alienating the very people they needed to listen to'.[146]

G-Scene, the newly launched scene magazine from 1995, spearheaded a campaign to fund a far-reaching survey of gay life in the town with an eye to more effective strategies for HIV and AIDS prevention and care. Entirely funded 'from below', the resulting Project Zorro (1996–1997) was a powerful further example of community mobilization in Brighton. The 1,576 questionnaires and interviews yielded important information on sex and risk and also flagged many of the coordinates of the gay male community in town – a community to which 79 per cent of survey respondents felt they belonged.[147] This was closely related for them to the St James' Street scene and nearby Duke's Mound cruising spot (visited regularly by two-thirds of respondents) as well as to shared reading matter (87 per cent read *G-Scene*), support services and special interest groups (including the Lancers gay bikers group, Ourstory and a choir).[148] The exclusive focus of Zorro on men and on men living in Brighton meant that the community outlined in the ensuing report was less mixed and inclusive of visitors to the town than the versions of queer community emerging through

Ourstory, BAAAC28 and *G-Scene* itself.[149] The Zorro data nevertheless signals a tight network and also showed that the town continued to exert a powerful draw: 91.6 per cent of those surveyed were born elsewhere (compared to around 80 per cent of gay men surveyed in a study around the same time in London) and 50 per cent of these cited Brighton's gay reputation as their reason for moving here.[150] They also mentioned its bohemian, arty reputation and house prices, which, in the 1980s and early 1990s, were lower than elsewhere in the south (a picture that was very different ten years later). Many saw in Brighton the possibility of escape from homophobia; two men moved from Hastings 33 miles along the coast after suffering repeated attacks there, for example.

Our own interviewees underscored this sense of what the town represented and promised in these years. Sean visited Brighton in the 1990s after his divorce and recalls 'this lovely vibe, the welcomeness';[151] Dennis – on the cusp of leaving his marriage – visited from Plymouth: 'It just seemed to be acceptable [...] Going to Brighton I'm thinking "you could be gay, you could be gay" because Brighton was the San Francisco of the UK.'[152] This feeling was surely underpinned by the town's earlier gay history, of which, thanks to Ourstory, more people in the town and beyond were aware. But if in the 1960s and 1970s the emphasis was on a vibrant social and sexual scene, the tenor was different now. Community in the 1990s was driven by the AIDS crisis and anti-Clause 28 mobilization and it was anchored in well-established support networks and a reoriented and more visible scene mapped and celebrated in a new gay press.

Brighton transformed in the 2000s

By the time the next local LGBT research project, Count Me In, was inaugurated in 2000 and certainly by its second incarnation from 2004 to 2009 as Count Me In Too, local and national contexts had shifted significantly, including equalities legislation on the age of consent, adoption, civil partnership and gays in the military. Brighton and Hove were now a city (from 2001) – and one that was demographically more youthful than the two towns had been before. The number of over sixty-fives fell from 16 per cent of the population in 2001 to 13 per cent in 2011 – bucking the English national trend which saw a rise in this age group from 15 per cent to 18 per cent.[153] The city's reputation for pleasure and consumption grew further and the local economy was based even more on the service sector, especially as one in twelve Brightonians commuted to work in the capital by 2011 but shopped and went out near home (in 1970 the figure was

Image 7 Flyer for Brighton Bound, a weekend event organized by the Sussex Lancers MSC, a leather and uniform group which ran from 1980 to 2001

one in twenty).[154] Experiences of queer life and community in Brighton shifted alongside these changes and the sense of embattlement in the 1980s and first half of the 1990s receded significantly. AIDS-related deaths plummeted following the introduction of anti-retroviral therapies (trialled in Brighton in 1994 and 1995 because of the concentration of cases there), and though HIV infection rates continued to rise, Brighton was also better equipped to cope. This was not least because there was now a dedicated clinic for gay men in line with one of Zorro's key recommendations.[155]

While Zorro and Ourstory had been community funded in the 1990s, the local police, local authority and University of Brighton provided financial support for Count Me In Too; LGBT life was now seen to fall within the remit of these different bodies as national government pushed its equalities and inclusion agenda. With the repeal of Section 28 in 2003, local libraries and museums were freer to mark LGBT+ History Month and Pride, which had become an emblem of the city's supposed liberalism and inclusivity. Count Me In Too found that 90 per cent of their sample of 1,145 lesbian, gay, bi and trans people had attended Brighton Pride at least once in the previous five years, with 44 per cent attending every year. Pride, said one respondent, was one of Brighton and Hove's 'great successes'. It was 'a fantastic thing' – and a far cry 'from those early days when there were a few hundred of us dodging missiles around Churchill Square'.[156] The *Argus*, which began to dilute its homophobia after a change in editor in 1993, cheerfully announced in 2009 that the city and council were 'the most gay-friendly in England'.[157] LGBTQ+ life (the Q+ now a regular addition to the abbreviation) was folded positively into the story the city told about itself – and in ways unimaginable in the 1980s and 1990s.

The internet and, from 2009, smartphones changed community and ways of relating sexually, socially and politically, here as elsewhere. Specifically gay bars and clubs became less significant as people felt safer in mainstream and crossover venues and used apps to hook up for dates and sex. Many preferred going out beyond the commercial gay scene. In 2003, the Cowley Club opened on London Road as a social and resource centre for queer, feminist, trans, ecological, animal and worker activism. It was appropriately near those alternative and countercultural venues from the 1970s and at the foot of 'Muesli Mountain', as the studenty Hanover area of the city was now known. Club organizers aimed to capture some of the connective political spirit some felt had been lost in the city, not least by choosing to name it after Harry Cowley, a Brighton window cleaner who campaigned for squatting, homeless and anti-fascist causes between the wars and up to his death in 1970.

The name, like its location, signalled a reach to the past and for what some saw as more communal grassroots politics.[158] Given its embrace of those who felt excluded, the club also nodded to some holes in the now much-vaunted Brightonian ethic of acceptance and inclusion. As the Count Me In reports revealed, age, racism, poverty, homelessness and drug use and abuse meant LGBTQ people could still feel like outsiders here. Queer in Brighton (2013) and Brighton Trans*formed (2014) garnered testimonies to some of those feelings even as the overall mood of both projects was celebratory. Sabah, for example, observed that 'a lot of queer people of colour in Brighton don't feel really safe about being out and vocal about their identities [...] and backgrounds'.[159] Jess moved briefly to Brighton from Manchester in 2008 on account of its queer reputation but stayed only two years because of the racism she faced in a city that has remained overwhelmingly white.[160] She was disappointed in her direct experience of a place so widely trailed and long understood as a 'gay Mecca'.[161] Kate, meanwhile, chose to transition in Manchester in 2004 rather than 'posh' Brighton; it was Manchester's 'down-to-earth' credentials that allowed her to feel more 'at home' as she confirmed her gender – hinting at a rivalry between the two queerly notorious cities.[162]

More broadly, these surveys and projects emphasized the diversity of queer experience rather than the coherence and singularity of gay and/or lesbian community which came across in accounts of the concerted activism of the late 1980s and in the Zorro report. The new generation of projects suggested more directly than before the multiple ways of finding and experiencing identity and community in the city – including and extending well beyond specifically gay and lesbian venues and groups.[163] This was particularly the case for trans and gender non-binary people who were finding a voice here as never before. Some participants in Brighton Trans*formed described how the gay and broader pub scene could be anxiety provoking. Cass, who was born in Brighton and moved 'home' to the city after living in London and Manchester, described being exhausted by 'the stress, the social anxiety of just going into a pub' because of the stares, misgendering and abuse. Other spaces had been or were more important, and including the hippie Open Café in the mid-1970s and the hairdressing salon in Hove where a group of trans women met and formed the Clare Project in 1990. It met weekly first in the backroom of the salon and then in the Methodist Church in Dorset Gardens. In the years that followed the Clare Project became a mainstay of trans support and socializing, giving Alice the impetus to move to Brighton and Michelle her 'avenue to transitioning'. The open door offered by the Methodist Church for trans and LGB (lesbian, gay and bisexual) people was to be found also at the Unitarian Chapel in New Road and the Quaker Meeting House on Ship Street, as well as in other central Brighton congregations. Here, as in the other cities, church, temple and mosque mattered in many LGBT lives – though experiences varied: Joanna, a sixty-year-old trans woman, was excluded from her church after her GP, a fellow parishioner, outed her (she went on to find another church and another 'brilliant' doctor).[164]

Since 2010, resources for trans socializing and support have grown substantially, as they have in Leeds and Manchester. Brighton Trans*formed mapped and celebrated the trans groups and networks which have developed since then. The Clare Project was joined by Transformers, Allsorts, FTM Brighton (a group primarily for transgendered men and transmasculine people), Transwimmers and others.[165] The Transalliance umbrella was formed to link these groups, and from 2013 a Trans Scrutiny panel drew together the city's statutory bodies – the council, police and health services – to review policy and approaches. The first UK safer sex campaign specifically for trans people was pioneered by the Brighton Terrence Higgins Trust around 2012. More recently, Brighton Museum hosted the Museum of Transology (2017–2020), an exhibition forged through the community-driven curation of E-J. Scott. It began as a display case in the Marlborough pub with an invitation to trans regulars to contribute and then, duly enlarged, found space and a large mixed audience in the nearby museum, one of the city's leading cultural venues. In an adjacent gallery was the 'Queer Looks' exhibition (from 2018), tracing local lesbian and gay fashion from the 1960s on.[166] In these and other ways, Brighton's margins were becoming ever more visible and 'ordinary' in the city.[167] A tourism campaign of 2021 riffed on this idea of the ordinariness of difference or eccentricity here, boasting that Brighton was 'never normal'.[168]

The Museum of Transology, Transpride (from 2013) and Brighton Trans*formed saw trans people consolidating community and making themselves visible on their own terms and in ways that resonated with earlier moves by lesbian and gay Brightonians in the late 1980s and early 1990s. The testimonies recorded were generally celebratory and often harked back to what felt special about this city. Fox described the height of the drag king scene in the early 2000s, for example – especially at the Marlborough pub. It was, he said, a playful time in his trans journey: 'it was a safe space for packing and binding and putting on facial hair and doing all that felt really really great'.[169] In this he saw parallels between Brighton, San Francisco and Sydney and echoed some of the Ourstory interviewees who connected the Brighton of their youth to distant and idealized other places – it was, they had said, a 'gay Mecca', 'a paradise which in my wildest dreams I'd never seen as possible'.[170] Some suggest that the particular sense of queer fun in the 1960s, of countercultural ease in the 1970s or of activist and radical community from the late 1980s ebbed away as gentrification took hold and the city owned and celebrated its liberalism and tolerance more overtly. Pride became a 'commercialized' city-wide event, and for Melita it was Trans Pride that was now more 'authentic'; 'a scrappy little underdog of an event, all acoustic musicians and hand-made banners'.[171] Participants in our Brighton workshop highlighted some of the disillusion and difficulty experienced by LGBTQ people here in the present, and they did this partly through comparison with the past (evoking too, though, historic wounds, especially the enduring trauma of the AIDS crisis). But despite this, most still relished the queer pleasures Brighton continues to offer. The city's size and seaside reputation, its bohemian and arty history and its proximity to and difference from London have made it special and queerly particular. That those who were wide-eyed at their first visit also often moved here and stayed is testament to Brighton's enduring queer appeal. So, while Jill observed how escalating housing costs have forced some of her older lesbian friends out of the city, she added that they all 'continue to love and treasure the independent spirit of Brighton'.[172]

41

2

Split scenes in Leeds

Image 8 Leeds Pride, 5 August 2018, showing the rainbow bridge and Viaduct bar

Looking back to her move to Leeds in the 1970s, feminist Al Garthwaite reflected:

> I have [family] links to the north of England and it made more sense to go north to find somewhere to live with four of us and a baby and cats and things. And it was much, much cheaper to get accommodation in Leeds. [...] Near the countryside, possible to get to London. So that was why we came to Leeds [in 1973]. And there seemed to be quite a thriving political atmosphere in Leeds as well, a lot going on.[1]

Activist and artist Ajamu X remembered the following decade in the city:

> [In the 1980s] you had Rockshots. You had the New Penny. And then there was a pub not far away called the Whip. And the Whip was a National Front pub. [...] And then also – because some of the gay bars were still also predominantly white, there's a sense of, you're new meat. [... So] a lot of Black folks would not go into town [...] [In Chapeltown] even though you weren't out you were kind of safe.[2]

The New Penny Ajamu mentioned was, until 1969, the Hope and Anchor – or Grope and Wanker as some had it. In 2016, a blue plaque was unveiled marking its longstanding significance to gay life in Leeds and this southern part of the city centre not far from the station. A year later Network Rail repainted the nearby railway bridge in rainbow colours, flagging the area's LGBTQ credentials to all. This was now very clearly Leeds' queer hub, as it had also been in different ways in the 1960s and early 1970s. In the years between, however, wider networks and different places within and beyond the city often felt more comfortable for people like Al and Ajamu. Ajamu mentioned shebeens and reggae pubs in the poor inner-northern suburb of Chapeltown, an area of Afro-Caribbean immigration from the 1950s. The 'thriving political atmosphere' described by Al was associated with the areas around the University and Polytechnic on the northern edge of the city centre as well as in squats and housing co-ops in nearby suburbs, including Chapeltown. Both talk about the importance of satellite towns and cities – the feminist and lesbian networks anchored in Bradford or Hebden Bridge, for example, or the vibrant gay scene in Huddersfield where Ajamu was born and brought up. These other places and also events in homes, community centres and rented rooms of pubs were often more immediately part of everyday gay and especially lesbian lives in Leeds than the venues in the centre. This geography relates to deep political divisions and to split scenes, and this led me to do a double take in this chapter. I looking across our period first in relation to sex and socializing (section one) and then in relation to politics (section two) in order better to account for the distinct queer networks of this city and its surrounding suburbs, towns and cities.

There are various factors which made Leeds particular. With a population of 750,000 it was three times the size of Brighton and Hove and was in addition well networked by road and rail with nearby Bradford, Huddersfield, Wakefield and Halifax (see Map 5). None of these towns and cities are more than 22 miles away and form, with Leeds, the fourth largest urban area in the UK, offering multiple opportunities for sex, socializing and activism. There was, in addition, a significant growth in the number of students here from the mid-1960s, changing the feel of the inner-northern suburbs of Woodhouse, Chapeltown and Headingley especially (see Map 4). Clothing manufacture and engineering meanwhile slowed while financial and legal services grew. By the late 1990s, Leeds was second only to London for these sectors, fuelling the gentrification of the city centre, including the queer area adjacent to the station.[3]

There was a particular sense of danger associated with Leeds in the late 1970s and early 1980s, even when compared to Manchester and Plymouth, which could also feel edgy. The National Front was very active in these years, as Ajamu testified, and between 1975 and his arrest in 1981, Peter Sutcliffe murdered thirteen women and attacked many others principally in Leeds but also in Bradford, Keighley, Huddersfield, Halifax and Manchester. The so-called 'Yorkshire Ripper' killings and the misogyny which laced the press and police response fuelled feminist politics, action and separatism here.[4] Subsequently, 'town hall feminism' in Leeds gave some civic grist to battles for equality.[5] Labour's control of the council was less secure here than in Manchester, however, and this in part explains the council's lack of stridency on gay and lesbian issues compared to our city across the Pennines.[6] As this and Chapter 3 show, however, there were multiple other factors in play which distinguished queer life in these two proud northern cities.

Sex and socializing from the 1960s

Out in the centre

As a teenager in the early 1960s, David was living in a small village 15 miles outside of Leeds and would travel daily into the city for work at the Great Northern Hotel (see Map 3). He recalled his short walk from station to work vividly:

> I would walk over the bridge, [...] past the ticket office down in the concourse [...] . On the right was W.H.Smiths and when I was working I would go and pick my papers up from there. I can remember Peter [who was queer and worked there] very well, and along the same side was the British Transport Police Office and the back entrance to the Queens Hotel. [...] Outside in City Square opposite the Majestic Cinema, I can remember my very first film – [...] *The Sound of Music* – quite gay! On the corner was a newsagent and a barber next door, I used to go there, he was gay too, and opposite was [...] the West Riding Hotel. Jerry worked there. Jerry was probably in his 40s then, he was very camp and he introduced me to cross-dressing. He used to come to the Buccaneer Bar [...] [which was at] the Great Northern Hotel where I worked [...] as a night porter [... It was] a renowned gay bar.[7]

These places in Leeds city centre were each queerly significant to David. The transport police were on his radar perhaps because of the danger they represented: the force was watchful of the toilets at the neighbouring City and Central stations (the latter demolished in 1967) and there were arrests there for cottaging, blackmail and the sale of 'lewd' photographs.[8] As in Manchester and Brighton, stations were places of sexual possibility for men passing through and with time to kill. These men may not have identified as queer, homosexual or gay, though David knew people working nearby in hotels and retail who clearly did.

In the evenings, David visited Flamenco's coffee shop, the Hope and Anchor, Charlie's and the Mitre. He probably heard about these rough, mixed places from Peter, Jerry and others in their circle. Such knowledge bound them together and gave them a sense of belonging in the city centre. The Mitre closed in 1961 but until then catered to journalists from the nearby offices of the *Yorkshire Evening Post* at lunchtime and to sex workers and queer men in the evenings (especially in the upstairs room); a two-way mirror allowed 'police or talent' to be spotted as they approached.[9] At the Star and Garter on nearby Duncan Street 'there seemed to be three or four different sexes'. It was Pete's 'absolute favourite' at this time; 'I was never quite sure who was supposed to do what to whom', he said:

> There were the 'ladies of the night' plying their trade, they were a lively bunch; always laughing: their antics made the pub a fun place. Mingled in were the old 'down and outs' – old kids who had been in there drinking since the pub opened. [...] The floor was always swimming in ale and blood and you could feel broken glass forever grinding underfoot. I saw a lesbian give a guy a crack who was getting too familiar with her friend.[10]

There were pubs with this kind of eclectic mix of outsiders in each of our cities, though there were also more exclusively queer venues in each – the Lockyer back bar in Plymouth, the New Union in Manchester and the Regency (and others) in Brighton. Here it was the Hope and Anchor that was the mainstay. It gained notoriety when it was 'exposed' in 1968 in *Union News* (a relatively sympathetic student newspaper) and a week later in *The People*, a high-circulation national Sunday tabloid. Between them the respective journalists reported same-sex dancing, a butch-femme couple 'sit[ting] quietly together' having a drink and a mock marriage ceremony. One man was fashionably but 'not outrageously' dressed in clothes he had travelled to London to buy. He described the electric shock therapy he was receiving to address his 'deviant' desires. Another punter, Jane, who worked at a local mill (probably one of those just across the River Aire) would arrive and leave work 'before everyone else because they ridicule him so much'. At the pub '[Jane] gets most hurt if he is not referred to as "her" or "she"'.[11] 'My real name is James', Jane herself told *The People*, 'I'm wearing woman's tights and a kaftan so that it looks like a dress. I'm an exhibitionist [… and] bent'. She described having girlfriends ('for company'), lots of boyfriends and some 'normal friends'. The Hope and Anchor was a place where she could 'enjoy herself without feeling out of place'.[12] It seems to have been one of the only pubs in the city where such gender crossing was accommodated then or indeed in the three decades that followed.

The People interviewed a group of rugby players gathered at the pub. One, a regular of ten years, had not been 'turned' queer by the experience, while the landlord, a former rugby-playing New Zealander, claimed the queers 'are good for business' and 'cause no trouble' even though he 'finds it difficult to talk to them'. His wife told *The Union News* that 'it's being queer that keeps you young'.[13] She was 'like a mum' to the assembled crowd, said one customer; there was here, as at Manchester's New Union and Plymouth's Lockyer Tavern, a feeling of home and family. Such mutual support was important not least because of the surrounding disdain. *The People* branded the pub and its customers 'utterly

Image 9 Call Lane, junction with Lower Briggate, showing the Hope and Anchor pub (later the New Penny) on the right, *c.*1965

distasteful' and cited Lord Arran's 1967 appeal to homosexuals to behave 'with dignity' after the partial decriminalization of homosexuality in that year. This behaviour might be expected 'in sinful Soho or permissive Paddington', the journalist wrote, but not in 'the homely Yorkshire town of Leeds'.[14] A week after *The People* article appeared the Hope and Anchor was 'completely wrecked' amid running battles between Leeds and Glasgow Rangers football fans.[15]

The pub reopened some months later as the New Penny and endured as other bars opened and closed nearby. Homosexuals were banned from the Buccaneer Bar at the Great Northern Hotel where David worked in 1973. Flamenco's lasted through most of the 1970s: 'people would go on there after the pubs', Roy said. 'It was predominantly men [...], but quite a few gay girls would come in. It was famous for its frothy coffee, as we called it in those days. And cheesecake – the most wonderful cheesecake. It used to be packed solid.'[16] The nearby Peel Hotel (from 1976 The Square) on Boar Lane drew a queer crowd until it closed in 1984 and then there was the 'seedy' and 'pitiful' Charlie's club, which ran from an upstairs room in Queen's Court throughout the 1970s and until it closed in 1982.[17] 'It really wasn't very nice', said Robert, recalling the sex men had in the toilets downstairs; 'I thought "well, what's the point? You might as well go cottaging, if that's all it is to the gay scene".'[18] Gerry remembers the disco soundtrack (especially Donna Summer), a 'weird mix' of queers, 'pimps and prostitutes' and the 'tough' bouncers who could be 'brutal' – especially on Wednesday's women's nights if there were arguments or fights. Gerry had by this time joined the GLF and 'sensed a big divide' between drinkers at Charlie's and politicized gays who went to the Fenton and other pubs near the university. 'I used to go to both', he said, 'but there was a bit of disapproval on both sides.'[19]

In the latter half of the 1970s you could buy *Gay News* from a kiosk opposite the Corn Exchange ('the only place' in the city centre you could get a copy) while the public toilets at the nearby state-of-the-art Merrion Shopping Centre (from 1964) were frequented by 'a dirty minded bunch', according to the *Yorkshire Post*.[20] Ten minutes walk from this gay cluster, across the River Aire in what was still (just) an industrial area, was the Old Red Lion with its small queer 'end bar' (see Map 3). This was a regular spot for the CHE group in the 1970s – though it was later known as the 'old dead lion' once the younger gay punters started going elsewhere.[21]

The venues on this 'closed little scene' could feel uncomfortable or compromising for some.[22] 'There was quite a lot of straight people going round [to the New Penny] to see the freaks', Roy said.[23] Ted, a teacher, avoided it because 'everybody in the staff room knew about the Bent Penny [as it became known]; it was in folklore, so it wasn't a place that nice or respectable people went'.[24] He was also anxious after encountering a pupil's mother on his first visit to the Old Red Lion. John, who worked at nearby Yorkshire Chemicals, didn't go to any queer pubs. 'I always had to keep a low profile', he said:

> If you went around Leeds, you'd be seen and everything would be straight back [to work]. Your job would have been untenable. The attitude to homosexuality was disgraceful [...] Any of the rare occasions when homosexuals reared their head, you were sort of outed and ridiculed.[25]

Women could feel unwelcome in these venues too. In the mid-1970s Ruth would get off the train from Wakefield and hang out in the area by the station 'sort of looking for like-minded people'. 'Most of the people I could see [coming in and out of the pubs] were men', she said; 'there was very little outlet in terms of finding other women'.[26] There were also rising political tensions. Roy remembers an argument with a woman in the late 1970s at Flamenco's about a lack of mutual support between gay men and lesbians. At Primo's, a gay club that opened in the mid-1970s opposite the New Penny, the proprietor delivered 'caustic remarks' over the microphone about 'eight or ten feminist lesbians' who he then promptly banned, marking them out from the 'exceptionally nice' 'gay girls'.[27] Lou recalled 'trying to make contact' with these central Leeds 'bar dykes' in the late 1970s by inviting them to a women's disco at the Woodpeckers pub on York Road to the west of the centre:

> It was just the most excruciating thing because [...] you just came up against [butch-femme] roleplay. Like, you know, if you wanted to dance with a femme, she said, 'well, you'll have to ask so-and-so'. We just couldn't cope with all that. So it died a death really but there were one or two valiant attempts.[28]

Julie remembers that these women were from the same working-class background as she was but also 'tended to be quite fixed in butch-femme roles and traditional lesbian style'. She was, she said, 'more excited by the feminists because they were rebellious and naughty'. She found them in other parts of the city.[29]

To the (inner) suburbs and beyond

From the mid-1970s there were GLF discos at the Swarthmore Community Centre near the university on the northern edge of the city centre. 'You felt really relaxed [at those discos]. It was the equivalent of the village hall in a way', said one regular.[30] Volunteers from Gay Switchboard and Lesbian Line drank at the studenty Fenton pub nearby (on different nights: Lesbian Line was on a Tuesday). Some of the women would then go on to the Dock Green, a former police station turned pub in Harehills, and Roots, an Afro-Caribbean venue in Chapeltown (see Map 4). 'You could get from the Dock Green to Roots and make a real night of it', remembers Lesley (see Image 26).[31] 'In a way', said Jude, '[it] was [the women's] equivalent to the New Penny'.[32] The lesbian nights at the Trades Club in Chapeltown ran through most of the 1980s and drew crowds of 300 or more. Local bands often played; music was 'a big part' of the lesbian scene and 'sort of supplemented the [lesbian and women's] discos', Lesley said.[33] These nights at the Trades Club came to a halt in 1991 when 'proud SM dyke' Angela Jones went wearing handcuffs and carrying a whip. 'A riot' broke out in response. While the women who objected were 'reminded of their own oppression', Jones accused them of 'fascism' for trying 'to deny us our freedom of dress'.[34] 'We were talking about dress to impress not oppress' after that night, remembered Cerydwen.[35]

Minibuses took women from Leeds to the Checkpoint, a largely lesbian club night in the 1970s and 1980s at the Black and West Indian Cultural Centre in Manningham, Bradford's north-eastern suburb. 'It was a really important place for us. [...] Depending on your salary, there'd be three different entrance fees. [...] And it was all towards the babysitting fund. So that women who had children could come out and dance. [...] That's how political it was.'[36] The Junction, The Sun, and The Bavaria were other gay, lesbian or mixed venues in Bradford that drew men and women from Leeds for a night out. The Junction had a similar reputation to the New Penny. 'Don't go in there: it's full of pouffs', John's mother had told him when he was a teenager in the late 1960s; 'thank you mother', he had thought.[37] The Bavaria ran through the 1980s and 1990s as a largely lesbian pub until it was destroyed by fire during clashes between the National Front and anti-fascist protestors in 2001.

Huddersfield to the south of Leeds and Bradford was 'really hopping' for both gays and lesbians in the 1970s and first half of the 1980s. Novelist Steven Alcock remembers driving there from Leeds, 'sometimes half a dozen or more of us piled in the back of a transit van, or [we would] take the train'.

In the mid to late 1970s the Manchester gay scene hadn't quite revved up, Sheffield didn't have any regular gay club and Leeds only had the pitiful Charlie's and the occasional Gay Lib Disco. [...] Huddersfield was slap in the middle of the lot (as well as various other towns in the region) with fairly good transport links and fast motorway connections.[38]

49

Kees van der Merwt from the Netherlands found a tolerant town when he moved to Huddersfield from the Netherlands in 1973 and opened the New Amsterdam pub with his partner, who would regularly perform as Shirley Bassey.[39] The New Amsterdam 'was literally two terraced houses [knocked together]. God knows how anybody found the place, because you went through a warren of poorly-lit back streets [...] The place used to get heaving.'[40] At the mixed Gemini Club, meanwhile, there were 'men dancing cheek-to-cheek' inside and having sex in the yard at the back. 'When they heard there were suspect policemen in the building, the floodlight would go on [in the yard] and everybody would pull their pants up, literally', said Roy.[41] In 1981, the police 'got wind' of what was happening and made ten arrests for 'lewd behaviour' and 'gross indecency', including of men from Nottingham, Leeds and Blackburn in Lancashire.[42] The Leeds man had already been arrested in Manchester for a similar offence and was now trying his luck in Huddersfield. Twenty-two-year-old Iftikhar Hussain, meanwhile, kept his queer social life at the Gemini and work at the New Amsterdam in Huddersfield separate from his family life with wife and child 40 miles away in Blackburn. Aside from the arrests, the police had John Addy removed as the licensee because he had presided over 'a cess pit of sexual filth'.[43]

The raid on the Gemini was part of a wider operation in Huddersfield in 1981 which saw plain clothes police take to Greenhead Park over a three-month period, cautioning fifty men and arresting ten others to break what the *Huddersfield Daily Examiner* described as a 'vice ring' enmeshed in 'a web of homosexual activities'.[44] Kees lamented a shift in the tolerant atmosphere of the town in his letter to the *Examiner* and he and others came together to form a Gay Action Group (GAG) to tackle what they saw as new levels of harassment, including men being stopped and questioned, a diary confiscated, verbal abuse and an alleged police cell assault.[45] GAG's coup was the relocation of London's Gay Pride to Huddersfield in July 1981 – drawing 1,500 people from across the country to a march through the town. Many went on afterwards to the 'Carnival Against Racism' organized by the Anti-Nazi League in Leeds' Chapeltown; there was a clear sense for many that these battles against homophobia and racism were connected.[46]

Ajamu was aware of this mobilization as a teenager in Huddersfield before he ventured out himself. In the early 1980s he was a regular at a Black club across the street from the Gemini. He would 'look who was going in'; 'I was just watching', he said. 'And then this one night, March 3rd 1983, a Thursday night, the door opened and I just ran across the main road right into the Gemini

Image 10 Lesbian and Gay Pride in Huddersfield, 1981

Club. And there was only one Black guy there and he became my boyfriend that night.' Ajamu's detailed recall over 30 years later suggests the enduring significance for him of this dash across the street; his subsequent move to the present tense in his testimony underscores it: 'there were lots of white men in leather trousers and white t-shirts. And I'm not coming out with my sexuality, I'm worried, and they're all trying to take my t-shirt off', he said. On a later visit Ajamu met some other Black queer men who were on a night out from Leeds. 'Oh my God', he thought, 'there are more of us out there'.[47]

The Huddersfield scene began to wane around this time. 'Straights [...] started taking over'[48] at the New Amsterdam and the Gemini closed in the 1984 – partly because Mancunians were going out on the reinvigorated club scene in their home city and people from Leeds were often joining them there. Ajamu moved to Chapeltown and enjoyed the queerness of the 'packed', 'pitch black' Afro-Caribbean shebeens like the ones in Spencer Place. It was, he said, 'one of those small town areas; [if you're Black] you don't say "I'm gay"':

> But then the shebeens [there] were kind of diverse and bigger, you could think: 'oh, maybe they might be a sex worker, they might be queer'. It was a mix of Black folks in these spaces. [...] One of the ways that you got a sense of who might be queer was through rumour and gossip. [...] Within Jamaican culture they will say 'he is funny'. And then 'funny' means gay, basically. So I knew then, I'd hear rumours and you then go to the club and see [that particular person] and give a smile.

Ajamu was also part of a small group of Black queer men and women who met every Sunday in each others' homes in Harehills and around 'for food and a chit-chat'. This felt safer than going out on the central Leeds scene and was also more discreet – something that was important to Ajamu because he was living with his girlfriend at the time and 'sleeping with her and then having sex with men'.[49] For gay clubs he went to Manchester with the friends he had made earlier at the Gemini. He also met men there who had advertised in the pen pal section of the *Caribbean Times* ('broad-minded guy seeks friend', the ads would say). The flirting, code and network of different places within and beyond Leeds opened out social and sexual possibilities for Ajamu.

Huddersfield, Manchester and Bradford are mentioned most frequently in the Leeds interviews, but other places figure too. Roy talked about Doncaster and Sheffield, both around 35 miles to the south of Leeds. 'Every month, at Sheffield city hall [from the mid-1970s], there was a gay disco. And the integration between the women and the men, it was fantastic. There was the odd scuffle – usually, a well-oiled dyke could take exception to what some femme queen had said. But it was fantastic interaction', he said. In Doncaster in the late 1970s and early 1980s he described going to the Railway pub: 'On one side [of the bar] there were all the dykes. And every one of them: white shirt, black tie, black suit, black shiny shoes. On the other side were all the femmes, and you'd think something had come back from the 50s and 60s, with all the net skirts.' He met some of the dykes through his work in a local factory: 'talk about the butchest, manliest women you could wish to meet. But the most friendly and down-to-earth.'[50]

By talking up the 'old-fashioned' queer dynamics in these places, Roy highlighted what he felt had by this time been lost in his home city. Paul similarly pointed to the deficiencies of the Leeds scene in his descriptions of Manchester, which was, he said, 'a lot better than Leeds' in the late 1980s and 1990s. 'There weren't as many gay bars then as there are now but it was a lot more fun […] You could just be who you are: […] the excitement of it, somewhere different and being more open than you were in Leeds without the fear of being recognized and calling you a faggot.'[51] There was still fun to be had in the centre of Leeds in the 1980s though. At Rockshots II (the successor to Primos) one man remembers a 'meat-rack row of seats', 'pulsating high energy music' and the 'euphoric aroma' of poppers.[52] It was 'a dingy black hole', said Jane Czyzselska (later editor of *Diva*); 'thrilling and frightening in equal measure'.[53] Banana Bar ran from 1987 to 1994 and Primo's II opened in the early 1990s in nearby Market Chambers. Paul went out on this scene sometimes but 'didn't like admitting [it]'; 'it had a bad reputation'.[54]

MSM: men having sex with men

'If you met someone [in Briggate] and wanted to have some privacy you got the number 12 tram and went to Middleton Woods and then walked back to Leeds. Trams went from Leeds to the middle of the woods!', said one man of his adventures before the Leeds' tram system closed down in 1959 (buses could also get you there after that; its reputation endured).[55] Another man remembered growing up on a large 1960s council estate in east Leeds in the mid-1970s: 'when I was 16, I met a boy about a year younger than me [...] we would take advantage of the countryside on our doorstep to go off and spend time together. We would get an illicit thrill holding hands together as we walked through a farmer's field, never giving much thought that anyone in the nearby tower block would be able to see us!'[56] David remembers 'having sex with other lads' as a twenty-year-old living 'in the sticks' outside Leeds. 'I wasn't aware that it was illegal. I wasn't aware of anything. I was being me. People knew what I was doing but it was in the country and everybody knew I was a poofter.'[57] Young men fooling around were more tolerated in 'the sticks' than in the city at this point, David suggests.

In Leeds itself the council-run Union Street baths gained a reputation before it closed in 1964.[58] Stan's Sauna in the two following decades was geared more specifically towards sex and ran from two terraced houses (with damp carpets) in Marsh Street just to the east of the centre. Public toilets at the station, the Merrion Shopping Centre, and in the suburbs of Stanningley, Morley, Seaford and Guisley featured regularly in court cases.[59] As elsewhere these places were tinged with danger – and especially in the sexual traffic between queer and normal and between younger and older. 'You actually had straight lads having a bit of fun and then they'd beat you up', said David. 'I've been lucky in that respect – yes, I've been knocked about a bit but they don't expect queers to hit back – I do!'[60] Forty-one-year-old poet John Riley was murdered by two men at a toilet in the north Leeds suburb of Chapel Allerton in 1978. 'I got the impression that [Riley] was a queer and that he was giving me the come on', said one of the men in a chilling police statement:

> I went outside and [...] told [Colin, his friend] that there was a puff inside the toilets. The man walked out and straight towards us. We both booted him and I hit him with my fist about five times in the face [...] after we'd finished hitting him [we] decided to put him round the back. We were going to leave him but we just seemed to lose our temper.[61]

'Young and good looking' police, meanwhile, 'pretended to be gay, flashing etc., and then making an arrest' at the Merrion Centre toilets. The man who reported this to *Gay News* had been arrested there and pleaded guilty in court 'out of fear'; he was, though, 'amazed at the lies in the police statement'.[62] Blackmailing cases cropped up in the press well beyond the change in the law in 1967.[63] 'In those days [the 1970s and 1980s] it was older men who were blackmailed and they paid money to keep lads quiet', said David.[64] There was also in these years a cluster of cases of sexual exploitation and teenage prostitution. In an indicator that this endured, MESMAC (the charity working across the region on HIV, AIDS and sexual health from 1990) launched a dedicated project to support survivors in Leeds and Bradford in 1999.[65]

Tales of double lives, discretion and the careful navigation of bars, sex sites, home and workplace recur in relation to Leeds; more men were 'on the down low' (as Ajamu put it) here than in Brighton. Police investigating the murder of a Bradford postman in 1992 described their 'softly softly approach' in interviewing men in their 'haunts': 'many of them are married, in good jobs and keeping their homosexuality secret', said the case detective.[66] When MESMAC was founded in 1990, it deliberately avoided sexuality labels, instead adopting the acronym to stand for Men Who Have Sex with Men: Action in the Community. This approach was explicitly rejected in 1995 by the Zorro Project in Brighton where men who had sex with men were more likely to identify as gay.

Race, class, religion, relative wealth and mobility were all important factors in the ways people engaged in the central and wider sex and social scenes. Paul and Ajamu both felt uncomfortable in central Leeds – on account, respectively, of being visibly gay and Black. Paul was left unconscious and sustained two broken eye sockets in an attack after leaving a gay bar there in 1997; Ajamu feared racist assault on the streets and objectification in the gay pubs.[67] Women (and especially lesbians) were not welcome in bars here either while men were not allowed at most of the lesbian nights elsewhere in the city in the late 1970s and first half of the 1980s. Early signs of trans networks and support faltered at this point too, leaving many feeling excluded until a shift in the 2010s. A university postgraduate student and a local Beaumont Society organizer were behind 'Transvestites and Transexualism in Modern Society', a conference at Leeds University in 1974 billed as the first trans conference in the UK.[68] It brought together over a hundred trans people, medics and journalists for daytime discussion and more for a disco in the evening. A TV/TS support group had a Headingley postal address at around this time but with no trace thereafter, and at the St James Hospital in Harehills, with its reputation for plastic surgery, surgeon Philip Snaith was carrying out pioneering gender reassignments and associated comportment and speech therapy in the 1970s and

1980s.[69] It was, though, the tragic death post-surgery of a bus driver who travelled to Leeds from Northern Ireland for their operation that made the news in 1980. Sporadic reports in the local, national and trans press in the early to mid-1980s – of a trans burglar, a suicide, a wedding between two trans people and cancelled reassignment surgery – suggested trans isolation rather than community in Leeds, or else a desire to pass as normal outside queer circles. [70] The woman whose operation was cancelled described how she just wanted to 'find a partner', 'settle down' and 'have a child', for example.[71] Meanwhile the particular strands of feminism gaining traction in Leeds at this time could make it hard for trans people to be part of feminist and lesbian networks. 'Because of the lesbian culture at the time lesbians who might have had feelings around being trans, would not have revealed that', said Jude; 'it would have been quite risky'.[72] Lynn remembers how 'the lesbian community were really unsettled [when] men who became trans then wanted to be lesbian […] because of the history that they had come with'. 'They'd grown up as a man. And so experienced patriarchy', she said.[73] In the early 2000s Jasmine, who transitioned with the support of her wife in her early thirties, found that there were still few resources for trans people in Leeds or West Yorkshire. She would travel instead to Manchester for support at the 'absolutely amazing' Metropolitan Community Church there.[74] People of faith like Jasmine or some of the Muslim men MESMAC were working with may meanwhile have felt out of place on the decidedly secular gay and lesbian scenes in the city.

Sexual discretion remained important into the 2000s. When the Steam Complex opened in the western suburb of Armley in 2007 (see Map 4) the owners were asked only to admit gay men on account, the police said, of the position of the sauna in a 'Muslim area' with a local 'criminal fraternity'. The owners countered that it might not only be avowedly gay men that used the sauna, and moreover that gay and bisexual men might also be Muslim or indeed criminals. Leeds residents were said by the owners to be 'less likely to use the venue' than men from Manchester or Birmingham; men from Leeds might meanwhile travel in the opposite direction, 'preferring to use a venue outside their home city'.[75] The advertising for the central Basement Sauna in the 2000s meanwhile noted that trains to Manchester, Huddersfield and Dewsbury ran all night from nearby Leeds Station, and that the sauna had a discreet rear entrance. A MESMAC sexual health worker identified such discretion as particularly important to the South Asian men he talked to there. They tended, he said, not to identify as either gay or bisexual and also to avoid the sauna at peak 'gay' times – after pub and club closing.[76] Strong family networks, traditions and expectations might continue to militate against visible gay or bi identities, as also in family-oriented white working-class communities in Plymouth.[77] In response, MESMAC launched the Sholay Love sexual health project from 2018 aimed specifically at this group, taking its name from the famously camp, homoerotic Bollywood movie.[78]

Making a scene: gay, lesbian and feminist politics

Lesbian and gay

Leeds GLF gained some early publicity with a feature piece in the *Yorkshire Evening Post* in 1971. The hook was an interview with 'John', a 'shy' scientist living in Headingley. Speaking under an assumed name and striking a less than strident tone, 'John' described how he wanted to establish a group which was a 'secure' place for gay people to meet each other, and which would give them the confidence 'to go out and tell people that they are gay'.[79] There were initially around thirty people in the group (mainly men, mainly students) and they met in a Christian Centre near the University. It was a revelation for those involved. After his conservative upbringing on the south coast, Patrick's politics switched: 'I was absolutely bowled over [...] I thought this was marvellous.'[80] As a sixteen-year-old, Roy found in the GLF a way 'out of my prison, which was my home life'. He 'burst out of his shell' in a university rag week parade in 1971 distributing leaflets proclaiming 'gay is good'. According to local and national press reports, parents were 'outraged' at such 'filth', especially as one had apparently been 'thrust' into the hand of a twelve-year-old boy.[81] Though the GLF issued an apology ('incidents of this nature give us a bad name', a spokesperson told the *Yorkshire Evening Post*),[82] the group subsequently hit a more robust stride. There was a campaign 'to tell people about homosexuality', said Patrick:

> We produced these leaflets, and we decided we'd leaflet the big council estates [...] So we organized parties of people to go to Middleton, to Halton Moor, which was considered quite a rough estate in those days. [...] And we spent about five days leafleting. [...] And then at the end of that week, we'd organize a public meeting.[83]

There was in this a concerted attempt to educate as well as to protest – something the group also did a lot. They joined the CHE in picketing the Great Northern Hotel after it excluded gays and lesbians from the Buccaneer Bar in 1973. *Gay News* reported the 'neurotic fury' of the hotel manager and the arrests of protestors who were later acquitted because the police 'made up their notes'.[84]

A year later, GLFers led by radical author Don Milligan wearing 'a long blue slit-legged velvet dress embroidered with sequins' stormed the British Medical Association congress on 'Sexual Problems' at Bradford University.[85]

Awareness of the issues at stake in gay liberation grew as a result of these actions and Student Union engagement, as well as a vibrant local theatre and arts scene. *Union News*, the student paper, had made a pitch for tolerance of the 'one in twenty' in its coverage of the Hope and Anchor in 1968, and over the following decade the Student Union provided space for a Gay Centre, Gay Switchboard and Lesbian Line. It also hosted performances by theatre groups Gay Sweatshop (from 1975) and Bradford-based General Will (from 1971).[86] Yvonne recalls the impact of a General Will production of *Present Your Briefs:* '[It] actually made me go more into politics of sexuality and feminism rather than the general politics of working conditions and all that kind of stuff [...] Them plays brought a change in my head and considering the number of people who started going to GLF meetings it must have turned a switch on in other people's heads as well.'[87]

There was a heated debate in the letters pages of the *Yorkshire Evening Post* in April 1974 after the university's Young Liberals demanded that homosexuality be included in the sex education curriculum of Leeds schools.[88] Alongside a carefully argued letter of support from the local GLF, and others from the predictably outraged, was one from a 'worker teacher' at the Leeds Free School, which, like those in Manchester and Brighton, sought from the late 1960s to provide an alternative to the 'hierarchical' state school system. There was a need, this correspondent wrote, to 'build up an honest knowledge of ourselves and each other' and 'refuse to pass on the corruption of guilt on homosexuality'.[89]

The Free School intervention signals how sexuality was often woven into wider countercultural debate and politics in the city in this period.[90] This was clear too in *Leeds Other Paper* (1974 to 1991) which brought different groups, causes and campaigns into oblique conversation. Its 'Out in the North' section detailed lesbian and gay venues and events in Leeds and nearby towns and cities. 'The Women's Centre Newsletter', 'Medusa' (a lesbian feminist poetry and creative writing newsletter from 1979) and other alternative publications similarly connected feminist, lesbian and anti-racist politics across the 1970s and 1980s. These could all be found in the local alternative bookshops – Fourth Idea in Bradford's Southgate (1975–1982) and the Corner Bookshop on Woodhouse Lane near Leeds University (1976–1987). These places, plus the students' unions, the women's and gay centres, Fat Freddie's café in a bright pink shed by the railway in the centre and Cutting Camp, a hairdressers displaying pink and black triangles in the window of its Hyde Park salon, were visible queer alternatives in Leeds'. Fat Freddie's was popular with 'artists, punks and druids' in the 1980s and early 1990s,[91] and Ray remembers thinking when he first saw the window display at Cutting Camp that 'there isn't anything like this in any other city in the country. Nothing that's so overtly saying: "we're gay and we're here".' Jude remembers them 'singing and dancing when they were cutting hair' – rehearsing numbers from their wryly named rock band Dorothy's Cottage perhaps.[92] Hairdressers, at least here and in Brighton, turned out to be significant places for queer connection and community.

These places and the networks associated with them formed a bedrock for reaction against the strong National Front presence in Bradford and Leeds. 'The [National Front] was something that brought a lot of people together [in opposition]', said Yvonne. 'Really the only people who supported our community were the Black community and the only people who supported them were us and so like a very close link developed in the seventies, ad hoc, not official', she said. Huddersfield Pride marchers converged on the Carnival Against Racism in 1981, the Black and West Indian Cultural Centre in Manningham rented rooms out for a weekly lesbian night and Chapeltown's reggae pubs often had a queer mix. Yvonne remembers, 'fellas who used to run the Black clubs' in Lumb Lane in Bradford turning up to General Will productions with a barrel of beer. 'There was this one old guy […] called Tiger, your typical sort of calypso, in his sixties, lovely fella, and after a play he'd get up and make a little speech about how we've all got to stick together.'[93] There was a sustained Anti-Nazi League campaign which involved plastering posters of teddy bears proffering anti-racist and gay and women's liberation messages across the two cities. The bears were meant to signal a peaceful pushback against the National Front, whose members ransacked (in 1973) and then burned down (in 1977) the gay centre in the annex of Leeds Student Union. 'Leeds ultra-right wing group have finally achieved their aim of driving gays from their base in Woodhouse Lane', reported the Student Union newspaper.[94] A year later 'a dozen young men wearing [National Front] badges' assaulted the GLF group drinking in the Fenton pub, part blinding one man.[95] The Corner Bookshop and Fourth Idea were attacked in the same year. The Gay Switchboard and Lesbian Line office went unharmed possibly because it was out of sight nearby in 'a really grotty basement […] underneath the university'.[96] Abuse came over the phone, though: 'we worked seven nights a week from 7 o'clock to 9 o'clock', said Ted; 'we were available for people to ring us up and also ring us up and abuse us, tell us what poofs and perverts we were'.[97]

The initial intention was that the switchboard would cater to gays and lesbians, but there was a strong feeling that women should know that they could call and speak to another woman. Some had 'terrible, terrible stories', remembers volunteer Julie: it was important, she said, to 'recogniz[e] that gay men's agenda [wa]s not our agenda'.[98] And so from 1978, Leeds Lesbian Line ran for one evening a week sustained in part by fundraising discos at Dock Green. This split led to tension – both in terms of the division of resources and the way some gay male callers felt they were treated if they called on a Tuesday. Patrick 'heard quite a few stories that if they rang up on Tuesday, they really got a bollocking from the women'.[99] Lesley said that men were 'politely asked to ring on another night' and underscored the importance of holding this space for lesbians: 'the fact that we had one night and they had six nights meant that those two hours were kind of precious'.[100] Leeds was not unique in having separate gay and lesbian phone advice and information lines, or having split gender groups, bars and socializing. There was, though, more rancour over such division than in the other cities and a deeper rift between men and women. This relates to the particular trajectory of the women's movement here.

Feminism and lesbianism

A Women's Liberation group first met at a house on Linda Street near to the university in 1969. They sent a delegation to the first Women's Liberation Conference at Ruskin College, Oxford, in February 1970,[101] and from then on support and campaigning groups proliferated. The Northern Women's Education Group in the city from 1971 'linked women right across the big northern cities';[102] Women's Aid, Rape Crisis and Justice for Women were set up soon after.[103] Many volunteers already identified as lesbian; others came out in the course of their involvement with these groups and also in workshops and conferences in the city and beyond. Lesley remembers the Women's Sexuality Conference in Leeds in 1978 being especially significant:

> There was a lesbian workshop, a straight workshop, which nobody went to, and a bisexual workshop. There were these sort of heavy-looking lesbians in the lesbian workshop, and about thirty women all went into the bisexual workshop. But within a year, I think, about half of those women had actually kind of gone through the process of coming out. […] Then from that event […] they set up three consciousness-raising groups. The Monday group, Tuesday group and Wednesday group […]. Those groups, I think, helped women to continue that process of exploring politics, feminism, sexuality and everything. […] After that, the floodgates were open.[104]

The Leeds Revolutionary Feminist Group argued the case for political lesbianism and lesbian and feminist separatism at the tenth Women's Liberation Conference in Birmingham in 1978 and a year later in a piece for *WIRES* – the newsletter established for information sharing at the national WLM conference in Manchester in 1975 and produced by a collective in Leeds until 1977 (and thereafter in nearby York). All feminists, the piece argued, should be lesbians – whether sexually active with other women or not; women who slept with men were 'collaborators with the enemy'.[105] Tina, who moved to Leeds to go to university in 1977, remembers that many of the women involved were 'ex-heterosexuals': 'they had a kind of, a baggage, right, which I didn't, I wasn't bothered about that. But it was also like, we sit around going on about violence against women, this and that, and why would anybody want to have anything to do with these bastards? So that was the kind of trajectory I suppose.'[106]

This was taking place in the context of Peter Sutcliffe's horrific attacks and murders of women in Leeds and its hinterland. Wilma McCann, from Scott Hall in Leeds, was the first woman he killed in 1975; his thirteenth and final victim was Leeds University student Jacqueline Hill in 1980. Women's mutual support and activism became urgent, especially with the victim blaming and denigration of sex workers by the press and police. Al noted that 'we didn't [campaign] because of Peter Sutcliffe but it […] certainly gave a focus'. 'You either became very afraid, or you got angry. And I suppose the fear fuelled the anger', said Lou.[107] Women came together in Reclaim the Night marches in the city from 1977 and three years later Women Against Violence Against Women (WAVAW) was founded here.[108] 'More people joined WAVAW than might have in another city. So of course [Sutcliffe had] an impact, and it meant that authorities were more inclined to take it seriously and make provisions'.[109] Neither Reclaim the Night nor WAVAW were specifically lesbian but many women describe these and other initiatives in Leeds being part of a shift in the way they saw their sexuality and identity. In 1984, WAVAW protested at graphic and degrading representations of women at the Polytechnic Art Gallery by smashing windows and some of the artworks.[110] A subgroup, the Angry Women, were allegedly involved in arson attacks on seventeen sex shops in the city in 1983. These actions were covered in the international feminist press; 'Hot Lesbian Put in Cooler' ran the headline of one piece in New York's *Womannews* after the arrest of the women allegedly involved.[111]

Leeds feminists by now had a wider reputation for strident activism in the face of male violence and also for a thoroughgoing women-only resource and support network. One local initiative was the university's women's minibus service which provided safe transport for women students. It was the first of its kind in the country and was launched partly because of the fall in the number of female university applicants in the context of the serial murders. 'It was very much a lesbian-organized service', Ruth remembers. 'I just remember a tape that was played in the women's minibus many times. It was: "any woman can be a lesbian, there's no penis between us friends. Any woman can be a lesbian". We used to go around playing these tapes. It was quite clear, the sexual orientation of the drivers of the minibus for many years.' This was a further way of making social and political connections:

> We were giving out information about the Lesbian Line and about events that were happening. And some of those were, you know, video nights at my house or somebody else's house. So we had *Desert Hearts* nights, things like that. *Killing of Sister George*.[112]

The particular strength of feminist networks in Leeds fed a drive to live out this politics – both in terms of the relationships women were having and also family, work and domestic lives.[113] Women's Centre newsletters in the 1980s advertised a range of weekly activities – usually including at least one women-only disco, a political or artistic workshop, and special meetings (of a women's anti-racist or young lesbians group, for example).[114] The radical arts scene grew in relation to all this activity. Leeds Animation Workshop (from 1976) and Video Vera (from 1981) ensured strong feminist and lesbian representation in the wider upsurge in radical collective film-making in Leeds.[115] In 1983 in Woodhouse Moor near the university the pavilion was converted into a collectively run centre for feminist and lesbian artists and photographers. 'There was a lot going on [at the Pavilion Gallery]', remembers Jude:

> And we'd have discos there. There was a lot of work with girls at that time, a lot of lesbians were working with girls in girls' groups. And we had a lot of photography projects linked to that, as well as in a lot of working-class communities. [We were] using photography as a tool around empowerment, promoting political awareness and understanding.[116]

Ruth recalls 'a sort of creativity and artistry, that was about being out [in Leeds]'.[117]

Leeds' creative and radical feminist politics drew women to the city and allowed 'everything [to be] women only' by the early 1980s. 'We didn't engage with men', Miriam said, 'and I don't really understand how we managed that. But we were big enough to do that. I mean there were some tame men, in sandals and with long hair, on the fringes somewhere […] but actually all of our attention was focused on women, and it was quite separatist really, one way or another.' The Women's Education Movement in Leeds and Bradford trained female mechanics, plumbers and carpenters. East Leeds Women's Workshop was set up on Harehills Lane in 1981 to train women for jobs traditionally done by men and in specific response to the closure of Burton's tailoring factory in the late 1970s (part of the broader decline of the textile and clothing industry in Leeds). Some of the big houses on Sholebroke Avenue became (see Map 4) feminist and lesbian squats, co-ops and housing association houses. 'Chapeltown always had quite a big feminist community, basically because it's cheap, inner-city, and had these big old houses that you could live in collectively', said Miriam. 'The geography of the city made quite a big difference. […] [It] shaped the politics in a city like Leeds.'[118]

Women's nights had reduced rates for those with children and there were collectively run crèches and shared childcare. In the early 1980s there was controversy over admitting boys to separatist crèches, but then 'women started having boy babies, [so] that was the end of that discussion'.[119] This was around the time children from earlier heterosexual relationships were joined by others conceived through artificial insemination networks. A go-between in Headingley ferried sperm from willing donors (including from members of an anti-sexist men's group) to lesbians who wanted to conceive – an arrangement 'exposed' by the local press in 1983.[120] Jude knew of twenty children conceived in this way in her circle of friends alone.[121] Alison explores some of these and other home and family arrangements in Chapter 6.

Many women from Leeds travelled across the UK and beyond for women's conferences and events. Lou went to Lancashire, London and Edinburgh – sharing lifts and sleeping on floors. Al set up a Women's Holiday Centre at Horton in the Yorkshire dales, about an hour and half's drive from Leeds. 'It was just a place, really, to get together, for women and children without much money to get away from men. Get our own space, recharge the batteries. It was really important to do that', she said.[122] Ruth was involved in women's projects in Liverpool, Bradford and internationally, and like others from Leeds and indeed Brighton, Manchester and Plymouth, took part in the Greenham Common peace camp in Wiltshire. The friendships and contacts that led her to these places and causes originated for Ruth in Leeds – though not its male-dominated city centre scene where she had made early forays from Wakefield.

This social and political network was far from harmonious. Class and its relation to different strands of feminism was often at issue, with a particular value placed by some on working-class roots. Julie described 'feminists from every single split-hair strand':

> You'd have the squatters who lived on Sholebroke Avenue, who were really involved in working-class politics, then you'd have some of the socialist feminists, then you'd have just some of the liberal feminists, some of the lifestyle radical cultural feminists, the vegetarians, you know, the 'If we live life like this, we'll move the revolution on apace'. And then you had the revolutionary feminists, who were more focused on an analysis of male power.[123]

Julie noted and also reproduced some of the judgements associated with class in her testimony: 'They decided that I was middle-class', she remembers, 'probably because I was a revolutionary feminist and that wasn't the way you should be, you should live at Sholebroke Avenue, squatting, with horrible snotty nosed babies and hanging used sanitary towels on the back of the toilet door [laughter], to signify you're a proper working class woman.'[124]

Though for many there was a feeling of liberation and rupture from constrictive norms in Leeds at this time, Rachel felt that there was 'a lot of pressure on gay women to be [...] separatist'. Gilda agreed: 'there was always an aggressive element to Leeds [...] what I recollect [is a] butchy gay [saying] "you're the traitors". There was an aggressive element to that.'[125] Sarah, describing her involvement in Women's Liberation in Bradford, remembers hearing 'about the horrors of Leeds': 'there was this massive, awful thing about, not only had you got to be a lesbian but you had to be a working-class lesbian as well'.[126] There was, she said, a divide between the two cities: 'when I came to Bradford, you never mentioned Leeds [...] there was always this impression that the women's movement there was, they were more into intellectualising politics and everything, whereas we felt we were more into doing things'.[127] The Bradford Dykes group had a particular 'impatience with feminist theory' and their split with gay men came later there than in Leeds; the GLF remained significant for women like Yvonne for longer. [128]

The trajectory of Leeds feminism fundamentally shaped lesbian life in the city for the women directly involved and for others too. Some women describe this period and their experiments in living as exciting and transformatory. Al moved here partly because of its 'thriving political atmosphere' and quickly found a sense of belonging beyond her family ties in the north. It was harder for others and some moved away to less pressured lesbian communities in Bradford and also Todmorden and Hebden Bridge further west (see Map 5). Trans people in the city could, as I've said, feel especially excluded in this context. 'I don't think it can be underestimated the pain sometimes caused to people who were trans and to the women as well', said Ruth, reflecting back. Meanwhile, although some gay men in the city saw themselves as lesbian feminist allies, the gender split here was more pronounced than elsewhere. 'There were no women [in CHE ...] – we were apart', said Roy, and Patrick saw a similar pattern in the local GLF:

> It was probably sort of fairly heavily male-dominated. One of the feelings, not unreasonable, from a lot of lesbians was that gay men's groups didn't particularly involve themselves at all in any women's issues. Whether it's abortion rights, custody rights, anything like that. [...] Whereas on some of the legal issues, lesbians were supporting [the men].[129]

David insisted in interview that 'the male gay community need to know that it was the lesbians who led the way [in terms of equality]. It's the lesbians who fetched us in and then it was male chauvinism that drove us apart.'[130]

'Town hall feminism' and Section 28

The feminist movement in Leeds helped shift the tenor of local government in the 1980s. There was an active women's committee from 1985 which championed women's rights and to an extent lesbian issues. 'We managed as lesbians [...] to get some resources because it was under the women's banner. That's how we wangled it', said Jude.[131] Cerydwen remembers that the women's committee 'was powerful, it had money, it had resources, and it had influence'.[132] Miriam welcomed this. With mainstream funding Leeds' feminism became, to her, 'a bit less whingey and weird'.[133] Julie, on the other hand, saw it heralding 'the demise of the type of feminism where you could live on unemployment benefit and do your activism sort of stuff. [...] Pretty much activism as we knew it was gone, and these women got jobs in town halls, doing their feminism in paid work time and very much on the soft end of the equal opportunities stuff [...] and it got to the point where I thought, "I'm just not engaging with this".'[134] With the rise of 'town hall feminism' 'it became more difficult to do community organized feminist conferences, because people's expectations were higher', said Sandra.[135]

The feminist work of the council was predictably not without its detractors. There was opposition from Conservative councillors amid wider national 'concern' about the 'loony left' and political correctness. The 1984 women's committee directive against pin-ups of women in council offices and against lesbian discrimination 'opened the council to ridicule', according to the only male member of the women's committee, Conservative Councillor Keith Loudon.[136] In what the national *Mirror* newspaper described as one 'granny's war on "gay girls"', Councillor Iris Favell battled what she saw as the council's 'gay agenda' and associated nefarious activities (two women snogging) in the city hall.[137] There was further councillor and letter-page opposition to small grants and then to the more substantial £67,000 1985 plan for a gay and lesbian centre in Kirkstall, the suburb to the south-west of Headingley. Kirkstall Labour Party passed a motion of support; locals interviewed on the street by the *Yorkshire Post* didn't object so long as there was no cost to rate payers.[138] The proposal was ultimately turned down and a year later in 1986 Labour 'moderates' on the council derailed plans to follow Manchester's lead in appointing lesbian and

Gay rights protesters flock outside Leeds College of Music as Clause 28 materialised yesterday.

Gay demo held over college row

HOMOSEXUAL rights demonstrators protested outside Leeds College of Music yesterday in a row between its director and its recently-formed Lesbian and Gay Society.

The 30 to 40 demonstrators were also voicing opposition to Section 28 of the Local Government Act which came into force yesterday, prohibiting local councils from promoting homosexuality.

The row began more than two months ago after Mr Joseph Stones was accused of trying to ban the society from the college by forbidding it to advertise on general notice boards or meet there except in common rooms or the Students' Union office.

Mr Stones has acknowledged that he does not want its posters on general notice boards, which he believes will be seen by children. He denies any attempt to ban the society from the college. He has suggested that it has only two members, its chairman and treasurer, Mr Clive Spendlove and Ms Madeline Holloway.

Police said the two-hour demonstration passed peacefully. Protesters handed out leaflets.

Mr Stones said that at most only two were students there. He denied saying he intended to sue the society for its allegations, which appeared in a student newspaper, but said he was taking legal advice.

● The BBC announced yesterday that it would make a "slight change" in security measures following Monday's invasion of the Six O'Clock News studio by four lesbian protesters. It is expected to increase scrutiny of callers at Television Centre in Shepherd's Bush.

Background — P.9.

Image 11 Leeds College of Music protest, 1988

gay officers and committees. 'The council was scared stiff, sadly', said Patrick; 'in the 80s, Leeds, compared with Manchester, was way behind'.[139]

Amid the intensifying debate about the 'exposure' of children to homosexuality in the run-up to the passing of Clause 28, the principal of Leeds College of Music (near the university) tried to ban the college's lesbian and gay group from advertising on the noticeboard and from meeting anywhere other than in the student common room. In a piece in the *Yorkshire Post* he protested that children frequently came into the college for music lessons and might see the group's publicity. 'Homosexuals', he said, 'are not doing themselves any good by going around waving banners saying "I am homosexual"'.[140] In the same year, Austin Allen, teacher and chair of Bradford Lesbian and Gay Switchboard, was dismissed from two consecutive supply teaching posts for 'coming out' to students. A local Conservative councillor demanded clear guidelines in the light of the case and the coming clause; meanwhile, Allen's colleagues at the Grange School in Bradford threatened strike action if he was not reinstated – as he ultimately was (the local education authority was relatively supportive in this case and others too, according to Ted).[141]

There was push back against Clause 28 and wider homophobia from various quarters. The *Bradford Telegraph and Argus* theatre critic drew the measure into his review of *Kiss of the Spider Woman* in 1988, questioning whether such productions could survive at publicly funded venues like the Bradford Playhouse.[142] Bradford Central Library pointedly provided space for an exhibition on the history of the local Gay Switchboard just as Clause 28 was coming into force.[143] In Leeds, Jude remembers internal dissent: 'the council sent out a directive to all council staff about Section 28, which basically said: "watch yourself, be careful, don't be seen to be promoting homosexuality". And I know a lot of council workers who received that just said, "well, that's a load of shit, I'm not going to follow that".'[144] A call from Conservative councillors in Leeds for the auditors to be called in to determine if a £100 grant to a lesbian group was in breach of the legislation got nowhere.[145]

If some felt wider communal activism had waned during the years of 'town hall feminism', Clause 28 reignited it. Women Against the Clause organized a march through the centre, drawing a mixed crowd of between 2,500 and 4,000 people (estimates varied) and including some new to activism. 'If I ever "came out" it was with about 4,000 other people one Saturday morning, here in Leeds. [...] I marched down the Headrow [a main city street lined with some of the city's grand civic buildings] demanding gay rights much to my own surprise', said Ted.[146] Cerydwen remembers 'walking with men for the first time' at the protest. 'That was the first time I had actually been in a room with men, where we were talking about joint efforts about being lesbian and gay, that was new and scary.'[147] Jude saw it as the start of more collaborative activist and support work – around Clause 28, HIV and AIDS (including a local ACT UP group) and also other specific campaigns. Two hundred men and women came to a public meeting Jude chaired at the town hall in support of the sixteen men imprisoned in 1991 for having sadomasochistic sex together in a house near Manchester in the so-called Operation Spanner case. The mix at the meeting was because it 'was sort of post-Clause 28', said Jude.[148] This became more the norm. The biannual Victor-Victoria costume balls were, said Cerydwen, 'huge events […] significant not just in their scale […] but because they were with men. It was new.'[149] The Pink Picnic held annually on Woodhouse Moor near the Pavilion Art Gallery in the early 1990s was similarly mixed; separatism in the city had passed.

The later 1990s saw the emergence of mixed social, sports and arts groups and projects in Leeds – including the Lavender Café orchestra (from 1992), Yorkshire Terriers football club (1997) and two choirs (Gay Abandon, 1997; and LGB Inclusive Choir, 1999). It was around this time that the areas adjacent to Leeds railway station – Lower Briggate and the Calls – began to gentrify. City centre living was becoming generally fashionable again and new and converted warehouse apartments near the station appealed especially to those who were travelling to and from London because of their work in Leeds' growing financial and legal sectors.[150] Trendy bars and restaurants followed as did new and somewhat more mixed gay venues like Queen's Court and Bar Fibre. The more male-dominated Viaduct followed the glass-fronted trend of Canal Street in Manchester and Soho in London. In 2012 Wharf Street Chambers, an anti-capitalist workers' co-operative began operating in an old hosiery factory nearby and partly in reaction to the local commercial gay scene. Discussion and support groups met here and it gained a particular reputation as a safe and welcoming space for trans and gender queer people in the city, somewhat like the Cowley Club in Brighton. It hosted club nights Love Muscle, borrowing the name of the infamous Brixton Fridge night in London in the 1990s, and BE LGBTQ which boasted 'New York c.1980 and eclectic contemporary Shoreditch sounds'.[151] These parties traded in the iconic 'alternative' status of these other times and places as well as the transatlantic traffic in queer culture and music.

A range of groups met at MESMAC's base in Blayd's Yard in this area – including Action for Trans Health, Non-binary Leeds and Gendered

Intelligence, three of at least six trans support and social groups that have emerged in the city since 2010. Health services for trans people in the city have also improved with the launch of the Gender Identity Clinic at the Seacroft Hospital in east Leeds (reportedly under strain by 2015 because of growing demand).[152] Leeds Council supports an LGBTQ umbrella organization which brings together these and other commercial and community groups for a quarterly meeting at the Cosmopolitan Hotel in Lower Briggate. And Pride has been celebrated annually in this area since 2006, drawing crowds of around 40,000 from the city and well beyond. It has very clearly become Leeds' queer hub again and there is a sense of return in this, even though the shape and dimensions of community have shifted dramatically since the 1960s. In the years in between Leeds' queer life flourished mostly beyond this part of the city – in the suburbs and satellite towns and cities and through social and political networks converging in people's homes, community centres and the upstairs rooms of 'regular' pubs and clubs. 'The scene was always underground in Leeds', said Ajamu, and as a result for people like Colin, from Plymouth, 'if you said a gay city, Leeds would not have come to mind at all'.[153] That the queer scene here was less visible until recently does not diminish its significance to those who were involved, however; for many women especially it was utterly transformative.

3

Gay and civic pride in 'Madchester'

Image 12 Paradise Factory's 8th birthday, 18 May 2001

In 1966, a young man standing on a central Manchester street corner caught the eye of journalist Barbara McDonald. He was wearing make-up and had dyed blond hair – a look sufficiently arresting for her to stop and record an impromptu interview with him. The man was unapologetic: he told her he was waiting for his boyfriend and that, yes, he was a homosexual. 'I'm quite happy with the fact', he said, adding that he was lucky because 'where I work they know and they don't mind. If I tried to hide it would mean I was ashamed of it.'[1] Earlier in the 1960s, Luchia heard about the 'pansies' who drank at the

New Union pub. 'I stood on Canal Street looking at all these people going in and out […] I saw men dressed up as women and vice versa […] I'd never seen anything like it in my life.' She plucked up the courage to go in and found a new 'family' there.[2] Another group of homosexuals was gathered together by former Labour councillor Allan Horsfall at Church House in Salford in 1964 for the inaugural meeting of the North-Western Homosexual Law Reform Society (NWHLRS).[3] Paul Fairweather, who was the first gay men's officer at the 'loony left' Manchester City Council (MCC) from 1984, placed Horsfall in a longer lineage – 'of Peterloo [… and] the Pankhursts'. 'There is a sense', he said, 'of Manchester as a radical centre.'[4]

These stories capture some of the straightforwardness and solidarity which interviewees frequently associated with being Mancunian and being a queer Mancunian.[5] They harked back to strident CHE, GLF and anti-Clause 28 campaigns in the city; to the LGBT+ Centre which, under different guises, has run uninterrupted since the mid-1970s; and to the solidly Labour council which pushed a radical equalities agenda from the following decade. And they refer to the cutting-edge music, dance, theatre and drag scenes which played out in old warehouses, factory buildings, pubs and clubs – what sociologist Katie Milestone has described as a particular local 'working class Bohemianism' in the city.[6] The gay village from the late 1980s, the TV series *Queer as Folk* (1999–2000) and ever-growing annual Pride festivals have meanwhile put Manchester decisively on a national and international gay map. Mancunian 'spirit' and 'cheekiness' are writ large in accounts of 'upstart' LGBTQ life in a city large enough to have lots going on but, '[unlike] London', small enough to be 'completely manageable'.[7]

In this chapter I explore the multifaceted queer story of this post-industrial city in three main sections. 'Northern Soul' charts overlapping queer, trans, lesbian and gay social, political and sexual scenes in the 1960s and 1970s. 'Safe Spaces and Battle Lines' is about draconian policing and the concerted resistance it provoked and also about the council's pro-lesbian and gay work from 1984 which helped fuse civic and gay pride here. The final section, 'Shifting Scenes', explores the dynamics of the UK's first gay village and the alternative scene that grew up around and in reaction to it in the late 1990s and 2000s. Each section speaks to particular experiences in the city at different moments, but together they help to marshal something of the collective sense of what it means to be a queer Mancunian.

Northern soul: queer Manchester in the 1960s and 1970s

Setting the scene

Manchester was a proudly working-class city in the 1960s: 47 per cent of men worked in manufacturing in 1961, 12 per cent above the national average. The sector was in decline, however, and, with central slum clearance, the city's population was shrinking – falling dramatically from 661,791 in 1961 to 379,529 in 1991 before beginning to grow again (the wider Greater Manchester area was steadier – fluctuating around the 2.4 million mark over the same period).[8] Ideas of local working-class stoicism, grit and community were tenacious and related to an industrial and radical past and present.

The early TV soap *Coronation Street*, set in a fictionalized Salford (Manchester's twin city just across the River Irwell), entrenched these 'northern' qualities in the minds of a national audience. It was filmed in the vast new Granada Studios constructed on the western edge of the city centre in 1953. The studios provided some economic ballast as the mills and factories closed and were an early sign, for good or ill, that the city was modernizing. There were other indicators too. High-rise council blocks replaced dilapidated terraces in some of the inner suburbs in the late 1950s and 1960s; a multi-storey car park went up behind Canal Street in the early 1960s, conveniently adjacent to the already queerly notorious New Union. A motorway (now the M60) opened in 1960 encircling Manchester and Salford and easing access to the satellite towns of Middleton, Oldham, Ashton-under-Lyne, Stockport and Bolton (see Map 5). This new motorway, plus the five city centre stations (two of which subsequently closed), meant Manchester was, like Leeds, a well-connected place in the 1960s. Unlike Leeds, though, it was the rough, hollowed out industrial centre rather than the suburbs and hinterlands which became key to queer life here.

Manchester in the postwar years was known for its cinemas and dance halls. Northern Soul took hold at the Twisted Wheel in Brazennose Street near the town hall; Calypso played at the Reno in Hulme, the inner suburb to the south, which, with neighbouring Moss Side, were areas of Afro-Caribbean immigration from the 1950s. Youth culture was thriving in this city, and, as in Brighton, was causing concern. The *Bolton Evening News* noted that Manchester's coffee shops were becoming night-time magnets for dissolute teenagers. 'Such moral decadence [in] the city tonight, happens in the small towns [like Bolton] tomorrow', it warned ominously.[9] From 1959 a new chief police constable of Manchester, John McKay, initiated a crackdown on such 'antisocial' people and the places they frequented. Afro-Caribbean immigrants and queer men were particular targets. There were just three prosecutions for male–male importuning in Manchester in the four years prior to McKay's appointment – the result, according to the new chief constable, of a deliberate and misguided policy of non-engagement. In the four years that followed the total was 506.[10]

Police routinely put queer venues under surveillance and brought charges for lewd dancing or other licensing infringements. They would 'turn up to try and sort out who was gay and who wasn't' at the Trafford Bar of the 'lush' 1930s Gaumont Cinema on Oxford Road in central Manchester (see Map 6) where 'half the blokes were wearing make-up' and some spoke polari (the queer argot associated more with the London theatre scene).[11] Double doors led from the Trafford into the Long Bar, which was popular with American servicemen stationed until the early 1960s at Burtonwood some 20 miles to the west of the city; there was almost certainly some social and sexual mixing between the two groups as there was in Plymouth. The Trafford Bar itself retained its queer gloss and the attendant interest of the police until the cinema closed in 1974.[12] The police were also on the case of the two landlords who began running the Rembrandt Hotel on nearby Canal Street as a queer venue from 1962: they found themselves in court and fined for running a disorderly house in 1965. The landlord of the neighbouring New Union was jailed in the same year for allowing his pub 'to become a canker at the heart of this great city'. The court heard that he had 'exploit[ed] abnormality for personal gain' and allowed 'men dressed as women' to 'writhe in a sexy way' on stage and to tell 'filthy jokes'.[13] Luchia remembers the drag queens there too but tells a very different story about this landlord who, with his wife, had welcomed and supported her when she arrived at the pub as a teenager. They found her a place to live with other lesbians and got her work at Club Rouge, near the Twisted Wheel on Brazennose Street, a 'classier' queer venue where *Coronation Street* stars sometimes drank.

Chief Constable McKay stepped down in 1966 but his draconian policies endured. Club Rouge had its licence trimmed and the manager fined and fired after plain clothes policemen observed same-sex dancing there in 1968. The court heard that the police had danced together too lest their cover be blown.[14] In the same year a bookshop popular 'with art students' on Victoria Street by the River Irwell was raided and the bookseller charged under the Obscene Publications Act for selling American physique magazines which, the prosecution claimed, might 'excite homosexual sentiments'. The prosecution failed; times were changing perhaps.[15]

Image 13 The Rembrandt Hotel, *c*.1966

These and other cases reveal a vibrant queer life in Manchester in the 1960s, though they of course also signal associated dangers. Luchia remembers that 'the police and the gay bashers were always hanging around and you had to run the gauntlet' between the New Union, Club Rouge and New York (another queer venue). The climate was, she said, 'vicious and a disgrace and it took its toll: every six months or so we'd hear of someone else who had died and who took their lives. And we couldn't even go to the funeral.'[16] Luchia didn't mention the Moors murders in her interview, but she was certainly on this scene when Ian Brady visited the Rembrandt and New Union to watch 'the maggots [...] running their hands through their hair, posing, waiting, giving the smile'.[17] In 1965 Brady picked up seventeen-year-old Edward Evans at Manchester's Central Station (a ten-minute walk from the New Union and a cruising spot before its closure in 1969). He took him by car to Myra Hindley's grandmother's house half an hour away in Hyde, just east of Manchester, and abused and murdered him there. There was less sympathy in the press for Evans than for Brady and Hindley's other victims. He was, as one Fleet Street journalist had it, 'a queer' who 'drifted from one haunt of homosexuals to another'.[18]

It was in this derisory context that a working-class community of queers, queens, lesbians, drag queens and sex workers tightened; 'we had to t[ake] care of ourselves', said Luchia. 'As [our numbers] got bigger we got bolder and we would step out together onto Canal Street with our drinks', she said. 'Queens' would stand 'at each end guarding us' and they also escorted Luchia to work; they were 'vicious' in the face of queer bashers, she said.[19] Other customers advised Luchia against, and gave her the confidence to resist, the lobotomy her GP was pressing on her to combat her desires for other women.[20] (That doctor would almost certainly have been aware of Manchester's Crumpsall Hospital, a prominent centre for aversion therapy which received a donation in 1964 to become the first UK centre for research into the treatment of homosexuals.)[21]

The notoriety and sense of community at the New Union was a considerable draw. Luchia was living and working 17 miles away when she first arrived from Ireland but she still travelled into the city to visit the pub every week. In a 1962 case, it transpired that the two men police spotted 'kissing and cuddling' in a car in a quiet lane in Middleton (to the north of Manchester and just off the new motorway) had met in the pub earlier that evening.[22] In this decade and beyond such mobility was important: while 'straights just went two doors down to the[ir local] pub […] a lot of gay people used to travel', said Carol.[23] From the mid-1960s members of the New Group of lesbians would come from right across the region to attend socials in the upstairs room of a 'terrible, filthy pub' amid the 'dark Victorian maze of streets' off Shudehill, on the other side of the centre from the New Union (see Map 6).[24] Judith remembers about fifty 'professional' and mostly 'butch or middling' women coming together there. 'I used to enjoy it because I had pretty dresses, had a whale of a time […] and all scrupulously moral', she said.[25]

The New Group meetings on Shudehill were fairly middle-class affairs and the Rembrandt on Canal Street in the 1960s was 'a country pub in the city' where the men were 'very well-dressed'.[26] Other places were less so. The New Union was 'too rough a do' in the 1960s for Judith's girlfriends to take her there.[27] The Picador and the Bus Stop café (an all-night haunt of young queers and sex workers near the Gaumont Cinema) had a similar reputation. Joyce hankered after a more sustained 'respectable' venue for women; the lesbian scene in the city was 'terrible' in the 1960s and 1970s, she said. She found a place in Ashton-under-Lyne, seven miles to the east of Manchester city centre, and opened it as the Gaslight. It was made up of two upstairs rooms, 'the seating was sort of leather [and] the DJ was one of the most popular in Manchester', Joyce said. 'I had mirrors so placed that I could see everything […] If the police came there were signals from downstairs – [though] we had nothing to hide.'[28] Carol remembers the 'culture shock' of seeing women in suits at the Gaslight in the mid-1970s – a very different style to the one emerging in the new studenty venues in the city centre.[29]

Politics

By this time the CHE was well established across the Greater Manchester area. It had made more of a mark here than in our other cities because this is where it all began. Allan Horsfall was writing impassioned letters to the local and national press in the early 1960s. One of his first came in 1963 in response to the prosecution of a group of men who had met through a pen pals club and worked at Bolton General Hospital – evidence of queer networks forged and sustained well beyond the pub scene.[30] Dozens more such letters followed, signalling to queer and normal readers alike that there was plentiful queer activity in Greater Manchester, that the police were active in response and that there were some, like Horsfall, who were prepared to speak out. He co-convened (with social worker and 'married father' Colin Harvey) the first meeting of the NWHLRS in 1964 in response to local policing and as a grassroots antidote to the more top down and London-based Homosexual Law Reform Society (launched in 1958 to push for the recommendations of the Wolfenden Committee). By the end of that year the NWHLRS had distributed thousands of leaflets arguing the case for law and police reform to Greater Manchester's councillors, social workers, magistrates, trade unions and newspapers.[31] Horsfall called for a centre for homosexuals in Manchester – something which finally came to pass a decade later. Inspired by the national network of working men's clubs, he also laid ambitious plans for Esquire Clubs for homosexuals which would serve as an alternative to the pub scene.[32] The plans faltered after an application to open the first Esquire Club in Swinton on the western edge of Manchester in 1969 was turned down by the local councillors; 'I don't want these people here', said one bluntly. More successful were the groups that formed after the NWHLRS was redubbed the CHE in 1971. In Oldham the 105 CHE members held regular discos and social events in a local church hall. The *Oldham Chronicle* carried the sensational news in 1976 that 'Churchmen Don't Oppose Homosexual Discotheques'.[33] The church council (which included a CHE member) had voted to allow the discos to continue despite reports of men kissing. Via the CHE, men and some women found piecemeal local acceptance and also some solidarity through protest, including against Manchester Piccadilly Radio for

Copy.

PRESIDENT : NIEL G. C. PEARSON, M.A.
VICE-PRESIDENT : MAURICE SILVERMAN, M.D., D.P.M.

NORTH-WESTERN

HOMOSEXUAL LAW REFORM COMMITTEE

Chairman : Rev. F. Bernard Dodd
Vice-Chairman : T. Colin Harvey, M.A., A.M.I., M.S.W.
Secretary : Allan Horsfall

3 Robert Street,
ATHERTON,
Manchester.

Telephone : Atherton 2982

18 September 1965

Dear Sir,

It disturbs me that homosexuals who complain of robbery are
not allowed by some courts to give evidence anonymously in the
same way that those who allege blackmail are invariably permitted
to do.

The distinction between robbery and blackmail can be a very
fine one; and parasitic crime directed against homosexuals is
now rife. Eight years of public discussion of the Wolfenden
Report unaccompanied by the necessary action has created a situation
in which the homosexual is looked upon as fair game by the hooligan
and lunatic fringe.

Action must be taken soon to change the discredited homosexual
laws, but meanwhile greater consideration for the needs of victimised
homosexuals is equally overdue. *within the courts.*

Yours sincerely,

Allan Horsfall
S E C R E T A R Y

The Editor,
Bolton Evening News,
Mealhouse Lane,
B O L T O N,
Lancashire.

Image 14 Letter from Allan Horsfall to *Bolton Evening News*, 18 September 1965; inset: Allan
Horsfall *c.*1965

broadcasting a 'poofter' 'joke' in 1975 and the MCC in 1978 for its failure to include discussion of homosexuality in its plans for school sex education.[34]

Angela found the CHE group at Manchester University staid and male-dominated when she went to a meeting there in the early 1970s. She moved on quickly to the newly formed Manchester GLF, and this group and another at Lancaster University (65 miles to the north) began to shape her activist politics. She took part in snog-ins at regular venues on studenty Oxford Road and picketed Samantha's Club in the city centre after same-sex dancing was banned there in 1972. Late night slogan painting saw 'lesbians are everywhere' and 'we're here we're queer and we're not going anywhere' daubed on the sides of city centre railway bridges. 'The first time they did this was late on a Sunday night', said Angela. 'On Monday there was chaos: people were getting out of their cars and honking their horns. They couldn't believe it.' 'We made ourselves known everywhere', she said.

Inspired by the growing critique of the 'exploitative' gay scene, Angela and a friend went to the Picador Club 'to see if we could convert and talk to some of these gays'.[35] Luchia was there that night and remembers overhearing some 'posh' women discussing politics. She asked to join their conversation and then invited them to come to one of the regular meetings she had been organizing in the room above the New Union. 'We started to break down barriers – we were all equal [and ...] we started to educate each other', Luchia said.[36] Angela remembers that this was where she first met 'a proper lesbian'; at the university, barely a fifteen-minute walk away, 'it was cool to be bi', it fitted with being 'a student and a hippie [in a context] where people were talking about liberation'.[37] Community at the New Union was meanwhile forged in the face of ongoing police harassment and street-level abuse.[38] 'We were all outcasts', Luchia said: 'a lot of the women were escorts, on the game', and there were petty criminals and drugs – used here 'to get blocked' rather than to 'open minds' (as university students were describing their drug taking). By 'com[ing] together' in that upstairs room at the New Union there was an attempt to create a sense of solidarity between these different networks within a broader 1970s context of 'less isolated' class cultures.[39]

In the mid-1970s a nascent gay centre emerged in a Student Union-owned basement in Waterloo Place near the university. When Grassroots Books moved out in 1975, the year-old Gay Switchboard moved in. It had already taken 1,200 calls and this increased fifteen-fold over the ensuing decade (to $c.18,000$ per year).[40] The Manchester Gay Alliance began operating from the same cramped basement later in the same year. It comprised Manchester Lesbians Group, the TV/TS group, Manchester CHE and Friend (the lesbian and gay counselling service). The trans group Jenny-Anne attended met in the university chaplaincy, also on Oxford Road, 'in a not very nice room downstairs.' 'Its big merit', she added, 'was it was right by the car park. So for people who were nervous, you could just arrive, come in the back door and nobody knew you were there.'[41]

The University of Manchester, Manchester Polytechnic, University of Manchester Institute of Science and Technology (UMIST) and the University of Salford often provided space for lesbian and gay groups and also drew growing numbers of students to a shrinking city,[42] changing the tenor of nightlife and counterculture here as in Brighton and Leeds. Salford University Student's Union outraged a local councillor by running a week of gay liberation events in 1976, and in the same year its students were among the 'shrieking homosexuals' who disrupted a Christian rally addressed by the new chief police constable, James Anderton.[43] Each of the Student Unions had a gay and lesbian disco; Subversion at the Polytechnic Student Union bar on Aytoun Street just south of Canal Street was especially popular. It provided an 'alternative' to the nearby commercial scene which some 'superior and patronising' gay activist students 'would call "the straight gay scene"'.[44] Gay, a member of the Grassroots Books collective (after it moved from Waterloo Place to more central Newton Street), remembers Subversion for the 'sticky floor [and] 70s music [...] A really wide mixture of people [and] quite a lot of group dancing [...] It wasn't terribly sexual, it was more social [... and] it was a safe place, of which there weren't that many [in Manchester] at that point.'[45]

Though socializing and activism remained relatively mixed, a separatist strand did emerge. Women left the GLF in 1972 in Manchester because men often dominated meetings and sidelined women's issues – a story repeated in Leeds and Brighton. In addition, said Angela, 'the way [the men] expressed their sexuality was cottaging and it was so alien. We found it hard to relate.' The Women's Centre in Brook Street became an alternative hub for women's and lesbian politics, support and campaigning from the early 1970s. Luchia and Angela moved into the building so that the centre's rent could be paid through their housing benefit – a necessity given the lack of wider funding. From here the pair and sometimes others offered support and advice over the single pay phone as well as organizing benefits and protests. There was by now a good number of one-off, weekly or monthly women's and lesbian nights in upstairs and back bars around Oldham Street and in central Salford. 'There'd be blokes in the bar downstairs: they didn't seem to bother – and they were getting the money out of us!', said Angela of the ones she organized.[46] 'We would have discos where we would only play women singers – almost impossible but it brought a different perspective.' Angela and Luchia were also making and playing music as part of the Northern Women's Liberation Rock Band. It was, she said, 'a vibrant experience' of women trying to 'define themselves' through music and at a distance from a male-dominated music and gay scene. One of their gigs was at Manchester's women's prison where Luchia encountered women she had known from the New Union and Picador. 'I was setting up my drums', she said, 'the next minute I heard someone shouting "Luchia are you alright?" I turned round and there were all my old buddies.' They were inside for 'shoplifting, prostitution, cheque fraud. All that sort of thing.'[47]

The separatist strand to feminist and lesbian politics in Manchester continued to play out in squats and housing associations and in community and council work. There were separate community-led papers, *Lesbian Express* (1979) and *Mancunian Gay* (from 1982), and from 1984 there were separate gay and lesbian officers and committees at the council. Separatism in Manchester wasn't as sustained or as intense as in Leeds, however. Rosie moved here for that reason, having been 'driven mad' in Leeds.[48] Manchester, said Jess, was 'more inclusive'; 'there was more debate […] and more fun'. 'We don't always need to be doing things which are really heavy.'[49] Perhaps as a result there was more inclusion of trans people. Angela thought the fact that one member of the Women's Liberation Rock Band was a trans women 'went largely unnoticed' and when Stephen Whittle, an early member of CHE, transitioned he found support from the radical Manchester Lesbian Collective he had helped set up in 1974.[50]

Mixing it up: socializing in late 1970s and early 1980s

In 1979, 'poofter terrorists' threw pink painted bricks wrapped in Gay Activist Alliance leaflets through the windows of the Cavalcade pub in the southern suburb of Didsbury after it banned gays and lesbians from drinking there on a Sunday. Others followed the pub's exclusionary lead, though there was also an ongoing tradition of equivocal accommodation in some venues.[51] In the centre Pete Shelley, the bisexual lead singer of the Bolton band the Buzzcocks, remembers that the Dickens, 'a real dive' near the main post office depot in Oldham Street, provided a space 'where you could go and be what you wanted' in the late 1970s and early 1980s.[52] 'You got Post Office workers; a lot of very butch and femme lesbians playing pool; lots of transvestites. And gay men, rent boys', said Paul.[53] Jenny-Anne remembers it being 'very friendly to the trans community. Among the people there were the drag queens, particularly Foo Foo Lammar [...] I felt it was somewhere you could go and be free, and be your real self.'[54] Paddy's Goose, Tommy Ducks and Blooms Hotel were other central and nominally regular bars which were popular with queer and trans people. 'If I went to The Goose [on a Wednesday], I'd be sure to find some other trans people to spend the evening with', said Jenny-Anne. These places provided some space for self expression and exploration – and perhaps gave Shelley the confidence to write with gender non-specific lyrics for the Buzzcocks, a band which, like others on Manchester's indie and punk scene, eschewed machismo and suggested the scope to be different in the city.

In Moss Side shebeens were often easy-going venues for late night and after hours drinking. 'They were run by Black people for Black people, but they didn't give us any trouble', remembers Josie.[55] 'It was a sort of class thing', said Paul. 'They were very rough actually. Rough, illegal drinking. [But] people were ok about lesbians and gay men being there. We wouldn't have gone had we not felt relatively safe, really. A bit of a sense of commonality against the police, I suppose.'[56] These places, like the lesbian private members clubs on Oldham Street, came and went as 'the police came and closed you down'. They would set up elsewhere, though, and 'you just went and joined another club, as happened many times'.[57]

Such queer tenacity was a feature of Manchester's drag scene too. Drag had long been on the bill at Manchester's working men's clubs and at central venues like Band on the Wall and the New Union. Frank Pearson as Foo Foo Lammar performed between queer and normal pubs and clubs from the late 1960s. He went on to run various clubs, including the Picador for a spell from 1970, but it was Foo Foo's Palace on nearby Dale Street from 1980 that cemented his local celebrity. The *Guardian* reported in 1981 that during a recession that was biting hard in Manchester, Foo Foo's Palace was 'pulling in the coach parties' and offering 'an evening of ecstasy for two quid on the door'; a report on TV's *Nationwide* in the same year offered some footage of Foo Foo, the packed club inside and its run-down exterior.[58] The largely straight audiences lapped up Foo Foo's act but others found it offensive; Paul regretted taking his colleagues from the council there for a night out in the middle of the decade.[59] When Pearson died in 2004 his story was rendered in the *Manchester Evening News* as one of Mancunian 'pluck': this former boxer and son of a rag and bone man had come from the tough side of town to become a 'Manchester great'.[60] In other venues in the 1980s vampire queen Rosie Lagosi was offering up her lesbian cabaret and goth band, deliberately challenging what she saw as the narrowness of feminist and lesbian politics. 'There was pressure on me to adopt a stereotypical view of what lesbians looked like', she said. 'Some of the politics were mad […] and women felt oppressed by my leather trousers [and interest in sadomasochism]'.[61] She and Foo Foo were part of a Mancunian tradition of irreverent performance which echoed down the years to come.

Around Canal Street in the early 1980s, Heroes and High Society joined the New Union, Rembrandt, New York and Napoleans, where a police raid in 1978 exposed yet more 'licentious dancing'. In the same year the Gay Centre moved from Waterloo Terrace to Bloom Street, one block back from Canal Street, on the back of a £6,200 Urban Aid grant. The centre now had more space for meeting and socializing and a growing reputation for youth work and parent support – spearheaded especially by Joyce Layland, whose son was gay, and after whom the centre was named in 2010 before becoming the LGBT+ Centre in 2014. The centre provided an alternative to the nearby commercial scene and for those who were under age especially. Peter remembers: 'put[ting] on little sketches, plays and things, comedy, […] we'd play table tennis and have tea and coffee like anybody else does. So it was where you could be, you could be normal.'[62] On his first visit he remembers being welcomed by Joyce and seeing 'two lads […] they were partners and they, erm, were kissing each other and I'd never, ever seen that. And I was like, erm, wow and then my very next thought was a tremendous sense of relief, and yes this is where I fit, this is right, I've come to the right place, this is definitely me.'[63]

From 1982, *Mancunian Gay*, produced collectively by men who had met at the Gay Centre, began (literally) to map this scene and its associated politics – though largely omitting those mixed and nominally 'normal' rough bars and shebeens and (given that this was a magazine for men) the women's and lesbian nights in back and upstairs rooms of regular pubs. Other networks, word of mouth and the all-important noticeboards at the gay and women's centres and bookshops continued to carry information on these. There was a sense overall of growing lesbian and gay confidence and visibility; the city's 'homosexuals', wrote one club reviewer, 'can threaten to take over any venue to which they are attracted in large numbers'.

Safe spaces and battle lines

Such 'provocative' homosexuals took to the streets in 1981 for a demonstration organized by the Joint Committee Against State Repression of Lesbian and Gay people. Around 11,000 protestors from, among other places, London,

THE MANCUNIAN GAY

No. 31 April Issue 1984   30p

SPORT STARTS ON PAGE 26   **Weekend Radio**

Eyes down, folks

BINGO

WINNER
Page 11

NUMBERS
Page 24

PERVERTS!

EXCLUSIVE

HABITAT ZAP!

Outraged members of the Greater Manchester and Salford Revolutionary Gay Men's Action Gang (GMASRGMAG) picketted Habitat in Manchester last Saturday in protest against their refusal to stock His and His and Her and Her towels. This they claim is totally sexist and anti gay.

They paraded outside the store carrying placards with slogans such as "Habitat is a Haven for the Self Oppressed", "Chic Out—Socialism In" and "Out of Habitat Onto the Streets". Passers by were stopped and asked to sign a petition, and to write a letter of protest to President Reagan.

Eric Todd from the group said that "By selling His and Her towels Habitat are encouraging traditional gender roles and reinforcing the power of the patriarchial state. Our picket shows that lesbians and gay men are everywhere and that we reject all attempts by multi national corporations to control our lives."

Future zaps of heterosexist institutions are now being planned. So Safeways and Laura Ashley, you have been warned.

POOLS CHECK

HETEROSEXUALITY — A GROWING MENACE
Are our children safe? Web of vice revealed — the inside story

Image 15 Mancunian Gay front cover April 1984

Huddersfield, Nottingham and Edinburgh marched through the centre to a rally and two discos (one mixed, one women only) at the Student Union of UMIST.[64] 'The town was packed with shoppers so there were lots of people around to see the march; their main reaction was one of total amazement', reported *Peace News*.[65] The demo was a response to Police Chief Anderton's escalating 'war on gays':[66] 426 men had been arrested for homosexual offences in Greater Manchester in 1979. These included the Labour MP George Morton, three teachers in Bolton (who lost their jobs) and the owners (one a former policeman) of the Fennel Street Sauna near the cathedral following a twelve-day under-cover police operation. Nineteen men were arrested over a three-month period at city centre public toilets, which had, according to police, become 'a cess pit' and a 'magnet for homosexuals and muggers', prefiguring language Anderton used later in relation to gay men and AIDS. [67] The arrest tally rose to 575 the following year (1980), partly because Stockport's undercover police team had swung more decisively into action, arresting 187 men chiefly at a cottage adjoining the Vernon Street court house. [68] This was the year of the raid on the Gemini Club in Huddersfield to which many Mancunians travelled to party in the 1970s and early 1980s.

Peter recalled a particular sense of danger in the city at this time because of the risk of arrest and because the police didn't respond to gay bashing. 'People walking home [...] got attacked all the time. And [...] nothing ever happened, nothing ever got known.'[69] This oppressive local climate coupled with the broader resurgence of homophobia and the AIDS crisis led many to despair and sometimes suicide. The Albert Kennedy Trust, dedicated to supporting young LGBT people who were homeless or living in a hostile environment, was founded in Manchester in 1989 in this context. It was named in honour of care leaver and Gay Centre regular Albert Kennedy, who died aged sixteen.

Manchester's anti-gay policing hit the headlines locally and sometimes nationally and drew protest letters – including one from the National Union of Students to the *Guardian* suggesting police time might be better spent in the hunt for the Yorkshire Ripper (who had already struck once in the city) and another from Horsfall, who called on police to 'come out from their miserable broom cupboards and sneaky spy holes'.[70] In 1979, Jack Straw, the new Labour MP for Blackburn (about 45 miles north of Manchester), introduced a failed bill to parliament to limit the power of chief constables. In his speech to the House of Commons he referred specifically to Anderton's overreach.[71]

While some Greater Manchester councils aligned themselves with the chief constable, the MCC began to move in the other direction like some in London and elsewhere. Between 1980 and 1984 'there was a big battle [...] where the Left gained control of the [Labour] party [and council]', displacing, said Paul, 'sort of old-fashioned, municipal socialists [... who were] very right-wing on social issues'.[72] There had been previous piecemeal council support for gays and lesbians. They endorsed the display of gay and lesbian helpline posters in the city's libraries in 1978,[73] for example, and supported the Urban Aid grant (from central government) for the gay centre in the same year. From 1984, however, there was more concerted action under the direction of new council leader Graham Stringer who appointed gay and lesbian officers, reporting to two new dedicated committees. Whereas the abolition of the Greater London Council in 1986 disrupted the equalities drive in the capital, the dissolution of Greater Manchester County Council (GMCC) in the same year had less impact on Manchester in this respect. This was because it was the MCC not the GMCC that was developing and implementing the more radical agenda. The MCC also 'had a lot more money and a lot more power' than in later years.[74]

Labour councillors accused Anderton of 'wasting time and money entrapping homosexuals'. He retorted that police–council relations in the city had, by 1986, become unworkable and were marred by conflicting world views.[75] While Anderton on AIDS was all moral condemnation, the council had, by 1986, set up a specialist AIDS unit with paid staff working on training, policy and support issues. This was well ahead of our other cities and most of the rest of the country and was due in part to the internal pressure exerted by the gay and lesbian committees and officers. One of these, Paul Fairweather, also volunteered at the gay centre and helped set up the AIDS Helpline, which later morphed into the George House Trust, the main HIV/AIDS support charity in Manchester. Crucially, the council did not see such voluntary mobilization as relieving them of the need to respond decisively (as seems to have been the case in Brighton during this period). In addition, the council had to nail its policy early on after a serious misjudgement. In 1985, twenty-nine-year-old Roger Youds was admitted to Monsall Hospital – a former fever and infectious diseases hospital in north Manchester which was designated a regional centre for AIDS patients in the initial phase of the epidemic. Youds, like others, faced fearful hospital staff who would leave his food outside his room, and in addition he was forcibly detained on the recommendation of the council's director of environmental health and with the assent of the chair of the Social Services Committee. 'They thought he was going to go about clubbing and infect people', said Paul; 'it was an incredibly traumatic experience [for him]'.[76] He was released after a few days following a swiftly organized campaign which ignited debate about the personal rights and freedoms of people with HIV and AIDS. The council shifted gear rapidly and in line with an emerging national policy of voluntary rather than enforced testing and treatment.[77]

At around the same time the council began allotting flats deemed unsuitable for families to students and single people, including a large number of gays and lesbians. Their case was being made by gay and lesbian housing groups on the council attuned to queer experiences of family breakdown, rootlessness and homelessness. This partly explains the developing queer reputation of the inner southern suburb of Hulme: '[It] was a place', said Paul, 'where people lived because it was incredibly easy to get council accommodation. You'd just go and they'd give you a flat [there]' (see Chapter 6 for more on housing in Manchester).[78] Jen said: 'it felt safe and secure' in these 'fairy towers' because of the number of gays and lesbians living in them and because the council was 'taking us seriously'.[79] Similarly, when a purpose-built Gay Centre – or, as the national *Daily Express* had it, 'a £118,000 gay club on the rates' – opened on Sidney Street near the university in 1988, 'the fact that it was there meant something; the fact that the council funded it in the face of opposition, that was important'.[80]

The MCC gained a national profile for its work on lesbian and gay rights on its own account but also because surrounding local authorities acted as a reactionary foil to the steps it was taking even before Stringer took over as MCC leader. Rochdale Council banned advertising for lesbian and gay counselling and support services in its libraries in 1980 while the MCC permitted them;[81] Bury Council sacked its leisure services director in 1980 after he was prosecuted for cottaging just as the MCC Labour group was pledging support for MP George Morton who had committed the same offence.[82] The councillor in Trafford who said that a bullet through the head was the best way of dealing with the homosexual 'problem' became mayor there in 1981.[83] Five years later, the MCC elected lesbian Margaret Roff to that position, sending the national press into a sexist spin about the elevation of a 'left wing spinster' and 'gay rights girl' (Roff was ultimately unable to take up the post).[84] After Clause 28 came into force in 1988 the Ecstatic Antibodies exhibition at the part council-funded Viewpoint Gallery in Salford was summarily withdrawn; the MCC meanwhile ploughed ahead with its support for the Gay Centre and funding its gay and lesbian officers. The reactionary patchwork circling Manchester made the city itself look particularly unstinting in its support of lesbians and gays. This was a source of pride for several Mancunian interviewees, who saw themselves bound into a civic compact with their local authority.

In Manchester, Clause 28 was thus not only an attack on a sexual minority but on the work and ethics of the council. The MCC secretly helped the anti-clause campaign by providing an office in the town hall – at least until it was discovered by the Conservative group – and aligned itself with the especially vociferous movement in the city. [85] The high point was a march and rally in July 1988 which drew 20,000 people from across the country, including on the specially commissioned 'pink express' train from London. It was the largest ever lesbian and gay demonstration Britain had ever seen and put Manchester firmly on the country's lesbian and gay map. This was a further source of Mancunian and northern pride. 'I welcome[ed] the fact that there was something outside of London. Feeling that that was good for the region, or the North as such', said Ruth from Leeds.[86] The march culminated in the star-studded 'Never Going Underground' rally in St Peter's Square (see Image 22 and inside back cover). Afterwards protestors converged on the cluster of venues around Canal Street which were marked on the map included in the official programme. This was the year the tag line 'gay village' was first used in relation to this post-industrial pocket of the city centre.[87]

The protest took place amid escalating homophobic attacks in the city and especially around this nascent village.[88] There was renewed opposition to the council's equalities policies – with some questioning the legality of council support for the anti-clause Love Rights festival of 1989 and of an apparently innocuous flower planting in Piccadilly Gardens the same year to mark the twentieth anniversary of Stonewall.[89] The display was roundly denounced as 'a magnet to vandals', 'disgusting', an affront to parents and children, a waste of money and a further encroachment on 'normal' space in the city. It was vandalized after only a few days.[90] A queer colonization was apparently also evident in an AIDS benefit at Stockport's Davenport Theatre – 'a family venue' which had on that night been the scene of 'a gay orgy'. The *Manchester Evening News* described, in shocked tones, how people had passed beer between them during the show and how men in drag had used the women's toilets.[91] There was more of such depravity to come.

Shifting scenes: in and out in the gay village

The village

Until the early 1980s, the area around Canal Street 'was full of cotton workers by day and prostitutes by night', recalled Peter Bessick, the former landlord of the Rembrandt. Though manufacturing had by this time entered a steep decline it was still a substantial employer in the city.[92] Thereafter, 'the warehouses emptied and only the prostitutes were left' on this edge of the city centre between the rail and bus stations.[93] Unoccupied buildings here and others in what is now known as the Northern Quarter (in and around Oldham Street; see Map 6) provided openings for new businesses, for ad hoc gigs, raves and parties, and for new club venues. The Hacienda on Whitworth Street ran from 1982 to 1997 with iconic acid house and ecstasy-fuelled nights from the late 1980s. On August Bank Holiday 1990, 1,200 women showed up for the Summer of Lesbian Love, a night which spawned club promotion company A Bit Ginger (playing on the hair colour of the duo who started it and on 'ginger beer', rhyming slang for queer). They went on to create Flesh, a monthly Hacienda night, which ran from 1991 to 1996 and fused 'out there' Madchester with camp flamboyance; 'Queer as Fuck' and 'Practice Makes Pervert' proclaimed the flyers posted around the city.[94] Inside, wrote one club reviewer, 'clones in jackboots and spray-on hot pants wiggle moustaches and buns next to trannies with attitude; tank girls pogo alongside voguing queens; and cut dreadlocked boys Saturday night feva [*sic*] with tattooed dykes'; no longer 'did gays have to gate-crash straight clubs to get off on the music hijacked by hip hets'.[95] At Flesh and Paradise Factory (from 1993) 'the management retained the right to refuse known heterosexuals',[96] and door staff tested prospective punters' queer knowledge and limits (would they snog their mate to get in?). Kate said it was 'the queers [who] kick started cool clubs in Manchester' and there was some delight in turning the tables and waving that hip queer upper hand.[97]

Paradise Factory was Carol Ainscow and Peter Dalton's second venture. Their first was Manto on Canal Street, which opened in 1990 and was modelled on bars in Paris and Barcelona[98] to 'introduc[e] a bit more sophistication' to the scene. Despite the fabled Mancunian straightforwardness, punters were initially 'nervous of the plate glass' for fear of being spotted in a gay bar.[99] This and further developments in and around Canal Street were fostered by the Central Manchester Development Agency (CMDA, 1988–1996), funded in part by central government, and working together with the MCC to regenerate the emptying city centre. They supported flexible licensing for pubs and clubs, pedestrianization and new lighting and street furniture.[100] Cruz 101 opened in an old textile warehouse in 1992, and Metz, Velvet and Via Fossa were operating in a similar vein to Manto by mid-decade. Mineshaft and Chains, leather and fetish bars for men, opened in 1994 and 1998 respectively, joining the Archway with its 'strong macho image' as part of that scene. The latter, also known as the Brickhouse, opened in a 'splendid' railway arch on West Whitworth Street and was inspired by the stripped back interior of Heaven in London.[101] Follies for lesbians endured from the 1980s and Fish at Manto and Woman's Own at Paradise Factory ran from the early 1990s. 'Up until then', said Jen, 'Manto and Canal Street was very male and very hi-energy';[102] these nights shifted the balance. On the other side of the Rochdale Canal from Canal Street the CMDC laid out Sackville Gardens in 1990 (see Map 6). It became, from 1991, the focal point of the annual fundraising Carnival of Fun and of Pride weekends – an elaboration of the earlier fun days and jumble sales held outside the Rembrandt to raise money for AIDS charities. [103]

In the early to mid-1990s there was for many the feeling of something new and exciting emerging in this part of the centre. Kate describes lots of queer people moving here around this time. The population of the city was only just past its 1991 low point after a forty-year decline, rents were cheap and city centre living didn't yet have a wider appeal. 'The only people who seemed to live in town were queer. [...] We didn't even have a supermarket [...] there was something about not just moving to Manchester but living in the centre of it. We didn't want to have to get taxis. We just wanted to be right in it, and be it, be part of it', said Kate.[104] She lived in India House, just off Princess Street and a five-minute walk from Paradise Factory, the Hacienda, the new gay village venues and a deserted warehouse which for a time was a notorious place to go for sex. A decade later Greg moved into neighbouring Lancaster House. A quarter of the people living there were queer, he said, as they were in Jenny's block a little further south in Brunswick.[105]

All this was bound up in a particular sense of pride in Manchester and its 'cosmopolitan' patchwork of city centre 'communities' – the gay village, adjacent Chinatown and 'curry mile' to the south – which the tourist office was beginning to promote as part of the city's appeal. It was, according to a mid-1990s focus group of gay men, 'a progressive place', where community and 'friendliness' were part of longstanding industrial and working-class traditions. The village, said one, was something Mancunians and not only gays and lesbians were proud of: 'I think it's our gay village, not their gay village'. It was for this reason a good place to come to be gay and a positive place to come out: 'You find that people aren't quite so positive about their sexuality [in places] like Huddersfield, Bradford and Leeds – smaller cities', said one participant (unaware perhaps of Huddersfield's 1970s gay heyday).[106]

If there was strong 'emotional investment' in the idea of Manchester as a tolerant and diverse city, the focus group participants also described the need for 'strategic calculation' in navigating the city and its suburbs.[107] Certainly queer bashing remained rife and the police were still active in targeting gay men and gay venues, though after thirteen men were arrested for gross indecency in a raid on the Mineshaft in 1993 there was an attempted rapprochement. The new chief constable, David Wilmott (from 1991), appointed a 'village bobby' (Inspector Tom Cross) who met 'gay leaders' to discuss policing in the area in the Rembrandt, 'the gay village hall' as the *Manchester Evening News* later had it. Cross was keen to emphasize his own normality as he took on his new role: 'I don't like [homosexuality] and I don't think it's natural', he said, though he claimed not to 'regard homosexuals as oddballs or perverts'.[108] In 1994, police attempts to censor a stripper and to control access at Cruz 101 brought a swift end to the gay 'honeymoon with police'.[109] In an echo of scandals in Brighton and Plymouth, the Manchester force admitted in 1995 that its database included a field to record the (homo)sexuality of those it came into contact with.[110] From this point on, though, there was more concerted change, especially following an MCC-sponsored national conference on the policing of lesbian and gay communities in 1995, subsequent police representation on community bodies and a presence in Pride parades from 1997.[111]

The second half of the 1990s saw shifts in other respects too. The CMDA spearheaded the reuse and redevelopment of buildings and land across the city centre, including the construction of the state-of-the-art Bridgwater Concert Hall adjacent to the huge GMex exhibition centre (formerly Manchester Central station) in 1996. In the same year a massive IRA bomb ripped through Corporation Street in the heart of the city – an event which, Greg said, 'galvanize[d] Mancunian identity around resistance, community and pride'.[112] The devastation forced further regeneration of the centre while the coming Commonwealth Games (in 2002) provided another spur for renewal in a city that now seemed to be on the up: people were moving here again and Manchester was repositioning itself as a national and international hub.[113] New shopping centres and hotels, the redevelopment of those old industrial quarters around Canal and Oldham streets and the renovation of iconic buildings like the Royal Exchange (also damaged in the bombing) changed the look and feel of the centre. The People's History Museum moved into an old pump house on the riverfront in 1996 (see Map 6), and, along with the redeveloped Museum of Science and Industry in the old Liverpool Road Station and national football museum (which relocated to the city centre in 2012), provided grist to the story of Manchester as an innovative global city of radical, industrial and footballing firsts.[114]

These years saw further celebration of Manchester's queer credentials. The early 1990s had put the city at the cutting edge for bars and clubbing; the international Queer Up North festival from 1992 did the same for LGBT arts, theatre and film. By its final year in 2007 it was the largest such festival in Europe.[115] The sheen of the pink pound was especially evident in this city; it was reportedly worth £200 million by 1995 and propelled new ventures.[116] In 1996 a fifteen-unit gay shopping centre, the Phoenix, opened on Princess Street. It included a clothes outlet, a hairdresser and a ceramic shop run by trans woman Julia Grant. The complex foundered on the now much higher rents and the absence of daytime customers in an area better known for its night-time economy; the nearby gay bars and clubs, the taxi services and sex shops fared better.[117] Grant took the whole Phoenix complex over and opened the Hollywood Showbar there in 1997. She maintained a couple of outlets, including a café and clothes shop for trans women, which was – Jenny-Anne remembers – much cheaper than the Manchester branch of Transformation in the northern suburb of Prestwich (run by Stephanie Booth, the trans 'girl in a million' as she styled herself).[118] The café 'would be open from about 4 o'clock in the morning, and people could go and have breakfast or a coffee to sober up before they went home. And of course people coming into the city, early workers, would use it.'[119] The Showbar closed in 2002 and was replaced with clubs AXM and Alter Ego. Round the corner Vanilla, a bar in the Manto mould and touted as the 'lesbian mecca of the north', opened in 1998.[120] Coyotes, a 'cruisy' lesbian bar with 'a fantastic atmosphere' followed in 2004.[121] The village remained male and youth oriented but there was now more of a mix than before and the series *Queer as Folk* had made it *the* place to visit. Paul would travel from Leeds: 'You could be just who you are. It was the excitement of going to Manchester where you could hold hands with your partner and kiss him in public in the gay village.'[122] Cerydwen, also from Leeds, found it 'liberating [...] exciting to have such a place'.[123] Jo contrasted the 'bright lights' of gay Manchester with 'parochial Plymouth'.[124] But Alan, also from Plymouth, felt let down. 'My whole impression my whole life was based on *Queer as Folk*. The Mecca. This is gonna be the Land of Oz.' 'I remember saying to my other half: "it's just a load of pubs on a street." And he said "well what did you expect?"'[125]

Alan was not the only one to be disappointed. Village venues could be explicitly exclusionary. Jenny-Anne went to the Hollywood Showbar with a young lesbian friend and the friend's mother:

I went to go in, and they all said, 'hi Jenny. And you can come in'. They let her mum in. But they wouldn't let the young girl in. And the guy on the door said, 'you don't look like a lesbian'. I said, 'what does a lesbian look like?' And then [...] one of the other door staff was a big lesbian, and she said, 'like this!'[126]

At Milk one woman felt the need to modify her 'hippie' image to fit in with a butcher crowd,[127] while in other nearby venues 'if you look[ed] a bit butchy you just couldn't get in'.[128] Jen described Poptastic in the later 1990s having a 'no bisexuals' door policy: 'I knew people who would carefully pair up into what would look like same-gender pairs in the queue, regardless of what relationships were going on'.[129]

According to the *Independent on Sunday* in 1995, hen and stag dos and straight drug dealers working often through pub and club bouncers were 'taking the gay out of Gaychester'.[130] There were reports of homophobic and violent behaviour, and some gay men and lesbians resented straight people compromising 'gay' space.[131] Their comments could be laced with snobbish superiority and misogyny. One gay man railed against 'boilers': 'cheap women, in cheap shoes who drink like straight men'.[132] A bar manager at Manto made a distinction between straight 'trendy' women (acceptable) and 'the normal Sharon and Tracy' (not welcome). Via Fossa, Manto and Metz were grouped as middle-class

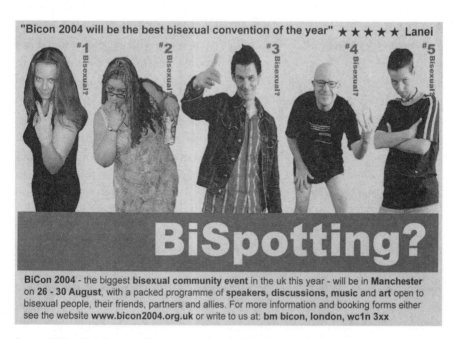

Image 16 Flyer for the 20th Bicon convention, held in Manchester in August 2004

venues by an employee at the latter; the New Union, Follies and now also the Rembrandt were seen to be rougher, more working class and for older men.[133] Class, money, age and style mattered in terms of who could feel included in the various village venues and indeed in the village as a whole.

Imagery associated with the village and broader gay scene was unthinkingly white.[134] *Mancunian Gay* had just one Black gay man on its cover in its four-year run. That cover featured American novelist James Baldwin rather than any Black gay Mancunians who, in an article in an earlier issue, were said to be poorly served by the city's gay scene. This, it said, made the monthly meet-up for Black lesbians and gays at the Gay Centre particularly important.[135] More than a decade later lesbian club promoter Claud Cunningham was still observing the lack of 'positive images of [queer] Black people' in Manchester and insisted that images of Black and Asian women were used to advertise her club night, Black Angel (from 1997).[136] In the new century, Jess sometimes preferred socializing at home to avoid racist hassle; Greg said that it only took 'very slight infractions [...] to expel people of colour from venues [in the village]'.[137] Sociologist Nina Held found trenchant stereotypes and presumptions about Black sexuality still in play among a number of white villagers in the 2010s.[138] Some queer people of colour felt more comfortable going to off-village venues as a result and also because the gay notoriety of Canal Street could be exposing. When Black Angel moved from Paradise Factory to the Green Room in Whitworth Street (nearby but at a sufficient distance), Claud noticed that more Asian women began to come because 'it was not known as a gay venue as such and was out of the village'. Taxi drivers, who might be part of extended family and community networks, would not know the significance of 'where they were picking you up and dropping you off', she said.[139]

The village has been criticized for being an exclusionary ghetto; for being too commercial, too young, too white, too straight, too gay; for not being queer enough. Perhaps because LGBT people 'had the greatest investment in the space' they have also often been its 'most critical users'.[140] While in Brighton there was a powerful reassertion of community in the 1990s, here the feeling for many was of community dissipating. The Gay Centre, a community hub in the area until 1988, moved to its new purpose-built home on the other side of the urban motorway to the south. The Lesbian and Gay (later the LGBT) Foundation, to which two of the Gay Centre's core services – Switchboard and Healthy Gay Manchester – transferred, did not open on Richmond Street in the village until 2002. Even then there was a tangible difference in institutional culture. In the mid-1980s Switchboard at the Gay Centre had seventy volunteers; at the LGBT Foundation Switchboard lines were answered by paid staff. 'They provide a much better service in a way but it's not community driven', said Paul.[141] This shift from a culture of make-do volunteering and community action to the expectation of professionalism was felt in other respects too. *Mancunian Gay* (which Paul helped establish at the old centre) and its successor *Gay Life* (from 1986) were 'radical, very amateur and ramshackle, but [were] the voice of the community'. Thereafter lesbian and gay scene information was folded into *City Life*, the Manchester listing magazine; 'it went from [...] radical to glossy and trivial'.[142] Pride celebrations meanwhile became less community driven. In 1999, charging was introduced and the village fenced off; for the first time no money was raised for charity. The ensuing backlash led Julia Grant and a committee of volunteers to reorientate Pride for 2001 and 2002 (as Gayfest and Mardi Gras) raising, respectively, £87,000 and £65,000 for LGBT charities. After that fencing and charging returned, however, leading to further criticism and boycotts; the commercialization of Pride in the new century was, for some, a source of shame.

'Alternative' scenes

The village 'phenomenon' provided some spur to an 'alternative' in the city, harking back to earlier music, queer and drag scenes. Club promoter Greg had twin reference points when he moved to Manchester in 1995. One was Lucy's, a queer bar in his home town of Blackpool, which he went to as a teenager and described as being 'like a Velvet Underground video'. 'It was really bohemian. [...] It was nothing like the gay bars that I went to after that. So there was a woman in a suit and a hat and a cigarette holder, sitting at the bar. And there was a beautiful shirtless Black guy behind the bar playing the tambourine. And there were people of all ages and sizes.' His other reference point was Manchester's indie music scene and the Oldham Street part of the city where Affleck's Palace, an old department store, served as an emporium for 'postcards, posters, books and bootlegs'. As a teenager travelling into Manchester from Blackpool this area gave Greg some sense of belonging: 'The walk from Piccadilly Station down to Piccadilly Gardens and up Oldham Street was kind of our walk, where we would hang out. [...] I started going to gigs [round there] when I was 13, but [...] had to start lying a little bit about how far I was going from Blackpool. [...] It was really exciting.'[143] These were formative experiences but they had little resonance with the village bars he started to go to once he came out and moved to Manchester as a student in the mid-1990s. He didn't find the community he anticipated there and neither did he find the music that mattered to him. He soon started going instead to the alternative and student club nights of the late 1990s – Club Suicide, Chips with Everything, Poptastic or Homoelectric, a club run by people who 'had been Flesh kids' and which addressed a mix of 'homos, heteros, lesbos and don't knows' from 1998.

Jayne Compton created Club Brenda in 1999 in the mould of earlier shebeens in Moss Side where, after the clubs closed, 'the after party would continue [...] until the early hours': 'it was just people coming together to party in spite of musical or cultural differences', she said. The music at Brenda was eclectic and punctuated with performance; 'people would just grab the mike and recite poetry; anything could happen'.[144] A Club Brenda night was the first time Greg had experienced being 'in a party that was evenly mixed between the sexes [...] And the dykes were dancing without any shirts on. It was punk as fuck. I was really excited about that.' David Hoyle, the Divine David, performed here and in other alternative Manchester nights from the mid-1990s as a radical 'anti-drag queen'. Like Greg he moved to the city from Blackpool and also like Greg developed a penetrating critique of the commercial village scene. 'I remember once I went to Club Brenda during Pride weekend', said Greg, 'and it was at the time when I was using both scenes. I was going to parties on the queer scene, but going to the village. And I had my Pride wristband on, and David Hoyle just cut the wristband off.'[145]

A lesbian scene meanwhile developed in Chorlton, a suburb 3.5 miles to the south of Canal Street. A local police station was converted into The Lead Station bar in 1995, followed by Bar Braw a few years later and other lesbian and queer-friendly venues along the main Beech Road. The area was by this time 'just full of lezzers', said a participant in a 2015 project ('Remembering Pride and Celebrating Place'); another scrawled 'LESBIAN MOTHERS' over the Chorlton area of a map of Manchester she'd been asked to annotate. She caricatured the area as one end of a lesbian timeline – starting in the village when women were younger, moving on to the Northern Quarter when they were a little older and thence to Chorlton with partner, baby and dog.[146]

A second generation of alternatives to the village was represented by Club Bollox (from 2007) which was, according to the *New Musical Express*, 'the Pied Piper of the Village', 'dragging more and more people away from the safety zone of Canal Street [...] and the usual thumping house or euro cheese'.[147] Greg at this time saw something particularly Mancunian in nights like Tranarchy ('very punk rock, very metal [...] a lot of drag performers cut their teeth there') and Cha Cha Boudoir at Cruz 101, a Canal Street venue.

'What they have really done is brought [...] a very queer kind of gender fuck political angle into a village venue', said Greg. 'Some people don't like that, and some people like me think it's great, because if there's something better than queering a straight space it's queering a gay space.'[148] The nights Greg was now running – Drunk at Vogue, Off the Hook and Queer Revue – took their cue from these queer alternatives. By using some venues of old (like Band on the Wall on Swan Street) and focusing on the Northern Quarter he self-consciously designed these nights to link with a particular musical lineage and ideas of local working-class and queer 'authenticity' which he saw as countering the 'generic' gay village.[149]

Drag Kings performed at Cha Cha and were not sidelined in the way Jenny felt they were at other 'queer alt nights' where drag queens tended to rule.[150] The Drag King scene took off in Manchester around 2010 with the formation of the Drag Kings of Manchester. DJ Wolfy, trading 'in that old school British humour', performed in queer and regular venues, including a working men's club.[151] Two more recent drag houses in the city – the House of Decay and the all-Black House of Ghetto – have twisted New York with English northernness. They 'have this thing that is probably quite Manchester', said Kate. 'They're not bitchy drag queens. Their whole philosophy is "you can sit with us" [...] you can be smart and clever and fabulous but you have to be welcoming. And I think that's a really beautiful Northern thing.'[152]

Queer Contact at the Contact Theatre on Oxford Road took up the mantle from Queer Up North in 2008 with smaller-scale events, keying into earlier traditions of community and grassroots art and theatre in Manchester. Mother's Ruin has produced queer performance there since 2009 as well as in old mills and established theatres and clubs – connecting with the industrial fabric of the city and both mainstream and fringe venues. The Black Gold and Spark Trans (now Trans Vegas) arts festivals, from 2015 and 2018 respectively, have more recently showcased Black queer and trans creativity amid ongoing racism and transphobia on the scene, including in the blackface used by Queens of Pop, a performance troupe booked repeatedly by gay venues and pride between 2013 and 2017. Rainbow Noir and African Rainbow Family (established in 2013 and 2014 respectively) have been significant in pushing back against such entrenched prejudice and in providing a space and voice for queer refugees and Black and minority ethic people in the city – including through exhibitions and the media.[153] 'You make a bigger impact here' than in London, said Kate. 'And you're supported in making that impact [...] I like that about Manchester [...] I've gone: "I'm going to set up a trans arts company [Trans

Creative] here." And suddenly, this funding became available.[...] Suddenly now that's happening.'[154]

These various bars, clubs nights, festivals and groups probably form the most expansive alternative queer scene in the country, pushing boundaries in terms of music and performance and in terms of gender and what it means to be queer. This scene came partly in response to Pride and developments in the village – the 'gay mainstream' or 'straight gay scene' as some had it. And yet 'alternative' promoters and performers share some of the same entrepreneurial 'give-it-a-go' spirit that underpinned the development of the village itself and which some, like Greg and Kate, see as a particular Mancunian quality. The village arose out of a set of local circumstances and a Mancunian 'bravado that has some substance' (as Greg had it).[155] It had its roots in those pubs we visited at the outset and which were sustained by landlords who refused to be cowed; its trailblazing development in the early 1990s helped put gay Manchester on the cutting edge. It is still a place of community and remembrance: the LGBT Foundation has its base here with its support services, workshops and drop-ins, the bars are still busy, and across the canal in Sackville Gardens are the Beacon of Hope AIDS memorial (unveiled in 2002), a statue of wartime code breaker (and latterly Wilmslow resident) Alan Turing (1912–1954) and a memorial to trans people lost (see Image 29).[156] Though the queer scene has fostered a strong and sustaining sense of community in the Northern Quarter and other parts of the centre, the village remains a lodestone for many within and well beyond the city.

Manchester is the biggest of our four cities and its queer history has been the most complicated to navigate. The interviews suggested different ways to tell its story – via bars, the longstanding LGBT+ Centre (soon to move again into a larger purpose-built premises), activist groups, appalling homophobia and repressive policing, the council, the village, the music, drag and cabaret scenes and also churches (mentioned as supportive by trans interviewees especially). The result is kaleidoscopic, conjuring multiple and overlapping ways of understanding the sometimes deeply fraught, sometimes euphoric queer life of this city. A single interview could conjure some sense of this. Ian, who was born in 1936, moved to Manchester in 1983 after losing his long-term partner in a motorbike accident in Paris. He has lived in the city longer than anywhere else in his life and has felt anchored here by his work, his local mixed friendship network in Altrincham (south of Manchester), his gay-friendly United Reform Church, the Rotary Club and the Manchester Leather Men (established in 1982 and of which he was president until he hit eighty in 2016).[157] When people from these disparate groups spotted him on local TV in full leather gear 'meeting and greeting' Pride goers at Manchester Piccadilly Station in 1997, Ian anticipated trouble:

> We had a member [of the Rotary Club] who was quite high-ranking in the Greater Manchester Police Force [...] And to be truthful I thought he was a right-wing homophobic bastard. And he came up to me at one of the meetings soon after and said 'Ian, I saw you on television'. I gritted my teeth and waited. And he said 'I just want you to know that if you have any trouble, let me know and I'll help you'. I was astounded.[158]

The story touches an enduring suspicion of a police force which had treated gay men especially harshly but also a Mancunian straightforwardness and solidarity which is part of the reason why Ian has stayed over a period which saw the reinvention of this industrial city and a related shift in its queer scenes. He, like Kate, Greg, Paul, Jenny-Anne, Jen and Luchia, attest to what is particular about this place and how being a Mancunian shapes ways of being L, G, B, T or Q here.

4

Naval gazing in Plymouth

Image 17 Tom Dancing, by Beryl Cook, 1976 (copyright John Cook 2021)

Ian, a Plymouth dockyard worker, told *Gay News* in 1976:

> I certainly wouldn't live anywhere else, perhaps because I was born here. I'll cope
> with living in Plymouth because it's well planned, easy to get at, close to the sea
> and the moors. Apart from the gay scene you couldn't wish for anything better.

In the same piece, the *Gay News* journalist described how Plymouth's queer
life was focused around the 'cramped nicotine stained and grim' back bar of
the Lockyer Tavern and one gay club 'or a third or two thirds depending on

the night you happen to be there'. After dark sailors and civilians partied on notorious Union Street, the road connecting the centre of Plymouth to the docks at Devonport (see Map 7). 'You have your joke, you muck about, but nothing else', said a seaman *Gay News* interviewed at Mr Harry's (that 'one gay club'; see Image 32). Though there was a CHE group by this time and though members agreed to be photographed on iconic Plymouth Hoe (see the inside front cover), *Gay News* identified queer life functioning largely 'below the radar' here. Homosexuality was still illegal in the armed forces and remained so until 2000; discretion was imperative for service personnel, their partners and their lovers. There was also a strong 'family thing' and 'vein of West Country conservatism' in this relatively remote, ancient city which had been replanned and rebuilt following the devastating wartime air bombardment.[1] When Jo moved to Plymouth from Manchester she found people who were 'very, very village provincial, old in their ways'.[2] This is part of what anchored Ian here, albeit with a certain resignation; the distinctive queer rhythms might have suited him. Another Lockyer regular, a teacher, told *Gay News* that 'Plymouth can be summed up best by the dockies who come into the Lockyer Tavern around 6 and order a mild and bitter. Later in the evening they'll order a lager and lime. And then just before closing time they'll ask for a dubonnet' – a temporary queer journey from butch to camp, snapping back to the docks the next morning.[3]

'You didn't see anyone from a different culture', said Alan, who, like Ian, grew up here.[4] There was more uniformity in Plymouth than in our other cities in terms of ethnicity, religion and also work. 'Because of its lack of diversity it tends to be less open to change', said a Lesbian Line volunteer when it launched in 1984.[5] Though there seems to have been tacit knowledge and even quiet acceptance of sexual permissiveness – cottaging 'was a phenomenal pastime in the town'[6] – this abutted a frequently articulated concern with 'what the neighbours might think'.[7] There was a desire and perceived need for Plymouthians carefully to negotiate established local, military and familial traditions and expectations. 'What the world does today, Plymouth does ten years later', the CHE secretary told *Gay News*; 'the best thing for gay people here would be if they all suddenly woke up with green noses. But then they'd probably start using makeup.'[8] This did not preclude a vibrant queer subculture – far from it – but it did create a particular dynamic in the 1960s, 1970s and 1980s for which, in the 2000s, there was real nostalgia. The LGBT scene of the new century felt 'sterile' and 'generic' to some; what was queerly exceptional about Plymouth had, they felt, been lost. In this chapter I chart this shift and tug a little at the story of Plymouthian conservatism. I start with the queer scenes from the 1960s to the 1990s and then double back to look at the dance of queer and normal in naval and civilian life over the same period. I look finally at the particular significance of other places and of people from elsewhere and also at a key turning point – not, as in the other cities, Clause 28 but rather the horrific murder of Terry Sweet in 1995 which, along with wider local changes in the 1990s, ruptured Plymouth's longstanding queer dynamics.

Queer scenes, c.1960–1995

The 1960s

Plymouth was, like Manchester, a working-class city, though here based around the navy and the docks rather than industry and manufacturing. It was more akin to Brighton in terms of size and had the most rural hinterland of our cities. It was also growing – from 204,409 people in 1961 to 239,452 a decade later. This was a trend which continued.[9] Plymouth was substantially rebuilt following the devastating bombing of 1941 with a special committee (dissolved in 1961) overseeing the construction of seventeen new factories (between them creating 10,000 new jobs) and swathes of new housing: 13,500 for the council, 3,500 private and 850 built by the Admiralty for the armed forces.[10] Plymouth had, by the start of our period, been remodelled as a self-consciously modern city.[11] Its centre was deliberately depopulated and reconstructed suburbs were zoned for supposedly more convivial family living. You were much less likely here than in Brighton to have a central bedsit a couple of doors down from a queer bar. Plymouth's culture, reputation and history revolved around seafaring, though the army and air force had bases here too (until 1971 and 1992 respectively). A full 40 per cent of men, 11 per cent above the national average, worked in public service of one kind or another, largely on account of this military presence; 25,000 people were employed directly in the dockyard or navy in the 1960s and roughly the same again in associated trades, amounting to a quarter of the city's working population altogether.[12] As a result, many Plymouthians shared a class and occupational background and identity. More people here than nationally were skilled and semi-skilled, with fewer in the professional and managerial or unskilled social categories.[13]

We get an oblique queer sense of this in the list of thirteen men who appeared in court on gross indecency charges at the end of 1959. Three were or had been in the navy (in the lower ranks); one was a military policeman. Of the rest there were three clerks, a mechanic, a demolition foreman, two labourers and a salesman.[14] Such men were always more liable to arrest than those in the middle or upper middle classes who had more access to private space, but the range and type of occupations nevertheless reflects that of Plymouth more broadly. It is likely that each of these men had some working connection to the docks or else the reconstruction work of the city. Michael was thirteen when this news story hit the local press, suggesting to him the dangers and possibilities of sex with other men in Plymouth. At around the same time his father, a jobbing musician, described a visiting singer to the Palace Theatre on Union Street as 'an old nancy boy'. Later he forbade his son from going to the Lockyer (on account of its 'nancy' clientele) and then also from Union Street itself (see Map 7). As a result these places were firmly in Michael's sights when, at fourteen, he 'was right out on the town. I was down at the Lockyer, I was down in the Palace, I was down Union Street, I was cottaging and sort of hooking up with anybody and everybody.'[15] He and his sister, who was also often out on Union Street with her boyfriends, had a pact not to tell their parents what they were up to.

The back bar at the Lockyer was a well-known queer hangout by the 1960s.[16] It was mainly men who drank here, and this is how Beryl Cook depicted it in 1976 (see Image 17). Lesbians came too, though, as did 'normal' customers

Image 18 The Lockyer Tavern, *c.*1960

who might wander through from the front bar – sometimes, said one woman, they 'stirred up trouble' or 't[ook] the mickey out of the girls or as they called them "butch women"'.[17] Ted, who was in his twenties when he began going to the Lockyer in the 1960s, described the regular lock-ins and drinks in the landlord's upstairs flat. He and the 'elegant' landlady 'were very nice to us [queers]' – rather like the licensees at the New Union in Manchester and Hope and Anchor (later the New Penny) in Leeds. He recalled too a camaraderie among the regulars and a playful competitiveness when visitors came from out of town. 'I remember a chap coming down from Brighton and he was an ex-Plymouth boy [...] he turned up in this big, flash American-styled car, beautiful car, and we were all looking at him in the bar and saying "I bet I can get off with him". [...] And anyway I did and we went out in the car to [the countryside].' Ted told another story of having sex with a visiting Londoner (a model 'photographed by Cecil Beaton') in his car on Dartmoor.[18] There was, he suggested, a local interest in men from elsewhere – and especially places with a certain queer sheen like Brighton or London; such connections carried some kudos. Burgeoning car ownership and the surrounding countryside offered Ted, Ian and others plenty of sexual and social opportunities. The local CHE group organized beach barbeques and horse riding on Dartmoor in the 1970s; later a gay walkers group and the hiking dykes took to coastal and moor paths.

Back in the city, Michael would pick up men at El Sombrero, a 'modern' coffee shop at Drake Circus popular with beatniks (whom his mother warned him against). On Union Street there was the 'elegant' long bar at the Palace Theatre which drew a mix of service personnel and queer locals, and Diamond Lil's, a venue remembered affectionately as a drinking haunt until well into the 1980s.[19] It was 'a sort of sailors' place with these drag queens', said Kevin, who was born into a Plymouth naval family.[20] For after hours drinking and dancing there was the nearby Paramount Club – entered through a doorway 'squeezed between these two pubs':

> You got up to this tall, really tacky room with a tacky bar where they played juke-box music. [...] And you got all the services, you got the prostitutes, you got the queer boys, basically the dregs of society ended up there [...]. And guys would dance with each other, and sometimes you'd get a drunken sailor [...] saying: 'Come 'ere darlin', I wanna dance with you!'[21]

Ted remembered that 'nobody took any notice if two men or two matelots [sailors] got up and danced together [at the Paramount]. It was okay.' He was nevertheless 'very wary of the advances of a group of five there on one particular night': 'they started to say, you know, "Come back with us" and I said "Where are you?" and they said "We're off the frigate. You can come back on board with us". And I said "No" and they said, "No, we're all right", and they all started kissing each other to prove they were OK.'[22] In his refusal ('you know, five! You can cope with one. Or maybe two') Ted perhaps had in mind the queer bashings in the city which sometimes involved soldiers and sailors. Ted didn't say so specifically, though, and what came across more in his interview was a sense of ease at the Paramount and also at the Mambo, another queer-ish venue nearby. He looked forward to 'blank week' at the latter – the days when sailors had already spent all their money 'on the girls' and so 'would come into the Mambo and [...] you'd probably buy them a coffee and get off with [one]'.[23]

This sex scene involving queer and normal men extended to nearby public toilets and cruising areas. Michael would regularly pick up sailors and married men: 'I reckon a good 50 per cent of my hook-ups were one-night stands with guys who identified as straight', he said. Among the other half were his first boyfriends, including one of two queer ex-sailors living together just off the Hoe and after that the 'first love of [his] life', Richard.[24] He was a former dockyard apprentice who had been bitten by the spreading 1960s travel bug and spent two years backpacking around Europe and North Africa before returning to Plymouth, getting a job as a security guard at the new Westwood TV studios and picking up Michael on the Hoe. Richard's story, like Michael's, speaks to shifting local possibilities and to wider social and cultural change. It shows too how cruising spots could offer more than fleeting pleasures. In Michael and Richard's case they led to love. A student new to the city in the early 1970s learned about the wider local gay scene through the men he met cottaging (*Gay News* – with its listings pages – was not stocked in any local newsagents or the library),[25] while Ted went to one particularly cruisy spot – Lion's Den Cove on the eastern edge of the Hoe (see Image 19) – to relax. This was a place protected from view by a dirty glass screen and a 'men only' sign in the 1960s; 'during the summer people would go up there and spend the day', he said.[26]

Such behaviour in Plymouth might be tolerated as long as it fell below the radar. Michael remembers his mum and dad being angry about a spate of cottaging arrests in the city: 'damn ridiculous, just let them get on with it', they had said. Despite their reticence about theatrical 'nancy boys', beatniks at El Sombrero and Michael's later 1960s preference for colourful shirts, they were also permissive in this sense and supportive of Michael when he introduced Richard to them as his boyfriend. They came to 'adore' Richard, and he, in

Image 19 Lion's Den Cove in the 2000s

turn, was astonished by their familial embrace: 'He was horrified when he came home [...] to my parents, and Christmas morning we all piled into my mum and dad's bed. My sister, her husband, me. He was standing there, "come on!" [we said].'[27] This was one of the ways the local family-focused culture was expressed, though Richard's own Plymouth family behaved very differently. He 'was not even allowed in his parents' bedroom' and Michael certainly wasn't; he was kept apart. At our Plymouth workshop a disturbing story surfaced of a father who badly beat up his son when he discovered he was gay despite the fact he himself had had casual sex with men.[28] Evident effeminacy or queerness – in this errant queer son or 'nancy' performers – might be derided even if sex between men was common and tolerated. In this military, 'male-dominated' city there was an especially thin dividing line between the casual sex men might have with each other and the associated queer and homosexual identities taken up by others which were beyond the pale.[29] Such lines were sometimes policed by the kind of violence this father meted out to his son.

The police were not as concerted as the Manchester force in addressing the 'queer menace' in the 1960s and 1970s and there was some equivocal accommodation. 'Various policemen would be up there [at Lion's Den Cove] – sunbathing. Nude, as well', remembered Ted. Recounting his prolific cottaging adventures, Michael noted multiple blind eyes turned and once picked up a policeman outside an empty public toilet and had sex with him in the police car. He also recalled a local 'Quentin Crisp character' called Rita who would put on make-up and go to the Lockyer and the cottage opposite. It was notoriously 'good for military' who might check in for some fun at the end of their night out on Union Street (the Lockyer itself was likely placed out of bounds to service-men by the military police). 'Everybody knew Rita', Michael said, 'which is why very often she wouldn't get caught. Police would just say: "for Christ sake Rita, go home! Put it away!"'[30]

Rita did 'get caught', however, and served time in Exeter prison. Michael's first fling was also convicted of a cottaging offence and was compelled to have electric shock therapy in lieu of a prison sentence; 'it ruined his life', Michael said.[31] Policing was inconsistent but it was not lax. The senior investigating officer in the Terry Sweet murder case of 1995 recalled that there had been anti-gay banter and jokes between colleagues ever since he joined the force in 1969.[32] Police had repeatedly gathered names of men in the Lockyer and, said Kevin, 'there were always rumours that [they] were watching the pub [… or] that there was a new barman that was giving police the names and numbers of people in there'.[33] In a notorious case in 1977 police made sixty arrests after picking up a nineteen year old and persuading him to identify men he had had sex with or who he thought were homosexual.[34] Charges were dropped after a complaint to the National Council of Civil Liberties was upheld; the police committed to referring men they encountered 'in the course of their duties' to the CHE. A year later, however, police were once more accused of a witch-hunt. Plymouth CHE 'blamed the West Country's rural atmosphere for its lack of big city broadmindedness' (though many in Leeds and Manchester felt such broadmindedness was distinctly lacking too).[35]

Other dangers lurked beyond the police. There was a trail of assault and blackmail cases in a city where the lively sex scene in Central and Beaumont Parks, the Hoe and city centre public toilets provided the mercenary-minded and the homophobic with clear places and opportunities to strike.[36] In addi-tion, there was a forces' machismo which might be played out on queer men – especially if the perpetrator had felt they themselves had stepped across one of those indistinct lines between queer and normal. An 'army deserter' 'stabbed a homosexual to death' in the city on New Year's Eve 1976 and a year later six ratings (naval apprentices) who had met and danced with 'two self-confessed homosexuals' at Mr Harry's called out 'degrading insulting remarks' and beat one of them unconscious outside.[37] The case was dismissively reported as 'a gay row' in the *Western Evening Herald*, one which, it said, 'cost' the ratings £510.[38]

Despite the frequent refrain that Plymouthians would not (and should not) 'put their heads above the parapet', there are examples of local stridency. A Lockyer regular of nineteen years' standing took out a writ against the new landlord for telling him to 'fuck off' because he was 'queer' in 1977. Earlier, Rita seemed not to have been cowed in their interaction with the police and Michael was clearly confident on the queer sex and social scene. He was buoyed perhaps by his youth, attractiveness and supportive family. He was also finding some anchor points for his identity and politics in his family's Labour politics and in queer-themed books and films. He saw *Victim* when it first came out in 1962 at the vast – but for this film virtually empty – 3,254-seater Odeon Cinema on Frankfort Street in the centre; for once he didn't stray to the projection booth for sex with the projectionist. Later he borrowed Peter Wildeblood's *Against the Law* (1955) from Plymouth's library: 'I read that and thought, wow, if anybody got caught with me I'd just tell the truth and say I belong to this as well.' 'To hell with what anybody thought', he said, in imagined contravention of a trenchant local culture.[39]

In the early 1970s around thirty Plymouth gays and lesbians came together to form the local CHE group. This was around the same time as in the other cities, but here CHE was primarily social. It met in people's homes rather than in pubs or the Student Union and was behind weekly discos in Devonport (near the docks), 'Call my Bluff' competitions, beach barbeques, a ludo championship and a 'vicars and tarts' party (see Image 27). 'Wallace' wrote in the national *CHE Bulletin* of the 'tremendous warmth' of Plymouth CHE and its 'terrific potential'.[40] The women's organizer was successfully building up numbers, he wrote, and probably because CHE was the only gay or lesbian group around.

Into the 1980s

One Lockyer customer described the loss of 'a home' when the landlord turfed out the gays in 1977 (and then everyone else in 1980 when the pub closed for good). The Gypsy Moth (later renamed the Yard Arm) took up the mantle, and down the hill in West Hoe Mr Harrys was by now notorious. Peter, from Dartmoor, remembers it being mixed gay/straight, men/women: 'it had always been very seedy, before it became a gay bar it was a prostitutes bar, you know that sort of place, the water came through the ceiling, the toilets didn't work, all a bit run down'. Sometimes, he went on, 'we had the National Front waiting outside Harry's and we had to kind of run the gauntlet of all this taunting, people were punched to the ground and stuff'.[41] Jo, who was a similar age to Peter and settled in Plymouth after a peripatetic RAF child-hood, nevertheless recalls feeling 'very looked after' at Mr Harry's – though possibly because lesbians were in a minority: 'the bouncers really used to take care of us because it was straight and gay. [...] It was fun, great disco [...] and we had the transvestites – it was everybody.'[42] In a city the size of Plymouth such mixing meant word could get out: 'You could dance away, and then sud-denly you'd have the embarrassment that it was someone you worked with before, or someone that knew your parents', said Kevin.[43] Plymouth was, said the CHE men's convenor, 'very much a small town where everyone knows everyone else'.[44]

By the late 1970s there was 'a big, big gay scene' for women – especially around the station and so at one remove from Union Street and West Hoe. Sharon remembered that 'we used to [...] designate, god, loads of the little pubs around North Road [near the station] – everyone would kind of gather on a Thursday night. [...] So [the landlord would] know we'd all descend on them on whatever night.' The Crown in Devonport was 'way out of the way' but was at least lesbian on Fridays and Saturdays – the nights when it was harder to colonize pubs in the city centre. The Penrose (on Penrose Street, also near the station) opened in 1981 and was run by a 'lovely' couple whose daughter was a lesbian. They were 'really good to us all and we used to have lock-ins. It was amazing', said Lynne, who was brought up in a Plymouth naval family.[45] Round the corner on Cecil Street was the Melbourne Inn, which hit the local headlines in 1979 after a street fight between two groups of women.[46] Generally, though, this scene was pretty invisible unless you knew women who were part of it.

New Zealander Prudence, who moved to Plymouth from Manchester in 1982 with her partner, Gay, set up the local Lesbian Line two years later partly because of this local 'ignorance of where to go for advice and for friendship with other lesbians'.[47] They were spurred to action by a letter in the national femi-nist magazine *Spare Rib* from a Plymouthian woman who felt she had 'nowhere to turn'.[48] Even so, Gay remembered that 'people [...] would phone up and want information and so on and there was just very little that we could tell them about. It was always a struggle.'[49] CHE was beginning to 'peter out', and though Plymouth Lesbian Network ran from the Virginia House Settlement in the Old Harbour area from 1986, it folded five years later after the council cut its £608 grant in the context of Section 28 and following the 'Cash for Gay Groups Storm' this funding provoked.[50] Woman's centre stalwart Sharon recalls that other women's groups ceased or moved on as new management at Virginia House raised rents and 'stifled the community focus'.[51]

The military presence and dockyard work declined from the mid-1980s and there was also less ease with queer–normal crossovers in the contexts of AIDS and the broader homophobic backlash. The Long Bar, the Paramount and Mr Harry's all closed in the 1980s and early 1990s, and, according to Michael, the city became 'less free and easy [...] from a slut's point of view'; 'more queer people were leaving the city rather than staying'.[52] The less military-oriented Old Harbour area near Virginia House, meanwhile, began to get a little gayer. Hawkins ran from the 1980s through to 2014 on one side and the Swallow opened in 1989 on the other (see Map 7). Its Mancunian landlords, Peter and Colin, were the first gay couple to have a joint tenancy in Plymouth. The dominant local brewery (Courage) had not been 'keen' to encourage gay bars in Plymouth – partly, said Colin, because they would have been placed out of bounds by the military police. But when, in the late 1980s, Courage started to shed their pubs so as not to breach new monopoly rules, Colin and Peter found an opening. The Swallow became the mainstay of Plymouth's scene for the 1990s and 2000s and drew a mixed crowd of lesbians and gays – though often grouped in separate parts of the bar. '[It] was always packed and you'd go in and all the men would be at the front and all the girls [...] would be in the back where the pool table was', said Lynne.[53] Hannah described it as a place where (in Plymouth style) 'nothing needed to be said' and she felt comfortable there as a mixed-race adopted woman both before and after she came out as bisexual.[54] Kerry, a trans woman who was brought up in the south-west, recounted being spat at on Drake's Circus and abused by customers in the city centre shoe shop where she worked. The Swallow was somewhere she felt safer. 'They've always been quite welcoming', she said.[55] The idea of providing some sort of haven had been on Colin and Peter's minds when they moved to the city and decided to open a pub: 'we picked [this spot] because it was sufficiently central, but sufficiently off the beaten track [...] people could get there easily but wouldn't be seen going in if they didn't want to be', said Colin. 'That was the prevailing attitude, that and the navy attitude.'[56]

Insiders (sometimes) out

In the navy

Dennis joined up in 1976 as a seventeen year old – partly to 'escape from life in the north-east'.[57] He and his fellow ratings had been told in training that 'if any of you people here are homosexual, the navy doesn't tolerate homosexuality, so pack your bags and go home'. 'I always remember that', he said. Dennis was posted to the submarine HMS *Superb* in Plymouth a year later and shared a room with three other matelots there; they became a forces family of sorts. 'Matelot' was local slang for sailor and in French translated as both sailor and bunkmate; in Dutch a 'mattenoot' meant the same. While precise origins and meanings had faded for most, Dennis still communicated a strong sense of such intimate comradeship with these men. Together they would explore Plymouth's 'backstreets, the places that you don't normally go on your own':

> From the bottom of Union Street right up to Derry's Cross, that was a hive of activity, with pubs thriving, activities happening. Different pubs, different genders, different classes. [... In Diamond Lil's] the people in there were a bit camp and a bit effeminate. [...] Other places that we went into, some of the nightclubs like Commodores, there was always an element of, if I look back on it, there was always an element of gayness. Not that I was aware of it then. You had other places which served the – where people would go for [female] prostitutes and things like that.

Dennis didn't then see himself as gay; these nights out were like 'stag dos': 'It was fun [...] You went in there knowing what it was. And you most probably accepted the innuendo or the banter that went on. Or the touching or the things that went on and were said. I can't remember things', he added evasively. 'I didn't go [to Diamond Lil's] on my own knowing there were people of interest in there. It was normally a case of a group of us going. [...] You go out together, you enjoy together, you are entertained. And you take it from there. You take it from there.' Though Dennis perhaps knew queer men were 'of interest', he guarded himself by only going out with his fellow matelots. They nevertheless together chose Diamond Lil's and similar venues over those places his peers would visit to meet women sex workers. There was something enticing for them about this queerer scene.

Dennis married after he returned from the Falklands War in 1982 and described 'a fulfilling and rewarding' relationship with his wife and their three daughters. An independent queer life meanwhile began to unfold elsewhere for him: 'It's quite strange really, because you know, I could have gone with a woman whilst I was away. But with a woman, you feel committed. But if you meet a guy […] you're there for the same reason. […] I could talk about up in Scotland, places I visited there [and] in Portsmouth [another south coast naval city].'[58] Dennis was again evasive; he 'could talk about' what happened in these places but didn't: the habit of Plymouthian and naval discretion endured.[59]

Colin and Peter, from Manchester, recognized this 'naval attitude' when they chose a place for their pub, as we've seen. Jonathan (Jono) Madeley – who moved from London to be with his mariner lover in the late 1980s – saw it too. Attitudes and behaviours in the city and on the scene were, he said, 'very much geared towards what the military might expect' and were underpinned by a related sense of risk. Jono noted that his partner's career would have ended if their relationship had become known; he described how another man had been kicked out of the navy after a former lover 'snitched' on him.[60] Colin had to deflect the military police on their visits to the Swallow at the end of the 1980s and into the 1990s.[61] In earlier decades the military police force would wait outside the Paramount and Diamond Lil's to spot drunken and/or queer transgression.[62] Jeannie, a member of the Women's Royal Army Corps, didn't go to any queer venues in Plymouth until after she left the forces in 1964 at the age of twenty-six. 'You more or less had to pretend to be straight', she said. The military police 'were always going through all your [things]; [you had to] scurry to hide everything under the lino […] all the letters and what have you'.[63] This close scrutiny endured. A handbook tutoring senior officers on how to spot homosexuals was still in use in 1987. They were told 'to keep an eye out for ratings "with feminine gestures"' and 'to conduct random inspections of sailors' private parts to spot signs of homosexual activity'. New recruits were also to be 'quizzed' about their sexual orientation when they signed up. When the *Plymouth Herald* reported on the handbook in 1993 it was said by the navy to be 'out of date'. Officers on Devonport warships apparently no longer needed to conduct 'random private part inspections' and homosexual servicemen and women were 'discreetly dismissed' rather than dishonourably discharged.[64] This is what happened to navy chef Richard Young in 1999 – probably one of the last men to be dismissed before the ban on homosexuality was lifted a year later. Richard 'knew he was gay' when he joined up at nineteen in 1993 but thought 'a modern navy would turn a blind eye'.[65] He was reinstated to the force after an appeal and the change in the law but just a year later was 'left for dead' on a Plymouth street after a horrific homophobic attack. Richard told the press from his hospital bed that while 'they have got no problem in the

Royal Navy, it is different in the streets'; 'I think the city needs to open up a little more', he said.[66]

The navy may have fostered homosocial camaraderie and contributed to Plymouth's distinctive queer dynamics, but it also caused considerable pain. It underpinned a culture of homophobic banter and bullying and created a climate in which abuse and sexual assault in barracks and onboard ship went unreported. That such things happened at all was evident only through occasional prosecutions. [67] Dennis testified to the hurt caused by homophobia in the navy beyond the legal change of 2000. He was having sex with men in his home city as well as away by then. His wife found out and rumour spread when she confided in a close friend. '[The friend] told her husband and he worked in the same place I worked and within an afternoon, the whole of the establishment knew about me. Things changed from then on', he said. His marriage ended and at work he felt he had no alternative but to come out to the recruits he was training. If there was an acceptance among this new generation of ratings in line with a broader shift in opinion,[68] Dennis sensed disapproval among his superiors. '[They] were asking questions of my suitability for the job [...] because some of the recruits were under 18 [the age of consent at the time]. And security-wise with regard to information I had access to. Would my sexuality or my position be compromised? All those things were going on in the background.' Well-worn narratives of the predatory homosexual and of queer treachery were at stake and Dennis felt edged out of his job by an enduring homophobic culture rather than by military law. Once his departure had been agreed, 'I remember just leaving, handing in my ID card and catching the bus home to my flat on the Barbican [by the Old Harbour]. No one had taken the time and effort to recognize my service [as was usual]. And I think, I do believe it was because of my sexuality.'[69]

On civvy street

While in Brighton many people had put a distance between themselves and their families by moving to the town, in Plymouth gays and lesbians were often locally born and negotiated their queer and family lives in the same place. Both might be strongly valued but many took care to keep them from crossing over – rather as some in Manchester's and Leeds' Asian communities did. There was, said a correspondent to the *Cornish Times* in 1984, an especially pronounced 'fear of what family and friends will say'.[70] Though Michael's family were embracing and the landlord and landlady of the Penrose seem to have taken their cue from their lesbian daughter, many others anticipated trouble in opening one world to the other. Joanna moved back in with her parents when she returned from South Africa but she took some time to tell them about her parallel involvement in Plymouth's lesbian scene. Kevin kept his sexuality and (from 1986) his HIV positive status from his parents. Their off-hand homophobic comments stung: 'they probably don't know they're hurting you. But those one-liners can [...] cut you like a knife. Very much so', he said. Others, like Dennis, married but didn't come out until later – a pattern which the landlord of the gay Clarence pub in the Stonehouse area said was common among his customers. 'Many of [them] have been married in the past for 10, 20 or even 30 years and are not out gay.' 'Many were not sure even until their fifties if marriage was right for them', he went on; 'they were bogged down by peer pressure. It's not just yourself you have to consider – it's the stigma you impose on your immediate family.'[71]

For some the culture of discretion created horrendously difficult situations. Chief Petty Officer Holyer's relationship with his wife – with whom he had lived in naval married quarters since 1974 – 'disintegrated' once she was 'exposed' locally as a trans woman in 1980.[72] Two years later Mr and Mrs Osborne were outed as 'two women' when the latter became pregnant by donor insemination. Neighbours were 'shocked', and the couple felt the need 'to flee'. In October of 1982 the national *Daily Star* newspaper reported that Mrs Osbourne had lost her baby in Torquay, the seaside resort 33 miles up the coast which had become their new home.[73] The story became a vehicle for local and national anxiety about single or unconventional motherhood, especially when it involved 'undeserving' calls on council housing. This was part of a broader pattern of sensational reporting and gives a flavour of the vituperative atmosphere for LGBT people in these years.

Anxiety locally about homosexuality deepened with the AIDS crisis. Lynne described it being 'terrible, really terrible at Clarke's [shoe factory] in the city' where she worked. Some refused to use the same toilet as a gay workmate; 'he was really kind of hounded about it', she said. Another colleague turned down her offer to go swimming at the newly opened city baths: 'I said "what are you talking about?" and she said "some of your stuff might come away and go into me and I might get HIV".'[74] Father Brian Storey, chair of the Cornish-based International Crusade for Moral Reform, and Dr Adrian Rogers from Exeter and chair of the Conservatives for the Family campaign, led a small protest in the city centre in 1987 against the sale and especially the free distribution of condoms; they advocated better moral standards instead.[75] In 1991 the Plymouth-based *Western Evening Herald* carried a letter in support of their 'Charter on AIDS', which included proposals to bar people with AIDS from certain jobs.

To come out or to reveal your HIV status could feel perilous. When Kevin joined the local buddy scheme organized by the Plymouth Health Authority (notably not by the local gay community) 'our meetings had to be secret because if people knew that we were meeting in a public building, there might be outcry [...]. It was like being in the secret service', he said. Volunteers at Sussex AIDS helpline had also felt the need to be keep the office address in Brighton secret, but in Plymouth caution and anonymity was even more pressing. A 'naval wife and mother' told the Mass Observation project in 1987 that there was 'local hysteria', citing the case of a dinner lady requesting rubber gloves to deal with a child who had fallen over in the playground.[76] Peter and his partner saw invitations to straight dinner parties dry up after the first AIDS case, even though the infection rate in Plymouth was the lowest of our four cities – and remained so.[77]

Kevin and others nevertheless testify to an ethic of quiet support in the city and its hinterland. When he told two colleagues that he was HIV positive they were immediately and enduringly supportive. 'It was a terrible thing, but it brought [...] I would say a beauty out in people', he said. Though he never told his parents directly, his father was 'very very supportive' of his decision to become a buddy (his mother was more reticent – worrying, he said, about 'what the neighbours would say'). Some of those volunteering alongside Kevin were straight, as were volunteers for the Eddystone Trust which worked to provide support and advice from its offices near the Old Harbour from 1987 and then also in Exeter and Taunton to the east. The Plymouth AIDS helpline and Positive Action were run by a mixed group of local volunteers; on Bodmin Moor, 30 miles to the north-west of Plymouth, the Bethany Trust opened a fourteen-room respite centre in 1990 run by a group of nuns. The scope to get support outside the city was important for those wanting to keep their HIV status and what it might imply about their sexuality secret. More broadly we see that the absence of loudly articulated support was not the same as indifference or lack of action.

Other places, other people

The things that were particular about Plymouth often came into sharper focus when compared to other places. London was writ large in Michael's sense of what it meant to be gay, for example. His queer cultural reference points in the 1960s (*Victim* and *Against the Law*) centred on the capital, and when he and Richard moved there they found a gay politics that hadn't taken hold in Plymouth. They marched on the UK's first Gay Pride in 1972 and joined a CHE group in the suburb of Harrow. When Michael returned to Plymouth in the late 1970s he found he didn't fit in so well any more. 'I kind of breezed in [to the local CHE] a bit. And said: "I worked in CHE in London, in Harrow", and they were so unwelcoming. [...] I was invading their space', he said.[78] Other members perhaps resented being implicitly measured against a metropolitan yardstick. Ted described a similar feeling of disjunction when he moved back to Plymouth from London when his mother became ill: 'I had moved on and Plymouth hadn't', he said. 'I went into the Lockyer and they did not even know the word "camp" or "gay". [...] They were laughing and said "What do you mean 'camp'?" And so we had long discussions about "camp" and "gay". "Oh, that's London", they said.'[79] Ted and Michael both saw themselves as differently queer after their experiences in London. Both saw Plymouth as 'stuck' on their return. Later, Dennis enjoyed the queerly tinged homosocial camaraderie in Plymouth, but he noticed and half hankered after something different when he visited Brighton and Manchester – cities where 'you could be gay' in a way that didn't seem possible or desirable back home.[80]

Places nearer Plymouth were important too. Mr and Mrs Osbourne perhaps chose Torquay because of its seaside live-and-let-live reputation and its well-known queer credentials. Interviewees mentioned travelling there from Plymouth to go to the Meadfoot pub and the Double Two club from the late 1970s (subsequently renamed Rocky's and Candyfloss). The gay Cliff House Hotel ran from the 1970s until 2013; Alan, the proprietor, styled himself as 'Britain's oldest working queen'.[81] The market town of Totnes, 4 miles inland from Torquay, had a similar reputation, which extended into the 2000s when Dennis would go to socials organized by the group Totnes Queers. The town, he said, was different from Plymouth and had 'this cosmopolitan lifestyle of freedom and c'est la vie.'[82] The Metropolitan Community Church (an LGBT-friendly church founded in the USA in 1968) had a base here, moving from Plymouth in the early 2000s because of a shrinking congregation there. This was a loss to those, like Kerry, who had found a sense of community as part of the church and couldn't easily travel to Totnes.[83] To the west in Cornwall 'bohemian' Falmouth provided a contrast too: 'it has that feel', said Joanna, 'very open, very accepting'.[84] In Exeter, 60 miles in the other direction, there were a couple of bars and also a more active gay society at the university, including monthly discos which several Plymouthians went to. A feminist consciousness-raising group at Dartington College of Art between the two cities 'opened out everything' for Lynne; the College of Arts in Plymouth had no gay group until later, and though the Polytechnic Student Union held gay discos and hosted a conference for south-west gay groups in 1978, neither place drove the sort of radical agendas or bohemian possibilities we have seen in our other cities. Alan said people in Plymouth who wanted to go out in the 1990s and 2000s tended to go elsewhere. Joanna's friends would travel to some of these places so 'they wouldn't be seen'.[85]

Coming in the other direction, queer visitors and incomers to Plymouth often made a distinct impression. Ted, remember, talked about the different styles visitors from Brighton and London had. Michael's dad pointed out the touring 'nancy boy' at the Palace Theatre, while a different Ted, a former seaman, and his chef boyfriend Paul, specifically recalled the TV entertainer Michael Barrymore staying at their gay-friendly Scheherazade Guest House in the 1980s.[86] Such outsiders brought different perspectives and, if they stayed, might ring some changes. In 1982, the year that thousands lined the streets of Plymouth to watch a Falklands War victory parade and fly-past, Prudence and Gay opened their bookshop, In Other Words, on Mannamead Road in Mutley with much less fanfare (see Image 30). They had met and worked together at Manchester Grassroots bookshop in the 1970s and moved down to Plymouth having spotted a gap in the market there.[87] In Other Words, here and later in new premises in Mutley Plain (see Map 7), evolved into something of a community hub in the absence of sustained non-commercial community spaces elsewhere in the city. 'We always thought it was important to have these signs that said "Lesbian and Gay" so people would see the damn things [...] and we used to stock the free [gay] papers', said Gay. She described queer people coming in and scoping the shop out. The 'shy or uncertain' appreciated 'those magic words sitting on the shelf'.[88] Alan remembers that, to him, 'it was almost like an alternative reality [...] I was living in Plymouth, and I was living in the traditional Plymouth, but there were these little pockets of places [like In Other Words] that I could access if I was brave enough'. Hannah felt something similar:

> You could pick a book up on feminism and you could pick a book up on bisexuality. It was brilliant. And then they had that coffee shop for a little bit downstairs. I say coffee shop [...] it was literally just a coffee machine. But it was lovely, it wasn't just a place with feminist books. It was LGBTQ, it was a place to feel at home really. [...] I was always going to [...] In Other Words, even before I came out, so these places were part of my life. [89]

Though In Other Words came a decade later than similar bookshops in the other cities, it served a parallel function in relation to wider community and political networks, linking the lesbian and gay movement to anti-racist, feminist and peace activism. Gay and Prudence were behind the Southwest Feminist Book Fair in 1984 which drew people from across the west country.[90] Others heard or learned more from In Other Words about the women's peace camps at Greenham Common and the local Plymouth Peace Forum. The latter set up a particular tension in a city where the economy and livelihood of many gays and lesbians and their families was so closely linked to the armed forces. Alan observed that 'Plymouth's historical dependency on Devonport Dockyard, and subsequently contracts for refit work on nuclear submarines meant any form of [peace] activism was viewed as anti-military, [...] as directly sabotaging the city's main source of income [...] It ran against an individual's civic responsibilities to question the presence of nuclear submarines in the city', he said.[91] Sharon and thirty others staged a lie-down peace protest in the centre of Plymouth in the mid-1980s: 'we were spat at, kicked, all sorts of things happened'.[92] Their visibility as peace activists – and perhaps also as lesbians – was an affront to local military culture. The local Young Conservatives group protested outside In Other Words in 1985 because the literature it stocked amounted (they said) to incitement to civil disobedience.[93]

As an isolated radical space in the city the bookshop was a lightning rod for controversy in other respects too. Susanne Bosch came to give a reading from her controversial children's book *Jenny Lives with Eric and Martin* (1983) – much cited in the drive for Clause 28. Adrian Rogers (chair of the Conservatives for the Family campaign) was outraged that the bookshop was promulgating such familial deviancy in this way and also by stocking leaflets explaining how lesbians might inseminate themselves. The result, he said (inexplicably) would be 'a wave of orphans'.[94] While in other cities there had been mass protest at Clause 28, in Plymouth the In Other Words window display at this time was pretty much the only marker of dissent. It was instead those who approved of the clause that spoke more loudly, fearing that gays and lesbians would start trespassing more visibly on public space and civic life if it wasn't enacted. The local press covered the Tory councillor's claims that known homosexuals had infiltrated Devon's schools and a local vicar's pleas with general election candidates to back restrictions on gay lessons if they were elected. They held up London's moral decline as a fearful example of what resulted from such horrors.[95]

When the trades union UNISON's gay and lesbian wing held its conference in Plymouth at the Holiday Inn on the Hoe in 1988, organizers were worried for the safety of the 600 delegates coming to a city not known for its lesbian and gay friendliness. Others were concerned about their use of the hotel pool – a full three years after transmission routes for HIV had been clarified.[96] In 1992, the Students Union of Plymouth University (until 1991 Plymouth Polytechnic) convened a debate on whether 'homosexuality should be promoted as a valid lifestyle' – riffing on Clause 28 and the ongoing national protest. Against the motion were Father Storey (who we met earlier) and the former mayor of Plymouth, Dennis Dicker. The proponents were Kevin Sexton, National Union of Students Lesbian and Gay Convenor, who travelled down from London, and liberal, lesbian theologian Dr Elizabeth Stuart, from the University of Glamorgan. The debate was held behind closed doors because of 'fear of a violent reaction from "a strong right wing element in the city"'.[97] Student Union organizers at least were nervous about how the debate would be received and also perhaps about the safety of these visiting liberal outsiders.

Alan said that it was people from beyond Plymouth who rocked the boat and who mobilized the lesbian and gay community in the 1980s and 1990s:

> Colin and Peter came [from near Manchester] to Plymouth and opened the [Swallow] pub. And Prudence and Gay came [from Manchester] to Plymouth and opened the bookshop. Jonathan [from London] at the time of the [1995 murder of Terry Sweet] went in the papers and stuff. But it was always the people from outside that were prepared to be visible. There were very few Plymouthians who stepped up.

With typical local reserve Alan didn't mention himself as one of those who did (as we'll see). It was meanwhile more straightforward for the incomers he mentioned to be visible in Plymouth. They were each distant from family and Colin, Peter, Prudence and Gay were also self-employed in queer contexts. They weren't fearful of losing their jobs or being shunned at work as others were in the city. These factors, together with their grounding in the different queer cultures of Manchester and London, allowed them to be more outspoken in a city which was, for Jonathan (Jono) at least, 'a bit of a culture shock'.[98]

Policing and Pride

Jono came to local prominence as a local organizer and community spokesperson in the wake of the brutal homophobic murder of sixty-four-year-old Frederick ('Terry') Sweet in November 1995 in a notoriously cruisy part of Plymouth's Central Park.[99] Fifty-three-year-old Bernard Hawken was left critically injured and brain damaged in the same attack. There had been a spate of earlier attacks in the same part of the park, including of a fifty year old assaulted with a hammer, but the particular ferocity of the Sweet case took it into the national press and provoked anxiety locally.[100] It 'blackened things for Plymouth', said Alan, keeping him in the closet for a further decade.[101]

Terry, the local press reported, was a divorcee and father who had lived with his 'devoted' male partner for the previous six years. He had also, according to his ex-wife, 'indulged in homosexual affairs' throughout their thirteen-year marriage.[102] Sweet's partner, Albert, had three children from an earlier marriage who had come to know Sweet as 'Uncle Terry'. Hawken was meanwhile one of seven siblings from 'a long established [local] family'.[103] He was subsequently pictured in the paper in a wheelchair with his young great niece.[104] These details oriented these men towards the family life which was so valued in Plymouth and flagged a relatively common local negotiation for queer people. Both men had married in line with strongly felt local expectation; both had come out later in life. Terry's ex-wife and the four children he and Albert had between them meanwhile seem to have accommodated the choices they had made – though the fact that Terry's ex talked about his affairs to the journalist suggests something of the hurt he had caused her.

Image 20 Graffiti in Central Park left after the murder of Terry Sweet in 1995. On the monument the first line reads: 'In memory of Terry Sweet. May he rest in pieces. Ha Ha'. On the pavement is scrawled: 'Please step over spilt AIDS'.

Fourteen months prior to the murder the police had joined a Gay, Lesbian and Bisexual forum to look at policing public space more effectively and sympathetically. Though there is little evidence of a change in policing in that period, it may have had an impact on the decision to hand over the murder enquiry phone line to 'the community'. Jono, who had been involved in the forum and who ran The Junction sexual health and relationship project in the city, was asked to coordinate it. This was a significant move by the police, ameliorating some of the concern queer callers may have had.[105] There was a legacy of mistrust and a fear for many of disclosing anything to a police force which had kept a list of 'known homosexuals' and used informants to pursue them. Previous attacks in Central Park had gone unreported because of what the national *Independent* newspaper described as the local 'stigma' associated with homosexuality and perhaps especially queer lives lived too openly in a city where there was a cultural, familial and naval impetus to keep quiet.[106] Jono noted in the press at the time that men cruising in Central Park 'might not be gay [and] may be husbands and fathers'; they were more likely, he said, to speak to him and the team he assembled than to a police officer.[107]

There was praise 'from the community' for the way the police handled the investigation.[108] Three men in their late teens, one with a previous conviction for part blinding a man in the same park, were swiftly arrested and subsequently prosecuted. They were, reported the *Plymouth Evening Herald*, from 'respectable families' but drugs had 'set them on a path to murder'.[109] Jono meanwhile started being recognized locally and received a generally positive response. He had 'stuck [his] head above the parapet' in Plymouth and not been shot down.[110] After the case Devon and Cornwall police introduced diversity officers and (in 1999) a lesbian and gay liaison officer for Plymouth. 'A more open dialogue occurred as a result of that crime', said the senior investigating officer.[111] In a newspaper interview following the trial in 1997, Jono nevertheless reflected on the enduring lack of local gay and lesbian mobilization: 'even after such a tragedy, the gay community in Plymouth are unable to have a voice – why I do not know. Possibly apathy and possibly fear'.[112]

He and Prudence (both non-Plymouthians) went on to set up Pride Forum in 1999 partly in response. It was 'a mixed group' with 'mixed ages', meeting monthly to network gay and lesbian groups in the city and to keep conversations going with the police and council. A dedicated council committee was convened to chart and network LGBT groups and resources in the city; the police began surgeries at a range of venues including the Swallow and at the City Hall. In 2001, Pride Forum was behind a community conference at the Virginia House Settlement titled 'What Will the Neighbours Think' (2001), riffing on that particular Plymouthian preoccupation. There were sessions on parenting, coming out, homophobia, trans experience and queer theory.[113]

Five years later the council supported a week of discreet indoor Pride events, including darts and a short film festival at Plymouth Arts Centre. Pride days followed in 2007 and 2008 at Plymouth Guildhall – inside, out of view, but attracting 1,500 and 3,000 people respectively. In 2009, the day included a short flag parade. There were, in these years, also Pride contingents in the Lord Mayor's Parade while in 2012 Pride was held in the open in Devonport Park.[114] 'If you held a (public) gay pride rally in Plymouth about five people would show up', Jono had said in 1995,[115] a sentiment echoed down the years by others. 'People had said [for years] there was no way we could have a Gay Pride in Plymouth, [...] people would just be too worried about being seen by employers and neighbours and all sorts', said Gay.[116] But these ideas could be self-perpetuating, and Plymouth's first open-air Pride, when it came, was a success. Significantly, though, Pride here resulted not from the community groundswell we saw in our other cities but from liaison between a small group of lesbians and gays and a council seeking to meet new social inclusion obligations set out by the New Labour government and to come into line with wider cultural changes.

The Pride in our Past oral history and archive project spearheaded by Alan from 2011 provided a further dimension to this new visibility, drawing out threads of the city's queer past and weaving some sense of community with them. 'I really felt a part of the community then', said Hannah; 'young people were involved, and generations. It was fantastic'. It also felt somewhat ephemeral, however: 'sometimes it's [...] pots of funding that will make that happen. It would be nice for things to be more sustainable.'[117] Alan suggested that previous queer generations in Plymouth had left too little to build on. In the interviews he conducted people would say: '"don't make a fuss", "don't draw attention to it"'. This, he said, 'left people of his [younger] generation with nothing to cling to really'.[118] In Manchester and Brighton youth and counterculture, partial decriminalization in 1967 and especially women's and gay liberation a few years later allowed some to feel more confident in being visibly different and defiantly political. Though beatniks hung out at El Sombrero and fashions changed with the times, counterculture didn't take so much hold here. Plymouth Polytechnic wasn't formed until 1970 and didn't develop the radical pulse we saw among students in Manchester, Leeds and Brighton. Gay and women's liberation didn't flourish here; the local CHE was more social than political and in any case faltered in the 1980s because there was a premature feeling of 'job done'.[119] This all related to a local conservatism and a disdain for the kind of radical and especially peace activism which was elsewhere twisted together with anti-racist, women's and gay politics. The growth in student numbers which altered dynamics in our other cities came later in Plymouth (doubling between 1991 and 2011 rather than in the earlier decades), and though students changed the feel of this city too, the era of especially fervent or visible student politics had by this time passed.[120] Plymouth's more expansive arts scene also only emerged more recently and didn't function as the kind of anchor and conduit for queer expression and thinking that it did elsewhere.

In 2014, Pride was held on the iconic Hoe for the first time. The former Lockyer barmaid (who had served at the pub when a new landlady 'with her nose in the air' had first tried to oust the queers in 1970) was there with her husband; both were enthusiastic about what they saw as a new openness in the city.[121] By now LGBTQ people were 'quite willing' to go to non-gay bars (as they had on Union Street in the 1960s and 1970s and around the station in the 1980s – though in a different context). Dennis and Kevin felt this shift was partly down to the decline in the docks, the reduction in the number of service personnel stationed here and a changing culture in the forces.[122] They also noted the studenty reorientation of the city. 'We were always known for being servicemen, service families and beer. Drinking. Pubs and clubs', said Kevin, commenting on these shifts. 'I never thought I'd ever see people spending so much on going out for coffee and meals.'[123]

These changes were laced with the kind of regret and nostalgia Alison discusses in Chapter 7. Ted liked the regularity and familiarity of queer 'family' life in the 1960s and early 1970s. He told the local paper that 'it was better when it was against the law […] we were like a big family; we all knew who we were and where we could go. You'd go out and visit people on a Sunday for tea and things like that. We always used to go for drinks on a Saturday night at the Lockyer Hotel. It was only a little place but we were used to it and the staff knew us all.'[124] Plymouth's heyday for lesbians had also passed, Jo felt. 'Manchester seems to have, you know, a scene that's ongoing. And Plymouth did have […] and it's disappeared.'[125] Union Street, said Kevin, had lost 'its sort of magic. I know people regarded it as rough and that, but there was a magic down there. […] Although there were fights, there was this great camaraderie of people.'[126] Dennis welcomed moves towards equality and the new openness but hankered after the homosocial comradeship he experienced when he first joined up:

When I was a junior rating, I shared a cabin with three guys […] And so we had that community feeling of, you look after one another […] And I think that's lost now, because everyone is an individual. […] They go back to their room and they shut the door. They just live on their own. […] The places, the pubs, the bars. They were probably frequented by sailors, be they gay, be they straight, or what have you. It's gone.

At the Swallow more recently, 'where 95 per cent of the people were LGBTQ', Dennis 'didn't feel comfortable [amid people] doing their own thing, being flamboyant, being garish, being loud'. The greater visibility of LGBTQ people has not led to a greater feeling of community for Dennis; like the people serving in the navy now, those in the Swallow were just 'doing their own thing'.[127]

In the testimonies gathered here, there was much tacking back and forth between Plymouth and other places, between the present and bygone days, as interviewees tried to articulate what was particular about their city and what had changed. In the process what emerged was the sense of a scene that only uncomfortably accommodated broader ideas of progress, visibility and pride. The queer temperature of Plymouth certainly changed in the 2000s but in ways that felt alien and 'sterile' to Dennis and 'inhibiting' to others. Things being more out in the open 'made it a little bit more frightful' for older lesbians and gays, said Jo.[128] Some also saw a local lassitude at play. 'We're trying to get together a few different things for people to be able to enjoy, partake in, which doesn't revolve around the pubs and clubs, so like we're starting our new coffee group [at the Theatre Royal but …]. It's that lethargy isn't it really, you know, they want it but they won't support it', said Martyn, social secretary of Plymouth Pride Forum until it folded in 2013 (Pride in Plymouth's coffee groups have since had more success).[129] Many still prefer to go elsewhere for a gay scene. Kevin mentioned friends who went annually to Pride in Manchester 'to be gay': 'they have four or five days to be drunk, dance, they have a World Aids Day remembrance and then they come back to a normal life down here', adding: '"Contribute down here too", you feel like saying!'[130] 'Being gay' in the sense of being visible and 'out there' has in Plymouth often been associated with other places. The nostalgia here is for identity, community and pride in a different key. In Plymouth, Alan concluded, there was a 'pride in passing'. And so, while it is tempting to seek something indicative in the photo of CHE members on the Hoe in 1976 (inside front cover) and in the first Pride there forty years later, what was happening elsewhere in the city in the period between these events is perhaps more telling: the way Kevin kept his queer and family lives apart; the quiet support offered by some in the contexts of AIDS and the Terry Sweet murder; or the local press celebration of longstanding gay couple-dom – of Colin and Peter at the Swallow when the latter died in 2006 ('Peter was Ginger to my Fred Astaire', the headline ran) and of Ted and Paul on their 55th anniversary in 2015.[131] When Prudence died in 2011, Gay received sympathy cards from their neighbours. If their relationship had been unacknowledged before it hadn't necessarily gone unnoticed or disrespected. In this we get some sense of Plymouth's queer dynamics and pride – quite different from those in Brighton where we began.

Maps

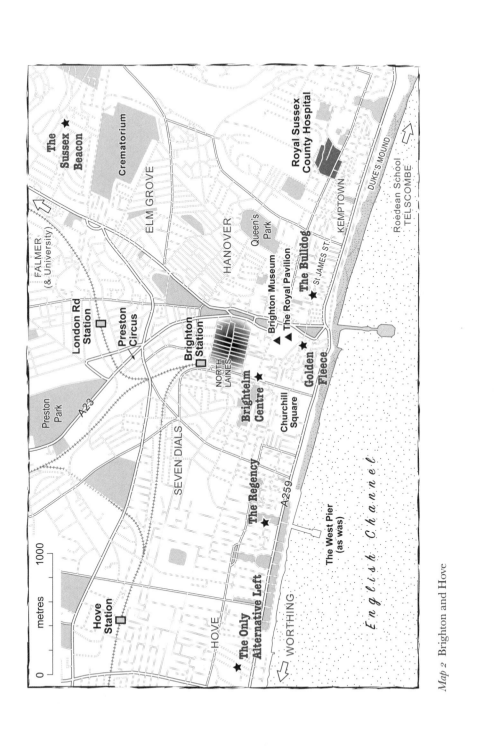

Map 2 Brighton and Hove

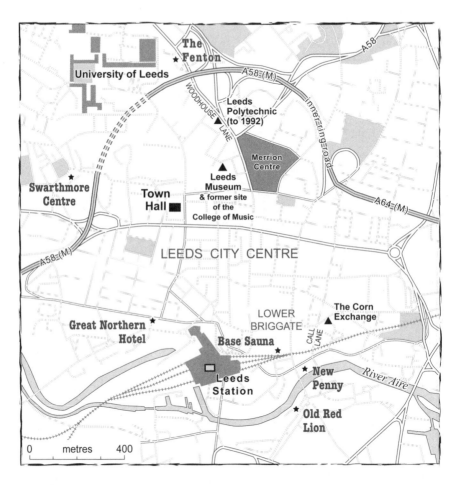

Map 3 Leeds city centre

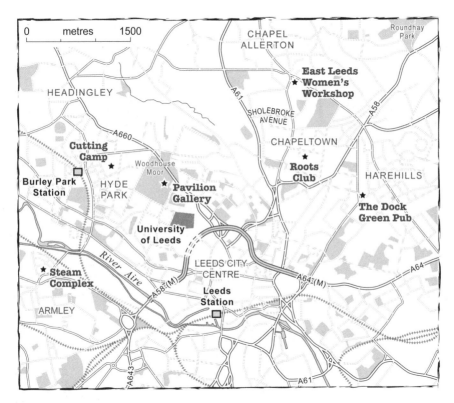

Map 4 Leeds city centre and inner suburbs

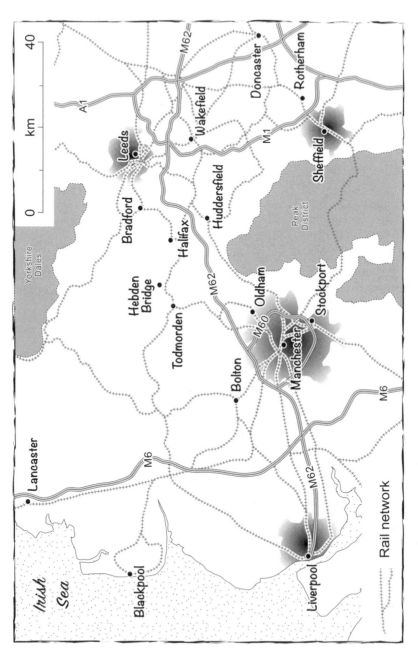

Map 5 Leeds, Manchester and surrounding towns and cities

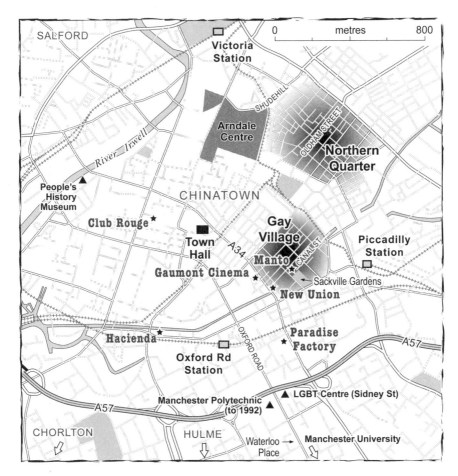

Map 6 Central Manchester

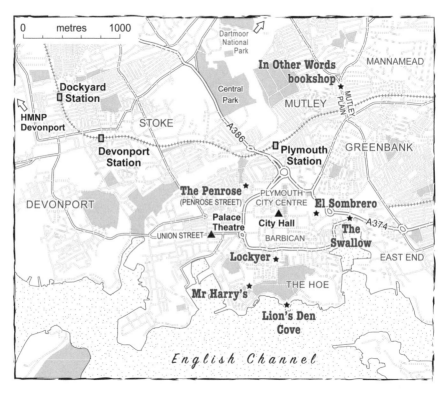

Map 7 Plymouth

Part II

Queer Comparisons
by Alison Oram

5

Circling around: migration and the queer city

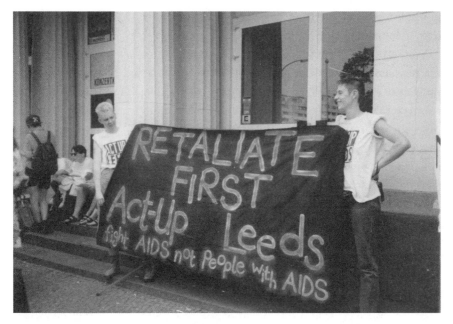

Image 21 ACT UP Leeds protesting in Berlin, 1993

Jenny-Anne initially migrated to the Manchester area from the south of England in 1974 when the company she worked for moved their offices to Stockport. At this time, Jenny-Anne was outwardly living as a married man with a family. She said, '[i]f you were trans in the late 60s, early 70s, it was very hard to find anybody'. Luckily, one of her friends knew of the TV/TS group which met in the Chaplaincy of Manchester University, and Jenny-Anne 'nervously went along'. A few years later she had to make further moves:

I had various run-ins with the police in the 70s, one of which destroyed my career [...] because they reported me to the company I worked for as being cross-dressed. And every time I got a new job, somebody would remember.[1]

Jenny-Anne moved back to the south of England in the early 1980s for better employment opportunities, not only for herself but for her children, yet continued to make trips back up north:

Manchester was such a liberal city, even in the 1970s and quite often although I lived firstly in Tamworth and then in Basingstoke – so a long way away – I would occasionally come to Manchester for events, rather than London, because I felt Manchester not only had better events but was a much more accepting city.[2]

Returning to Cheshire (and later north Wales) in the early 1990s, Jenny-Anne was able to pick up her Manchester life again and find trans networks and affirmation in the north-west.

Jenny-Anne's story shows some of the complex reasons why queer people migrate. Transphobic hostility forced her to move to find new employment a number of times. She describes gravitating back and forth towards Manchester over several decades as it continued to offer her more trans-friendly possibilities than the south of England. This process of moving around to find a city that fits, that is a comfortable place to live a queer life and gives a sense of belonging, is a recurrent theme in the migration stories of LGBTQ people who settled in Manchester, Brighton, Plymouth and Leeds. So many of the stories of migration involve not just straightforward moves from one place to another but a circling around. This is so common that it seems to be a particularly queer type of migration. Circling around might describe local or short-term movements, oscillating between heterosexual and queer environments, such as Jenny-Anne's commuting to Manchester from Basingstoke, from Cheshire and later from north Wales for the day, evening or weekend to find community. Queer people engage in plenty of national-level circling, too, as they check out different places to satisfy varying life choices and changes.

The period Jenny-Anne describes was one of increased movement for many people. Universities were expanding, drawing more young people away from their home towns. As the economy increasingly shifted away from manufacturing and towards service industries there was more mobility in the job market and people might migrate to follow work opportunities. The increase in car ownership and improvements to the road network aided these moves for work but also helped stoke people's desires to explore more of their own country and holiday abroad as well. Moving around and further afield became easier and more attractive, even if it also brought challenges.

Circling around: migration and the queer city

These social, cultural and economic changes affected many people, whatever their sexual and gender identities, but this chapter shows what was particular about these movements for LGBTQ people and what differences those moves made to them and to the cities they moved to. Because the oral histories were contributed by people now living in Manchester, Leeds, Plymouth and Brighton, there are inevitably more stories about why people moved into a city than there are about the others who left. Over three main sections I show that there were different factors in play pulling people into each city. In the first I look chiefly at the famously queer draw of Brighton, and in the second at the difference that the expanding universities made to Leeds and Manchester and their LGBTQ cultures. In the third, I look particularly at Plymouth, at how family connections as well as love and employment affected movement to and fro. When LGBTQ people move to a new city they may hope to find a congenial gay community. Yet the queer desire to move from one place to another is also prompted by everyday-life demands – to find work, to go to university, to join a partner or to start a business: reasons common to everyone, queer or not. LGBTQ people may also have stayed in a specific city (or returned to it) with a sense of belonging to that place and region. All of these comings and goings and queer arrivals ripple into a city's social scene and politics, helping to shape distinctive queer urban cultures. First, though, to some of the broader dimensions of movement for LGBTQ people.

Circling around

Perhaps there is something about movement, migration and travel that is especially attractive or necessary for queer people. Over a lifetime, many LGBTQ people engage in complicated patterns of movement, involving several different places or cities to which they belonged or where they lived for a while. At an individual and local level, the idea of circling around evokes practices such as cruising or flirting: moving back and forth, catching someone's eye and their attention and interest. In relation to places too, it is a process of checking them out – which place can happily accommodate the queer me?[3] Gay men have often been particularly associated with the pleasures of movement, be that smaller-scale practices of cruising city streets or the travel opportunities for work or for leisure.[4] But lesbians too (as we shall see) have also flirted with places, seizing and creating prospects for moving around, whether within the hospitable streets of queer-friendly Brighton or Manchester, or through nationwide networking and household moves.[5] Indeed, one of the themes that emerges from people's tales of national circling is how frequently lesbians moved home around the country, over long distances and often more than once or twice. In the 1960s and 1970s, there were widening opportunities for women of all class backgrounds to travel overseas and within the UK for work, while the growth of higher education especially benefitted women, increasing their mobility in employment, their independence and their capacity for sexual self-determination.[6]

In all four cities we found extensive evening and weekend travel as people socialized queerly in the hinterlands of their cities or further afield. Some of these journeys reflect a degree of caution and constraint. People circled away from their local neighbourhood for fear of being recognized in a gay bar, especially in the earlier part of the period. In Plymouth, for example, the nearby alternative was Torquay (33 miles away by road), which has a long-standing reputation as the south-west's 'gay Riviera'. Meanwhile, people from Cornwall would travel to Plymouth to go to the Swallow. 'The important thing was that you weren't known. [...] you're not going to bump into somebody.'[7] In the north and north-west there was a lot of circling around to escape local scrutiny or to enjoy new faces and clubs – to Huddersfield from Manchester and Leeds in the 1970s and early 1980s and then increasingly to Manchester as its scene expanded. A 1995 survey of gay men found there was 'considerable geographic mobility within the North West, with venues in Manchester and Blackpool attracting men from all over the region and beyond'.[8] Blackpool was a popular destination for both lesbians and gay men. Peter described how Manchester lesbian and gay youth group activities included day trips to Blackpool in the 1980s and 1990s.[9] Caroline, who lived in Manchester in the early 2000s, said: 'every so often Vanilla [a lesbian bar] would have coaches to take people to big events, night club events on a Saturday night, to Liverpool [and] Blackpool'.[10]

For northern trans people, the quest for welcoming clubs combined with anxieties about being outed created a longstanding traffic between Manchester, Liverpool, Cheshire and north Wales. Jenny-Anne recalled the 1970s and 1980s:

> There was a summer party in Ashton, that happened quite regularly, from Northern Concord. We organized events, the Beaumont Society organized events in Scarborough and in Harrogate and in Preston. And the one I particularly liked was in Deganwy in north Wales, near Llandudno.[11]

Now living in north Wales, but continuing her involvement with Manchester activism, she described how:

we get quite a lot of people coming to our north Wales group from Cheshire and the Wirral, because they don't want to be seen out in Birkenhead where there's a group, or across the water in Liverpool. And fortunately, our people from north Wales seem to be quite happy to come to us. Some of them do stray to the other cities. Obviously, when there's Sparkle [transgender festival], lots of people go to Manchester.[12]

Political activism was another reason for longer-distance journeys. Leeds lesbian-feminists talked about hitch-hiking or hiring cars in the 1970s and 1980s to get to London and other cities for feminist conferences, for the Patriarchy Study Group and so on, sleeping on friend's floors or 'you know, you'd go to conferences and sleep in a sleeping bag on the floor of a church hall'.[13] Lou remembered: 'We did demonstrate a lot. All the time. And we didn't have very many cars. When you went down to London you had about six in a car. [...] And you'd hitch. If you hadn't got a car you'd hitch.'[14] This mobility was expedited by the newly built M1 motorway, linking north and south, with a final section into Leeds city centre completed in 1972. Lesley recalled links with York and Wakefield and going to Manchester, Sheffield and London for Lesbian Line or Lesbians in Healthcare conferences; '[a]nd then you'd go out afterwards to a disco'.[15] The motivation for such journeys was often social as well as political – a chance to catch up with old friends and make new ones – and for some women these events and weekends away were an opportunity to discover their lesbian desires and come out.

Some Brighton lesbians travelled far and wide in the late 1980s to campaign against Clause 28. Melita described how

> I was invited by people in the London campaign, who had been hooked up with a Dutch group of artists and activists who had heard about what was happening and were absolutely horrified. And they organized this rickety bus to go round Europe with two gay men cabaret performers from Manchester, a group of lesbian punks from London in a band called Mouth Almighty, and a bunch of absolutely random people.

Returning from Europe, Melita and her Brighton comrades then organized a UK version of this anti-Clause 28 tour:

> I said, let's do this in England! It's easy peasy! So we did it. We organized a speaking tour, and we contacted lesbian and gay and bisexual societies at different universities. We contacted tiny groups in places like Lampeter in Wales and Hereford and Worcester and basically anyone who'd have us. [...] So we met great kindness and great support.[16]

This travelling charabanc from Brighton (and similar movements between other cities) extended urban activism around the country and beyond. Leeds lesbians and gay men formed an ACT UP contingent and demonstrated at the international AIDS conference in Berlin in 1993, for example (Image 21). This is a reminder of the transnational queer organizing that people in our cities were involved with. All this gallivanting around and coming together strengthened LGBTQ networks and a collective sense of being queer at a crucial time of antagonism towards gay men and lesbians.

The women's and lesbian and gay movements themselves smoothed the path of migration in the 1970s and 1980s, as they offered an instant community, a sense of purpose and friendships. These years saw the emergence, almost, of a sense of 'lesbian nation', giving women the confidence that they would find other lesbians across various cities and towns in the UK. Gay grew up in Bath in south-west England, went to university in Nottingham in the radical late 1960s, then lived in Leeds for a year to do teacher training, which she described as 'thoroughly miserable'. After two years in Norwich with a male partner, Gay then moved north to Manchester: 'life became exciting at that point'. Deeply involved in early women's liberation and living in a shared house with two gay men, Gay came out as a lesbian two or three years later.[17] She met her long-term partner Prudence (herself a migrant from New Zealand) through the book trade in Manchester and in 1982, as we saw in Chapter 4, the couple moved to Plymouth to open their own alternative bookshop, the first in the city. This was the last stopping point in Gay's circling around the country. After living in one place for several years, lesbians and gay men, including incomers, might develop an affiliation to a city, especially if they were active participants in its LGBTQ life, but this sense of belonging was not necessarily a feature of their earlier lives.

In many of the stories of queer migration in this chapter, there is a sense of forging a personal attachment to a new place or deepening an existing one. We can see this in the accounts of regional circling around a conurbation or its hinterland. For some contributors this was a desire to still belong to the place where they grew up; for others it was a continuing pull to their adopted city or region. This was sometimes expressed in terms of geographical location, for example identifying with northernness or with the south-west. Dennis, whom we met earlier, had been posted to various places while in the military but had retained a family home in Plymouth and lived much of his life there. He left the city and moved in with his partner near Totnes, 25 miles away, for four years in the 2010s, subsequently returning to Plymouth, partly to take active care of

Image 22 Flyer for Never Going Underground, 20 February 1988

his grandchildren.[18] Deb, who was originally from Exeter, described how she moved around several Devon towns:

> I didn't come out until '93, and I was very much split between Exeter, Torquay and Plymouth with my different social groups. So Torquay was where I started most of my social stuff. But I really enjoyed coming to Plymouth. I moved away and worked in London and Norfolk and Kent, but when I wanted to come back to Devon, it was very much for me about coming back to Plymouth and have a bit more of that sense of community again after having travelled round so much.[19]

As the largest city in the south-west for many miles, Plymouth acted as a gathering point for LGBTQ people who wanted to live near family, friendship networks and a gay social scene.

Queer heaven on earth: the dream city by the sea

In the early 1960s, Sandie and her girlfriend took a holiday in Brighton. Delighted by the queer welcome they found in the city, they moved there from Birmingham a few months later. 'We packed all our goods in a transit van and set off for Brighton without a second thought. Brighton seemed to be a gay people's town and moving there was like starting a completely new life.'[20] Sandie had acknowledged her same-sex desires to herself and broken off an engagement at the age of seventeen. Now in her early twenties, she had come out in terms of going to Birmingham's gay and lesbian pubs but she wasn't out to her family, who were putting her under pressure to settle down.[21] But more important than these push factors was the positive allure of moving somewhere where it felt good to be gay, where she had the opportunity to reinvent herself as a young gay woman:

> Before I came to Brighton [...] I had really led a repressed life. I was frightened and still very much under the parental thumb. It was like a metamorphosis when I came to Brighton. It was like casting off an old skin. A lot of it did have to do with the wonderful freedom of Brighton. When I went back to Birmingham, it was no longer my home.[22]

In her fear of her family's rejection and the sense she could find a better gay life elsewhere, Sandie encapsulates the sentiments of the classic queer migration story – that leaving one's home town is a necessary move to fully express queer desires and live a freer life as gay, lesbian, trans or bisexual.[23]

By the time Sandie moved there Brighton already had a word-of-mouth reputation as a gay resort, even before the existence of a gay press, and as well as its lesbian and gay social scene there were gay clothes shops and bookshops (see Image 3).[24] Gay people, said Sandie, 'seemed to be accepted':

> We'd never seen gay people *en masse* like that before and clubs that everyone knew were clubs for gay people which was unknown, even in a great city like Birmingham. We actually saw gay boys that we could identify as gay boys walking in couples along the shopping streets.[25]

Sandie's account is full of the tangible benefits that the move to Brighton achieved. But it is also a vision of an idealized place of gay acceptance and community. This imagined queer city is common to many stories of LGBTQ migration and is particularly voiced in relation to Brighton. Sandie clearly trusted that work would be available in Brighton but in fact homophobic employment

Image 23 The proprietor of the New Steine Hotel, Brighton, *c.*1978, catering to the gay tourist trade

references followed her down south. She was rejected for teacher training and experienced periods of unemployment without even enough money for food. Nevertheless, the almost magical vision of Brighton as a gay haven continued to be uppermost in the story she told nearly thirty years later.

As both a gay resort and an established queer city, Brighton hosted (at least) two types of LGBTQ migration – temporary visitors and permanent migrants. In practice, these moves often merged in people's accounts, as some visitors took opportunities to become full-time residents. Many told stories of visiting the city over many years as a place to relax from often more restricted lives elsewhere. People visited with new boyfriends or girlfriends, with established partners or for recuperation following a relationship break-up. Keith, a gay man, explained: 'We would come down from Leicestershire for three or four nights a few times a year and had discovered – I can't remember how – the almost perfect guesthouse in a quieter part of Kemptown.'[26]

Others were drawn by the promise of sexual freedom in Brighton, which often merged with its seaside setting in descriptions given by lesbians and gay men, 'enchanted' by its boundless horizons.[27] Temporary migration such as these holiday visits was aided, from the 1970s, by the growing pink pound infrastructure, especially the increasing number of gay guest houses. These were found not only through friends but via the gay press and phone lines. Jenny, a Brighton Gay Switchboard volunteer in the 1980s, remembered people 'ringing us up [who] would ask where can we go, where can we stay?' (and see Image 4).[28]

Short-term holidays in the city, for its gay pleasures or as temporary sanctuary, are part of the texture of Brighton throughout the period. Some visitors returned for good, citing the openness of bohemian Brighton compared to their repressive home towns, especially between the 1960s and 1990s. As Freddie explained:

> When I was in my twenties it was a lot more difficult. I lived in a small village in Oxfordshire and I lived a lie for many years. It was all hush-hush. I was beaten up a fair few times, queer-bashed. [...] I packed my bags and thought, 'I'm going to head down to Brighton'.[29]

Although Freddie also described attacks on his Brighton shop and hassle from the police in the 1980s, the fact that he was able to run a successful gay business combined with neighbourhood acceptance of him and his boyfriend meant that he saw the city as his true home. The everyday experience of being a full-time Brightonian might fulfil some of the dreams and desires nurtured by visitors who circled around before moving permanently, though there was violence and homophobia here too.

The decision to move to Brighton still involved weighing up real benefits and costs, as James' story shows:

> Well, we moved to Brighton in 1993, when I got together with my other half. We wanted originally to buy a house in London, but out of the question already money-wise […] [for work] we needed to be in London within an hour […] And settled on Brighton, because it was so queer, basically. […] We wanted to be somewhere where we could lead a comparatively normal life.[30]

James juxtaposes wanting to live in a queer place and the desire to be treated 'normally' as a gay couple. The move marked a stage in his life when he was settling down with a partner. James' antiques business depended on his having good transport from Brighton, as did his partner's work in the London theatre. The couple's choice of location was practical in terms of their professional needs – a decision that might equally have been made by a heterosexual couple. But James had been visiting Brighton since the 1960s, knew the gay male scene inside out and valued its proximity:

> St James' Street was very much queerer in the 80s and 90s than it is now. […] there was a backstreet sauna. There was a gay coffee bar and a bookshop and there was a tobacconist with a notorious notice board.[31]

Of our four cities, Brighton was consistently the most obvious destination throughout the whole period in which to seek queer community. Most of its LGBTQ residents were not born and raised in Brighton itself but were drawn by its liberal reputation and remade their queer selves and homes here. Of the forty people who gave their stories to Brighton Ourstory for the book *Daring Hearts*, published in 1992, just seven were born or brought up in Brighton, Hove or Worthing (the last a town 11 miles to the west). Brighton's magnetic pull as a 'gay capital' is also clear from the 1997 Zorro survey of gay men's sexual and social lives in Brighton. This found that over 90 per cent of gay men living in Brighton and Hove had migrated from elsewhere, mostly for gay-related reasons, including the availability of community, a social scene and knowing friends and partners.[32]

The attraction of Brighton for migrants did not essentially change over the fifty-year time period discussed here. Legal reforms, changing cultural attitudes and the increasing acceptance of LGBTQ people from the late 1990s meant the contrast between the welcome of Brighton and the homophobia of elsewhere lessened somewhat, at least for some queer people. Yet into the 2000s, the magic of Brighton as the promised land, with its sexual buzz and offer of a queer home, was often voiced by newcomers in very similar terms to decades earlier.

This was especially the case for trans and non-binary migrants in the 2000s, as their community in Brighton took shape and gained visibility, particularly after the establishment of the Clare Project in 1990. Around half of the two dozen people who gave their stories to the Brighton Trans*formed project in 2014 had moved to Brighton specifically to transition. A number had moved from elsewhere on the south coast, for example from the less congenial town of Hastings. But a fair few had already been living in Brighton for a while, whether as gay, lesbian or heterosexual, and had moved towards a new gender identity in that time, suggesting that the culture of the city could actively nurture an individual's migration towards a different identity. In their stories, some people, often from small towns or rural areas, echoed the classic queer migration story. Sarah was one who had made that journey:

> I came from south Wales and before that I came from Jersey and I know that it would have been impossible for me over there to kind of have the opportunities that I've had here. Just people walking down the street don't really stare at you, like they do elsewhere in the country. People see someone who's obviously trans and they just don't react, they just go about their daily business.[33]

Having friends in Brighton already was important to Sarah, as it was for many others, and she also evokes a romanticized vision of the seaside city:

> I remember sitting on the beach and there was the smell of barbecues in the air and the sun was going down and I just remember sitting there, thinking 'I could live here, it seems like a really cool place'.[34]

Reuben, one of the youngest narrators at twenty years old in 2014, told a similar story in starker terms, casting Brighton as 'the safe land for anyone' and a 'safe bubble' for trans people.[35] Like a number of other trans contributors, Reuben emphasized how Brighton enabled greater non-binary gender diversity, without pressure to conform to particular trans journeys such as gender confirmation.[36]

The search for a satisfactory place to call home was complicated for LGBTQ people of colour.[37] Already out as a lesbian, Sabah started at Sussex University in 2008. 'So, yeah, when I moved down to Brighton, it was like "Oh, yeah, like I can be gay" and I was the biggest gay they ever saw.'[38] Sabah, who described himself as South Asian, later began transitioning. At this point, he discussed the loneliness of being the only brown person in trans support groups while feeling anxious about reactions from straight people in youth groups for people of colour.[39] Interviewed a couple of years later he said he intended to stay in Brighton but pointed to reasons why London might also be a good choice:

I know a few friends who identify as queer and as people of colour and they've just got fed up with the lack of diversity and the lack of understanding and they're like, 'Oh I'm going to go to London because it's bigger and, you know, the communities are bigger', but in the same way they're still just as isolating. It's just you can just get lost for a bit longer.[40]

The weighing up of whether larger cities such as London (or Manchester) with more diverse communities could offer a more comfortable home than densely queer Brighton was a real dilemma for queer people of colour like Sabah, and also Jess, whose story we will come to later.

These themes of safety, tolerance of diversity and of a nurturing urban environment have become part of the narrative of Brighton's exceptionalism for recent as well as historic migrants and visitors. Caroline described a visit to Brighton in 2012 with a new lover, coming out as a lesbian for the second time:

We had come to Brighton to enjoy the 'scene' but what we found was acceptance everywhere we went, not just in the gay bars. The scene was all of Brighton for me. Eastern European girls with glinting eyes greeted us at the hotel reception, waitresses did not give us the questioning stares that we'd found back at home on the Isle of Wight. [...] [W]e walked, watching the roaring slate grey sea on that dark December night. [...] I was loving Brighton, it made me feel at home, welcomed me, a lesbian with L plates, in love! [...] I felt natural and free.[41]

In many respects this reprises the stories from the 1960s and 1970s. Caroline was rediscovering her sexual identity, and that identity was being endorsed, it seemed, by the city itself.

Brighton drew queer migrants from Yorkshire, Wales, Birmingham and further afield, and there was also much regional circling around the 'gay capital'. A number of people had moved to Brighton from further along the south coast, from places such as Chichester and especially from Hastings, which several people mentioned as a challenging place to be queer, especially in the 1970s and 1980s. But rising house prices and gentrification in Brighton had a contrary effect, propelling people out of the city. Sandie had moved to Eastbourne – 22 miles along the coast to the east – by the 1980s in order to buy a house, though still returned to see friends.[42] By the 2000s and especially the 2010s there is a sense of the region in a state of queer flux as people relocated to smaller and cheaper local towns, including Worthing and (ironically) Hastings. Others were nevertheless moving back to Brighton, suggesting the continued pull of the city,

Image 24 Flyer for the Brighton lesbian beach rebellion, *c.*1990

especially for those who were more affluent.[43] The Sussex coastline, east and west of Brighton, can be seen as a queer corridor of sorts, with people shifting back and forth according to their circumstances. The tide has changed a little now, rippling outwards as much as inwards.

University, politics and identity

An increasingly common migration from the 1970s was that of young middle-class people moving away from the family home to go to university or college. Opportunities also opened up for people from working-class backgrounds as access to higher education grew. By the second half of the 1990s, around 30 per cent of young people were entering college or university, most of them still moving away from home to do so.[44] Moving to a new city as a student and leaving behind communities that may have been experienced as homophobic was important for many young people who came to identify as LGBTQ throughout this period.[45]

Some young people chose which university to apply to on the basis of a city's queer reputation – as we have already seen for Brighton.[46] Rowena described how, in the mid-1990s, her friend Jane and her friends

> had actually researched their university choices entirely on the basis of gay scenes. They had decided that Manchester was the best scene in the country at the time. I think once I started to go to other cities, I think it was, to be honest. Nowhere else had that kind of – a whole street full of gay bars, and a heart to the gay scene, the way that Manchester did.[47]

But most prospective students did not research their university choices with such 'a decidedly gay edge'.[48] Those who were exploring their sexuality might hope that any university environment would provide a safe haven for coming out.

As student numbers grew from the 1960s through to the 2000s, these mass migrations to university had an impact not only on young people as individuals but collectively on cities like Manchester and Leeds where there were large student populations. In the first part of the period, universities were often perceived as places that were more liberal in their values than wider society. They were among the first institutions to offer meeting spaces to lesbian and gay groups – through their student unions and chaplaincies – and students began to organize 'Gay Socs' from the 1970s; by 1974 there were eighty across the country.[49] Indeed, Britain's gay liberation movement started in universities, at the London School of Economics in 1970, and the student movement was key in spreading ideas of gay rights across the nation.[50]

There was a strong connection between the growth of a city's student population and the development of its lesbian and gay politics and social scene. As well as students, other young people moved to those cities, drawn by their counter-cultures and left-wing, libertarian and sexual politics, especially in the 1970s and 1980s. Radical politics acted as a pathway to migration and new sexual identities, particularly to the university cities of Leeds and Manchester where there was already much activism from the mid-1960s, students there demonstrating against the Vietnam War and against apartheid in South Africa and Rhodesia.[51]

From 1968 the scale of student activism and dissent blossomed across the UK (as it did internationally), with dramatic protests against US policy in Vietnam at Sussex University and confrontations on race and UK immigration politics at Leeds.[52] Students increasingly applied liberationist rhetoric to questions of gender and sexuality in the WLM and GLF.[53] In this context, Patrick describes how he evolved as a young gay man at college in Leeds in the post-1968 years, as he embraced his sexual identity there. Originally from a conservative family on the south coast, he also 'completely turned to the left'.[54]

Leeds had a particularly intense political culture between the 1960s and 1980s, spawned by the city's radical traditions and closely tied to the '1968 moment' of student activism at Leeds University. Lou, who studied sociology here between 1964 and 1969, recalled:

> We were going to do it all, and we were going to do it differently. I think it was partly because of '68. We were in a general political turmoil and feeling that the world could be changed [...] The University was not the sort of size it is at the moment, there were only about five, seven thousand students there, but even at the time it was one of the largest red brick universities, and there was a strong Sociology department.[55]

Lou remained in the city, collectively setting up the first Women's Liberation group and the alternative *Leeds Other Paper*. The breadth and diversity of Leeds' alternative political culture, from anti-racism to campaigns highlighting male violence against women, attracted other young people to the city in the 1970s and 1980s. Lou refocused her politics from the libertarian left towards radical feminism in the 1970s, working in Women's Aid and coming out as a lesbian. Radical and revolutionary feminism subsequently drew a younger generation of women into Leeds and Bradford from the late 1970s.

The dynamism of Leeds' activist and lesbian scene continued to bring people into the city. Jude initially moved to Hull for art college in 1981, in order to get as far away as possible from their small town in south Wales; again, a classic lesbian and gay migration move. In the mid-1980s, Jude and their girlfriend relocated to Leeds, drawn, like other women before them, by its feminist politics. Jude's partner was already working at East Leeds Women's Workshop. As Jude explained:

[T]here was an attraction to Leeds. It was the place to be for particularly radical lesbians. I volunteered at Rape Crisis in Hull. And was involved in a lot of the feminist activities around challenging male violence at that time. And there was a lot here going on, obviously, around that.[56]

The size and diverse nature of the lesbian community in Leeds was a strong pull for Jude, who deliberately avoided London, preferring the political climate of the north.

[M]y partner and I got together in 82. And we'd actually been talking for a while about having children. But that was another reason for coming to Leeds, because we knew there was a very active self-insemination network here.[57]

There was also plenty going on in Leeds' feminist arts scene, supported by the University and Polytechnic, to which Jude became a longstanding contributor. While radical lesbian feminist politics was gradually winding down in Leeds in the late 1980s, there was continuing queer activism provoked by Clause 28 and its local effects.[58]

Meanwhile, across the Pennines, the size of the student population in Manchester, combined with the city's established gay politics and its rapidly developing club culture, came together during the 1980s to produce, by the early to mid-1990s, a nationally recognized queer city to rival Brighton.[59] Manchester's student population was the densest in the country. In 1991, over 4.5 per cent of its central city population were students, ahead of Leeds at just below 4 per cent; by 2001 that figure was 9 per cent compared to Leeds' and Brighton's 5 per cent.[60] LGBT people who migrated to Manchester in the 1980s and 1990s often came out as students and contributed to its growing queer culture. Nigel Leach moved here to study around 1980 and came out in the middle of his youth and community work course at Manchester Polytechnic when he was in his later twenties. That, he said, is 'a whole history in itself – about people who don't come out when they're young, they come out a bit later'.[61] The ease of coming out for young people as students may have related to the city they had moved to and also the courses they took. Manchester's, Leeds' and

Brighton's universities were each adding courses on women's studies, gender and sexuality in the 1980s and 1990s; the introduction of the University of Sussex's Sexual Dissidence Masters programme caused a furore in the press when it launched in 1990.[62] Nigel, like many others, stayed on in Manchester after graduating and was proud of his pioneering role as a youth worker at the Lesbian and Gay Centre in Bloom St in the mid-1980s, becoming 'the very first sessional youth worker for the youth group [...] in 1985'.[63]

Manchester students in the 1980s also helped to grow its queer club and arts scene, which was incubating in this period alongside the city's politics. Paul Cons came north from London in the early 1980s to study drama at Manchester University, subsequently working in alternative theatre. He secured a paid job at the Hacienda just as the club was taking off, later setting up the legendary Flesh monthly club night there in 1991.[64] Tanja Farman left Watford for Manchester University around the same time, and in 1992 co-founded the long-running queerupnorth arts festival with Gavin Barlow.[65] With its range of comedy, performance art, theatre, cabaret, literature and fine art, queerupnorth celebrated queer creativity and consolidated Manchester's claim to be in the LGBTQ vanguard.

Jess moved to Manchester in 1992 from Bradford where she had grown up. In her late twenties, she was drawn to the city by its political openness and its exciting club scene, but the enabling factor was starting a degree as a mature student at a time before tuition fees and when grants for students' living costs were still available. Jess felt pushed away by West Yorkshire's separatist lesbian politics and was drawn to Manchester's mixed gay scene. Her active choice to move to Manchester highlights the contrast in lesbian and gay culture between the two regions:

> Bradford was very much at that time segregated. That sounds quite harsh, but it was on lots of different fronts. [...] it was very much a separatist lesbian movement, and that's not what I wanted to do. [...] Whereas Manchester felt more open, there was much more debate. So coming to Manchester was much more about having fun and partying and going out and enjoying being around other lesbians, gay men, people who identify as queer.[66]

As well as enjoying the scale of Manchester's clubs (compared to Leeds' and Bradford's) and its open politics, Jess also valued the city's LGBT-friendly civic policies and its push to make the city more diverse and inclusive. She noted the council's support for the Summer of Lesbian Love in 1990: 'I think it was quite important. It was saying: actually, this is ok. [...] And looking at discrimination [...] for me, that was an important part of living in Manchester.'[67]

Jess traced further circles, moving to Brighton for two years in 2008, but 'experienced the type of racism there that I haven't experienced in years. [...] I was like, no, I've had enough now and came back to Manchester. [...] Manchester is still the place where I feel the majority of the time that I can be me and be ok. Both in terms of my sexuality and my racial identity.'[68]

Alongside the growth of its universities and club scene, the increasing visibility of MCC's support for lesbian and gay rights started to draw in discerning migrants from the mid-1980s. Charles, for example, had left Scotland in the 1970s, seeking greater tolerance in England, but returned to Glasgow to care for his ageing parents. Diagnosed HIV positive he moved to Manchester around 1988–1989 because, as he asserted in the mid-1990s, 'The medical services in Manchester can't, I believe, be surpassed anywhere outside London.' He went on to make a major contribution to HIV/AIDS organizing in Manchester.[69] Others came as Manchester's slow burn as a queer place burst alight in the 1990s and it became the gay destination on the cutting edge. Awareness of its civic politics increased at a time when the achievements of London's Greater London Council were being dismantled and combined with its gay village and partying scene to attract young people such as Rowena and Jane, as we saw earlier.

Not all colleges and universities were bastions of liberal acceptance and safe havens for coming out. A second period of university expansion during the 1990s and 2000s meant that a rapidly increasing number and proportion of young adults entered higher education, which at the same time became more market-oriented and employment-driven. Student political activism fell away during this time, and we can conjecture that as universities became larger institutions, their culture and values became more similar to the societies around them – reflecting, for example, the growing acceptance of LGBT rights from the late 1990s but also continuing homophobia.[70] Dan anticipated that Leeds University might be more gay-tolerant than his 'really claustrophobic' school and family in Cambridge. He said:

> I came to Leeds in 1999 and reason being that's where my course was and it was really, really far away, and you can kind of just could take on a new identity – you've not got all that past history, you can just be whoever you want to be and I came with a conscious decision that I was going to be really open with everyone.[71]

Yet when Dan arrived at university he faced immediate homophobia from a student flatmate and didn't come out in this new environment as he had intended. In freshers week he felt too unconfident to explore the LGB student society stall. It was instead a new friendship with a student who had grown up locally that allowed him to settle in and have fun:

> Because he had grown up in Yorkshire [...] he took me under his wing and showed me round so I got to see the wonder that is The Bridge, Queens Court, the New Penny and Poptastic which was heaven-sent really because we both really liked rock and indie music and there was this brilliant club that did cater for gay people but played the alternative music that we loved.[72]

The chain reaction of student and queer politics and cultures is particularly obvious in the northern cities of Manchester and Leeds, which had the largest numbers and concentrations of students. In contrast, the relatively late development of Plymouth's colleges and university (and the local focus on science subjects), has had such an impact only recently.[73] The queer culture of the city remained to a large degree influenced by its military and maritime economy. The growth of Plymouth Polytechnic (Plymouth University from 1992) and its student market was one of the business factors that persuaded Prudence and Gay to open the In Other Words alternative bookshop in 1984 (see Image 30). However, none of the Plymouth contributors moved to the city specifically to go to university here, though for some, including Jono and Hannah, the university offered the chance to retrain once they had settled here, in their cases in youth and community work.[74]

Work, family, love

When Judith got a job as a social worker and moved to Rochdale, just east of Manchester, to make a fresh start in the 1960s, she had not acknowledged her lesbianism to herself. 'I felt uncomfortable, that's all I can say, and removed from the boyfriends.' Born and brought up in Chichester on the south coast – 'a very Victorian and very sheltered upbringing' – Judith had been living in Brighton in the same house as a close female friend. When that friend went off with her boyfriend, Judith realized her feelings of loss were for her friend: 'I realised then, quite sickeningly, that it was her that I was missing and not him at all.'[75] Judith's move north to Rochdale prompted a personal crisis and she had a nervous breakdown. Fortunately for her in the context of the often highly punitive treatment of lesbians and gay men in psychiatric practice in the 1960s, Judith's psychiatrist not only helped her come out and feel positive about it but put her in touch with other lesbians in Manchester. 'From what I've heard of psychiatrists since, I must have just fallen on my feet.'[76] She joined the 1960s lesbian network the MRG via its newsletter *Arena Three* and rapidly became involved in Manchester's lesbian parties and its thriving homophile movement, including the CHE.[77] Judith's move to Greater Manchester, ostensibly for work, enabled her to come out as a lesbian and actively engage with Manchester's lesbian and gay culture. All kinds of everyday reasons might lead people to up sticks and move to a new city, for work or university, to join a partner or leave a relationship, or to look after family members. These incentives for moving among LGBTQ people mirror those of heterosexuals, though Judith's story and those of other contributors show how queer entanglements might also be in play.[78]

All four cities experienced job market highs and lows in this period, especially during the 1980s recessions. The two larger cities, Manchester and Leeds, appear to have offered LGBTQ people greater employment opportunities, simply because of their scale, and interviewees working in the public sector – in teaching, the health service or for local councils, for example – were especially able to move with their work. In cities where the local economy was quite specialized, such as Plymouth with its dockyard and military bases, or at particularly low points of economic recession, young people might be obliged to migrate away from home, irrespective of their sexuality.

People now living in Plymouth who told their life stories illustrate the significance of migrating for employment but also challenge the traditional narrative of needing to reject one's birthplace in order to come out and find lesbian or gay identity. For many born in Plymouth, customary entry-level work was in some branch of the maritime trades or the military. Ted started his working life with a couple of years in the merchant navy, following in his naval father's footsteps. He then moved frequently between London and Plymouth, having a wild gay time in early 1960s London, where he worked in a number of jobs, some with a queer reputation – in restaurants and menswear – which offered him a route into gay subcultures.[79] Another Plymouthian, Jeannie, similarly started in the military, in what was a classic form of escape for women who wanted to meet other women and develop independence and a set of employment-related skills. After leaving the army and living in Exeter, Nottingham and London she returned to Plymouth when she was about thirty, in the late 1960s, where she met her long-term partner Sylvia. Nevertheless, they had to move again to London as jobs dried up in Plymouth, though eventually they 'got homesick' and moved back down.[80]

Retirement from work is often a stage in life when people have more freedom to move home to somewhere they've often dreamed of living, whether that's a 'big gay city' or somewhere rural or coastal. For older LGBTQ people, such decisions are shaped by memories of earlier homophobia in particular kinds of places. Alison, from London, chose to retire to the sea but opted for the city of Plymouth rather than a seaside village. She had had a difficult experience of living with her girlfriend in rural Buckinghamshire in the 1980s. 'Obviously the gossip would have gone round because it was a very small little village, you know. And I just found that really uncomfortable and I couldn't handle it really.' Alison had visited Plymouth a few times, it was familiar, and in retirement there she valued 'the safety of the gay community even though [...] I don't do the pubs so much now [...] it gives me that feeling of security'.[81]

For Alison, as a retiree, the job market in Plymouth was not an issue in her move, but for both Ted and Jeannie the thin pickings there led to them leaving the city to find work in their younger years. Both felt a pull back to the city, in Ted's case to meet family obligations. 'I'd had a phone call from my two brothers [...] saying mother was ill [...] And because I was the only single one I had to come back to look after her.'[82] Familial caring responsibilities are usually seen as a reason why women cannot migrate so freely as men, but in twentieth-century English families this was an expectation of single people generally.[83] Ted was not in fact single, but his relationship with Don, whom he had met in London in 1960, was semi-hidden. After Ted's move 'home', Don would visit at weekends before making the move himself; at the time of interview in 2012 the couple had been together for fifty-one years. Ted's story contrasts with the classic model of the lesbian or gay child being rejected by their birth family, and it also shows how queer people are often seen as available carers, and assumed not to have partners, children or family responsibilities of their own.

Ted's circling back and forth is echoed in other stories from Plymouth, highlighting that city's strong culture of family. With a father in the forces, Joanna had moved around incessantly as a child, trained as a physiotherapist in London and then worked abroad herself in South Africa and Italy.[84] However she came back to Plymouth where her parents lived in 1978 when she was in her late twenties:

[M]y parents are both Plymouthians, [...] so, you know, in a sense [...] Plymouth is home base. [...] when my dad retired we got caught in defence cuts. So they decided to come back to Plymouth. [...] Came back here to really sort all my things out because I'd been away for a while, with a view to going back to Italy. Got a job here that worked with disabled [people], which is what I love, so I stayed. [...] So that's why Plymouth became my real home as such.

It was only then, in the late 1970s, prompted by an old friend, that Joanna made sense of her sexual feelings and emotional life and came out. Her parents were accepting of her sexual identity perhaps because they themselves had travelled widely and experienced single-sex working environments: 'I think possibly because they're military [...] For my father especially he was very open and I think in the military, you know, you live a different life so you are open to much more', said Joanna.[85] The wider horizons brought by migration can help with the social acceptance of queer relationships, even in a traditional city. Plymouthians were more prepared than families in other cities to do the work of negotiation around their queer and 'normal' lives. For some lesbians and gay men here, this enabled a closeness to family and a feeling of being at home in the city. Of course, the interviews only included people who had moved back to Plymouth and not those who migrated and stayed away, but the pattern is striking and distinct from the other cities.

Some LGBTQ people had to cut all ties with their birth families and create new lives and families of choice in a different city. But relationships change over time, and family breaches might be repaired. Paul grew up in the 1980s in the Dewsbury and Wakefield area of urban West Yorkshire where his whole family had roots. He was rejected by 'a lot of mates' when he talked to them about being gay and his parents first referred him to a psychologist and then kicked him out of home. '[I] didn't speak to my mum and dad for over five years. [...] I had contact with my brother at the time and then he started to become really homophobic.'[86] Paul found somewhere to live and got a job: ironically, given his father's threat to have him sectioned, as a psychiatric care worker. He found a lot of support from the LGBT youth group in Leeds and began socializing with them on the gay scene there, something he initially found quite scary. He met his first boyfriend, who worked as a chef, and they moved in together in the city. Paul remained in West Yorkshire and did not cut all ties with his birth family forever. In his moves to get away from them, for love and for work, he circled around the region where he grew up, and en route found new affiliations and friendships in a familiar location.

An important part of Paul's story is the sense of finding himself and his identity in Leeds with his new boyfriend. The desire to be with – or to leave – a partner is a powerful motive for migration and led people to move long distances. This was hardly unique to LGBT people but neither was their queerness irrelevant. Dan, whom we met at Leeds University, worked for a while in drug support services in the city after graduating before taking a job in London – partly because of a relationship break-up:

I'd come out of a very difficult relationship and I just wanted to get away from Leeds, you know when you're just sick to the back teeth with everything, and I had no responsibilities, I didn't own a house, I wasn't in a relationship, some of my good friends were in London so I thought, yes, sod it, I'll move down to London.

Love took him back to Leeds again, though. He met his new boyfriend, Richard, in a London club. They recognized each other, having lived in the same area of Leeds; 'we used to see each other on the train and I used to think "who's that handsome man?"' Richard didn't like living in London and moved back north, but the men forged a relationship despite the commute and in the mid-2000s settled together in Leeds. Dan affirmed: 'It's weird, my connections to Leeds are never going to be severed because I moved all the way down to London and yet got brought back by someone else that lived here.'[87] The emotions engendered by personal relationships can lead to major life changes, as they did for Dan in his long-distance migrations.

Moving for love, or out of a relationship, might also be a process of reinventing a new sexual self. For Jo, coming out as a lesbian was a long process: 'It was an act of finding.' Living in Manchester, there were plenty of opportunities, but 'being married at the time' she felt she couldn't 'go to a lesbian group, because how could you do that. They would all laugh at me.' It was moving to Plymouth in the 2000s that allowed Jo to make this migration towards a new sexual identity:

I actually came to Plymouth to be gay, to the provincial town, which is quite funny coming from Manchester. [Laughter] Popping down to Plymouth so that I could come out is hilarious really. But that's what I did, and it was a gentle place to come out.[88]

Jono moved to Plymouth too, from London and its much more visible and political gay scene. He came for love, to be with his partner who was posted there in the military. He loved the location: 'close to the sea, fantastic moorland around me, it was absolutely fantastic. I loved the idea of living in Plymouth. [...] surrounded by beautiful scenery.' But, aged twenty-six, Jono had to change career as a result of the move, from financial management to youth work, and faced a queer culture shock. 'I kind of brought my activist, political head down to Plymouth [where] the scene at that time, in 1988, was very, very different.'[89] Just a few years later, in 1995, when the Central Park murder of Terry Sweet happened, Jono became the de facto spokesperson for the LGBT community, liaising with the police. His story is one of bringing more outwardly facing politics to Plymouth from London, of his migration as an individual having an impact on the city.

Even a small group of LGBTQ incomers can make a real impression on a city, adding new layers of queer life, whether that was an alternative bookshop in Plymouth or a new kind of feminist politics in Leeds. Universal reasons for migration are shaped by people's queer identifications and emotional lives as they make choices about where to live, often flitting back and forth and circling around to find a place to settle in. The mass effects of young people's movement to university has particularly marked the LGBTQ histories of the northern cities of Manchester and Leeds, though their cultures of 'queer up north' are very different from one another. Once certain cities build a reputation for their queer scenes, more people are drawn into their orbit, reinforcing their LGBTQ variety and density. This is particularly evident in the scale of a city like Manchester but also in smaller Brighton. Manchester could increasingly accommodate a diverse trans and drag scene, a range of intersectional feminist and lesbian politics, and a queer arts programme. Brighton, meanwhile, has sustained its magnetism as the queer dreamland city where LGBTQ community might be found just the other side of the rainbow.

6

Urban accommodation: queer homes, households and families

Robert was looking for respite and change when he moved to Brighton in 1993. Living in cheap, precarious accommodation he found queer community all around him in the centre of the city:

> I was looking for somewhere to live in peace as a gay man. Brighton was equivocal in this respect. It was gay-friendly enough during the week and off-season, but at week-ends and during the summer it could become dangerously homophobic as crowds of Londoners poured off the train. [...] I rented a bedsit in a house in Waterloo Street shared by gay drifters: rent-boys, cabin crew, hotel management students. My room had a single bed, a shower and a Baby Belling stove. The carpet stank of poppers. I had never found London an easy place to socialise [...] and it was fun to find myself, all of a sudden, transported into a jolly alternative soap opera.[1]

Robert evokes the social aspects of bedsit life in Brighton, often portrayed elsewhere as lonely and isolated. Here he was living cheek-by-jowl with typical Brighton gay service sector workers. However, the key element transforming this multi-occupied house into a 'jolly alternative soap opera' – like San Francisco's gay *Tales of the City*[2] – was its proximity to Brighton's queer centre and the sheer density of the LGBT population living in that part of town.

LGBTQ people have long created new kinds of households by adopting and queering single-person homes, squats and collective housing, and family homes. In the first half of this chapter we will see that some of these kinds of households are emblematic of specific cities, the Brighton queer bedsit being one of them. In Leeds there are rich histories of collective households, many of them women only, while in Manchester and Plymouth, LGBTQ people negotiated the rights to social housing that were previously reserved for heterosexual families. Local politics and queer cultures, as well as city-specific housing markets, have influenced how people made queer homes. The second half of the chapter looks at

Image 25 Queer squatter protest, Brighton, 2013

how LGBTQ people fitted into more everyday patterns of home-making as couples and as families with children. How accommodating and accepting were urban residential areas to queer people in their quest to create secure and comfortable homes? LGBTQ families of varying shapes and sizes show that 'normal' suburban living arrangements were often less heterosexual and more queer than a first glance would indicate. Socializing with friends in the private home, discussed at the end of the chapter, has been vital for LGBTQ culture in each of our cities and further challenges ideas about home and household.

In material terms, the kinds of accommodation – the rooms, buildings, houses and flats – available for queer people to live in varied across the four cities. As Robert found, Brighton's gay scene was focused on a small geographical area in the centre, not only in terms of its pubs and clubs but also in terms of where LGBTQ people commonly lived, at least until the late 1990s when gentrification kicked in. The city has a distinctive housing landscape. Its centre is made up of Regency-era squares and terraces with an inner ring of various-sized Victorian houses. Council estates and middle-class suburbs form a semi-circle around the centre. Brighton's large old houses have lent themselves to multi-occupancy and division into bedsits and little flats to a far greater extent than is found in the other three cities. Young people elsewhere might describe moving out of the parental home into bedsits, but in a more utilitarian way, without the option of a central district of cheap housing close to a gay scene. In Manchester, at least until the 1990s, the shrivelling of industry from the 1970s meant that the centre of the city – which had never had a high residential population – hollowed out further. Cheaper commercial property facilitated the development of queer bars and clubs, as well as community centres, if not yet many queer homes. Unlike Brighton, most LGBTQ people in Manchester lived in the suburbs and neighbouring towns and came into the city centre's gay clubs and pubs from Hulme, Whalley Range, Chorlton and other districts that were at least a bus ride away.

The practice of squatting, common in the 1970s and 1980s, depended upon the availability of large or unused buildings (often local authority-owned) which were thick on the ground in the post-industrial inner suburbs of Leeds and Manchester and to a lesser extent in central Brighton. Leeds' LGBT population lived for much of this period in a 'doughnut' of older inner-city suburbs, particularly to the north-west and north-east of the centre. They also rented council properties interspersed across the city. Plymouth's postwar redevelopment, overseen by local and national government, followed modernist ideas of town planning which, in the 1940s and 1950s, imagined the heterosexual nuclear family as pretty much the only group for which housing was needed. This led to an emphasis on council housing stock suitable for such families and far fewer bedsits. The redevelopment also meant there were fewer unoccupied residential buildings in the city. In contrast, Brighton's proportion of council housing was always much lower than the national average throughout the period.[3]

Class and income are significant factors in the accessibility and choice of housing in Britain, with different effects on LGBTQ people than on heterosexual couples and families. The prospect of renting a local authority-owned home has declined considerably over the fifty years covered by this book, in terms of the availability of property and the criteria for eligibility. People with middle-class incomes have generally had sufficient resources to choose where to rent or buy a home and the likelihood of enjoying more space and greater privacy in relation to neighbours. Across all four cities, rising house prices and the decline in social housing have tightened the housing market and made homes more expensive. Some of the cheaper areas that were formerly districts of choice for lesbians and gay men have gentrified, while the regeneration of city centres has led to an increase in housing there, most notably in Manchester but also in Leeds.

Queering home

A gay time in bedsitterland

Craig left home at seventeen when his parents divorced, and he lived on state benefits in a central Huddersfield bedsit in the 1980s. Dressing effeminately he hung out with an alternative and goth crowd who, despite their meagre incomes, were able to make the most of West Yorkshire's queer scene. '[W]hen I was 17 I just lived to party. There was no two ways about it.' Their appearance often drew antagonism, 'but it was safety in numbers so that's why I think we all lived in bedsits all in one house because we all walked back together'.[4] Frequently evicted for noisy parties, Craig and his friend Martin 'moved into an even bigger house where there were even more gay people so we all went out together and there was a real sense of community'.[5]

In Manchester, city centre living in little flats was pioneered by a handful of queer people from around 1990. Here, it was quick, cheap and simple to move seamlessly between street, home and LGBTQ venues. Kate was a drag performer and describes sashaying through central Manchester streets: 'We did not have to go far to have a night out, I literally got in drag and trotted down to this brilliant night. […] [T]his tiny little dance floor.'[6] But in the 1990s, before gentrification, this could also be a perilous place to live. A gay man and his flatmate in the same block of flats as Kate were homophobically abused and burgled at gunpoint. 'They woke up to find a guy in a balaclava pointing a gun at them. They were totally traumatized for a long time.'[7] Despite the threat and edginess, cheap single-person housing enabled queer people like Kate, on a precarious income as an artist and performer, to claim space in the very centre of the city in this period between Manchester's industrial decline and its subsequent gentrification.

In Brighton in particular, city centre living in rented bedsits or small flats was a common lifestyle for young single LGBTQ people, at least until the 2000s when it became more expensive. Being very near or right within the gay scene gave people the freedom to live out their sexual desires and identities between the public streets and their private homes. This gave a strong sense of focused community, with sex and friendship on tap. Robert described the chaotic nature of his multi-roomed building:

> I lived in room 6 and there was a hooker working out of room 9. There was a 6 screwed to my door, but the upper screw was missing and it would sometimes flip down and become a 9. I was occasionally bothered by visiting johns, whom I would redirect to the floor above. One client came back downstairs to my room, naked and bleary, and explained that it hadn't worked out with Simon but he liked me very much and did I want to earn fifty quid? He was a natural blond. This was my opportunity to discover sex-work which, being priggish and ambivalent, I passed up.[8]

This sense of sexuality spilling over from the streets and between rooms in a house echoes the raffish history of Brighton as a pleasure resort for illicit sex.

The multi-occupied houses of Brighton were firmly established as part of the gay scene, as indeed they had been since the war and especially as the sea-side industry of hotels and boarding houses started to change. The facades of Brighton's Regency-era houses were often grand and imposing but many had been turned into tiny flats and bedsits which could be cramped and run down. They were nevertheless near the sea and near the queer bars and businesses in the centre. Arriving in Brighton as a twenty-two-year-old graduate in 1987, already out as a gay man, Alf described living in a series of bedsits or shared flats with friends, the first in Eaton Place just off Marine Parade. 'I mean, it was quite an interesting introduction to Brighton, as they had a top floor flat in Kemptown [the gay area].'[9]

Stories of bedsitterland in Brighton show how enmeshed different threads of queer life were in this relatively small city. Lesbians and gay men were often involved in creative networks and passed on rental accommodation to each other. Rebecca came to Brighton in 1995 and describes how, not long after,

> I joined a writer's group and made friends with Bella, who was a lesbian and Frank, intense and quiet with long black hair. I moved to a tiny seafront flat on Marine Parade when my artist friend Graham moved out. It was the perfect place for multi-tasking: you could make a cup of tea whilst having a shower [...] Unemployed, I busied myself painting the gunmetal sea of winter storms which rattled the window.[10]

The nearby gay pubs, bars and clubs offered greater physical comfort than a poky flat as well as a feeling of belonging and family. 'Your extended family was the gay scene', one gay business owner said of the 1970s and 1980s, which he saw as a particular time of mutual support. 'Everyone out there, like my brothers and sisters were different in their own little ways, so we looked out for each other as a family.'[11]

Often seen as lonely and dystopian – and there is a hint of this in the winter winds of Rebecca's Brighton – the city bedsit could also be a place of danger and surveillance for lesbians and gay men, especially but not only before partial decriminalization in 1967. Thin walls and close proximity meant neighbours and landladies might know more than was comfortable about their tenants and the lovers they brought back. George was fearful when he stayed at his boyfriend's bedsit – especially when overnight snowfall meant his departure was marked by his retreating footprints.[12]

But they were also sites of freedom, a 'room of one's own' where LGBTQ people could express their particular domestic styles.[13] In late twentieth-century Brighton the bedsit was often all those things and also part of a convivial culture of home that overflowed onto the landings and doorways of the building and into the streets and gay pubs.

Bedsit community might be essential for low-income renters to keep afloat. The six gay tenants in a subdivided house on Grand Parade worked together to feed themselves in the 1960s, as Sandie explained:

> [W]e were all desperately short of money and several of us were out of work [...] and so, I'm sorry to say, we took to pinching. When we were passing greengrocers' shops, where they were all out on the pavement, each of us had to take something different, maybe your job for that day was to nab a carrot or a potato. [...] And then into the stockpot it went and this vegetable stockpot kept us going for about three weeks at one stage.[14]

Robert's account emphasizes the casual and relaxed nature of these marginal gay lifestyles as they continued into his later generation. 'I was befriended by a couple of boys across the street who lived entirely for pleasure on almost no money. After many years of being obsessively ambitious I found their aimlessness soothing.'[15] His story of bedsit Brighton brings to life the mixtures of LGBT people who populated the city centre: a sense of lives being lived on the edge in some respects but also grounded in a familiar queer neighbourhood and its palpable threads of sex and pleasure.

Radical experiments: queer squats and communal living

Redolent of a particular time period (the 1970s and 1980s) and of some of our cities more than others, lesbian and gay collective households came to symbolize a powerful alternative form of family and home. The politics of squatting empty properties and challenging not only the conventional family but also the whole concept of property ownership was developed in the 1970s by left-libertarian, anarchist and other countercultural groups. From the early 1970s this critique was sharpened by ideas stemming from the GLF and the WLM. Their radical visions of home aimed to unpick the gendered tyranny of housework, to share childcare between men and women, to experiment with alternatives to the isolation of monogamy and to produce a model of co-operative life that was anti-capitalist and anti-consumerist. These new households would give people an emotional and physical alternative to the oppressive heterosexual nuclear family.[16] Single-sex shared housing was important in a feminist context as explained by Debs, who lived in a lesbian house in Brighton in the 1980s:

> It was a time when most young people lived communally, heterosexual or whatever [...] So instead of moving into a mixed communal house you moved into a women's house [...] If you were living in a house of women only, the conversations were different and I think this enabled feminism and feminist thought to flourish much better because women, especially then, and still are, talked down to by men.[17]

The lesbian and gay squatting movements of the 1970s and 1980s required a particular conjunction of political culture and available unoccupied housing to flourish. Both were thick on the ground in the post-industrial inner suburbs of Leeds and Manchester. On a smaller scale, in central north Brighton there were also plenty of derelict or unused buildings: 'lots of empty houses that were being squatted, lots of empty shops', said James; 'it was pretty grotty, actually'.[18]

Plymouth, on the other hand, lacked the radical thread of activism around lifestyle and housing politics to foster the idea of collective living. Because of extensive rebuilding it also had fewer empty properties.

This new politics of everyday living could encompass all aspects of people's personal lives, though households varied as to which ideals predominated. Communal living influenced sexual choices, it involved the politics of food and eating and it supported lesbian activism. As Miriam recalled, in the Leeds context of 1980s lesbian non-monogamy debates, 'there was every kind of household structure that you could possibly think of. There were collective households, there were people in three- and four-way relationships, there were people in ex-relationships with new generations of partners with them, there was everything going on.'[19] The politics of food, its type (often vegetarian), its preparation and the sharing of the evening meal around the table were all politicized in these households. Lynn's kitchen cupboards in Leeds were censored for inappropriate food when she came out in 1987.[20] She remembered 'a lesbian friend coming round [...] and going through my food cupboards and telling me what food items I should have. [...] "Oh no, you can't have that and you can't have that and that's not good for you". So that's my first recollection from that time.'[21] Lou described political debates at the dinner table:

> Everybody in our house got dragged into stuff to do with the [Leeds Women's Aid] refuge. [...] you know, it was like at communal meals and you're debating, we just debated what was happening, radical and political issues, it was just the stuff of life, you'd do that while you were eating the evening meal.[22]

Communal living sustained queer creativity as well as politics. The lesbians who formed the Siren Theatre Company in Brighton discussed how their collective homes in the late 1980s fostered their theatre and music making. This contributed to the town's thriving alternative culture which was separate from but overlapped with the lesbian and gay scene. Debs recalled: 'There were these connections between communal houses, weren't there? And the way that people met, you didn't have to go to a club or something because there were these connections through the university and through activities.'[23] Jude remembered rehearsing the feminist plays of Siren and the Theatre Against Sexism in Debs' house in Queen's Park Road: 'We were also playing in Devil's Dykes and then Bright Girls.'[24] The feminist ethos and the debate about separatism (that some Brighton women remembered as being particularly strong in the 1980s) didn't stop neighbourly crossovers: 'some men lived in the men's house on Queen's Park Road, so they were the new men, if you like. There was a sharing of equipment and that made a huge difference. There were lots of bands. Loads of bands. It was great fun.'[25]

In 1980s Brighton the squats and collective houses were particularly strongly linked to a cultural politics of sexuality and gender – to activism through music and theatre making – while in Leeds they were more hardcore in their politics. There were highly complex nuances between the ideologies of different lesbian groups in Leeds in the late 1970s and early 1980s which affected how and where women made their homes. Al explained what lesbian separatism was and why she didn't completely agree with it:

> I found the [...] radical feminism way of dealing with [patriarchy] was to [be] looking more at [...] removing yourself from [men] and setting up something alternative. And I'm not against setting up alternatives, I mean I lived communally, brought up children collectively, we tried to live a different life. But I suppose when you have children you have to engage with the mainstream rather a lot, and I thought separatism might be something you were prepared to do as a strategy to give yourself a power base, and not to have your energy leach away [...] But not as an end in itself. So my aim was never to go and live in Women's Land in north Wales, full stop, [to] just remove myself from it all as an answer to the issue of women's oppression.[26]

In Leeds, lesbian separatism was followed more completely by larger groups of women than in other cities outside London. It was aided by feminist training workshops for women in the manual trades, which enabled the complete exclusion of men even from stepping inside a separatist house to fix the plumbing. Women's squats, housing co-ops and collective households were found in the north-west inner-city districts near the universities, in Hyde Park, Woodhouse and Headingley, and in the north-east in Chapeltown and Harehills, which were poorer areas of sex work and Black Caribbean and Asian migration. Some of the 'Revvies', the revolutionary feminists, lived in Hilton Road in Harehills and also in Kensington Terrace. Other lesbians, including those who advocated both separatism and the importance of working-class identity, lived in Sholebrook Avenue, where around fifteen large houses were squats or short-life properties (leased from the local council) run by co-ops and collectives. Isis was the women's house, Wild Lavender the gay men's, while New Albion was mixed. A further grouping of lesbians who were more aligned with a cultural form of radical feminism lived in these areas and in Chapel Allerton to the north. They were derided then and since by other women for being preoccupied with moon cycles and co-counselling rather than direct action on the streets.[27]

As well as being a political ideal, collective households and squats offered women a cheap (or free) form of housing that enabled them to live and be activists on low incomes or unemployment benefit. 'I was on the dole', said Julie, 'and of course you got housing benefit then which was very important, so you could live. I mean I'd had no education, I couldn't get a job, there was nothing really that I could do. [...] And yes, it funded my activism.'[28] Similarly in Manchester, the housing benefit claimed by Luchia and Angela helped them maintain the women's refuge they ran.[29] These state benefits became increasingly difficult to access from the later 1980s, but up to that point were significant for sustaining alternative housing and lesbian activism and lifestyles.

There were paradoxical strands in Leeds lesbian politics which spilled into collective households. On the one hand, as activists they wanted to politicize and support other lesbians and welcomed new women into their homes as well as into their campaigns and community. Tina moved into Al's household of women (at that point in Chapeltown) as a young student. Meeting in a punk club, Al had said: 'I hear you're looking for somewhere to live, come live in my house.'[30] Households like this one, in the same area of the city as the women's discos at the Dock Green pub and the club nights at the African-Caribbean Roots, enabled women to live convivially and socialize across political boundaries. This sense of neighbourhood home and belonging parallels that in Brighton, but here in Leeds it was at a distance from the male-dominated city centre gay scene. On the other hand, the strength of Leeds' lesbian feminism,

Image 26 Dock Green, Stanley Rd, *c.*1980

the political disagreements between different factions and the atmosphere of fear and violence against women led to acrimonious splits and in-fighting. Several women interviewed much later referred to how the radical and revolutionary feminists hated each other, how class was often a trigger for hostility and how some experienced physical violence in attacks on their houses and cars. 'Because we were attacked by other lesbians in Leeds. [...] They were objecting to us being mouthy. [...] And that felt very weird. [...] so you're a lesbian under attack by other lesbians in this small political group.'[31] Home did not always feel like a safe space.

The revolutionary feminist house in Hilton Road, Leeds, broke up in the early 1980s but not before its politics had stirred up intense debate among lesbians and feminists across the country. And such experiments in alternative living had other legacies too. The gay men's house on Sholebrook Avenue, Wild Lavender, was set up in 1980 'by a group of gay men interested in living together [...] with ideals of nurturing each other and living co-operatively'. By 1984, 'the co-op members had learned a lot about honesty and acceptance'. Many of these gay men went on to form the Edward Carpenter Community, named after the British pioneer of gay rights, which runs week-long retreats for men to explore community-building, creativity and personal growth.[32] A number of squats, especially those in council-owned property, morphed into housing co-ops with more secure tenancy agreements. Others developed into housing associations, which could claim state funding and prioritize specific kinds of applicants such as women or single people, as well as lesbians and gay men. In late 1980s Leeds, Lynn moved into Tangram Housing Co-op and recalled others from that time, including Firelight, a lesbian housing co-op in Hyde Park and 'a separatist one, on Winwood Road'.[33] Several of these housing co-ops with feminist and queer beginnings continued to operate forty years later.[34]

Social class and social housing

LGBTQ people who struck out to create radical new forms of home and household may have been bold and enterprising. But it was no less challenging to try to live comfortably as a queer couple, family or single person in conventional housing in ordinary residential areas. Choices about the type of housing and the possibility of making a home in an LGBTQ-friendly neighbourhood have been largely governed by income and social class.[35] Jeannie, who we met in Chapter 6 with her partner Sylvia, had been out to her Plymouth family about her sexuality since her teens in the 1950s. 'There was no problem. [...] There were other situations that were more important to deal with, if you know what I mean.'[36] Here, Jeannie is referring to poverty and abuse in the family. Jeannie was not especially close to her birth family but they rubbed along and the couple looked after her elderly mother for many years. They went out on Plymouth's gay scene and were out to Sylvia's children. However, Jeannie was more anxious about their next-door neighbours. 'I used to tell some people that she was my sister. It was easier to live with because [in] certain situations, people question [you].'[37] Part of the problem was their perceived entitlement to the council house they lived in:

> [The neighbour] said 'I don't understand why two women get a place', this is a brand new building down in Weston Mill, twenty five years ago [c.1987] [...] And I said, 'I don't understand what you are talking about'. 'Well, my son' she said 'has been waiting for a place' and she made a big deal of this. 'Well' she said, 'how come two women', I said 'well she's my sister'. [...] Although they never came out with it, they didn't agree with the fact that we should be given priority over maybe so called straight couples.[38]

The chance of renting a local authority-owned home has shrunk markedly over the past few decades, and such housing has increasingly been seen as less desirable. In the postwar years, eligibility for council housing was based on a concept of housing need which took as its starting point the heterosexual nuclear family with children and largely excluded alternative households. Lesbians and gay men in the earlier part of the period who had stayed in the cities of their birth and lived in council accommodation may often have inherited tenancy rights through their parents or via a heterosexual partnership that had broken down. Jeannie doesn't explain the basis on which she and her partner Sylvia were awarded a council house in the 1980s. Both were from working-class backgrounds. Jeannie may have 'inherited' rights from her parents, and Sylvia had separated from her violent husband in the early 1970s. Sylvia also had chronic health problems and was on disability benefits in later life, which is likely to have given her extra 'points' in the allocation system.[39] Jeannie's anxiety about her neighbour's hostility vibrates in concert with considerable media antagonism to lesbians and gay men being given council houses in the 1980s.[40] During the AIDS crisis and amid widespread homophobia, the tabloid press represented queer people as usurping the rights of 'normal' heterosexual families and attacked the provision of lesbian- and gay-specific public services such as education, housing and medical care. (Young single mothers seeking council housing also received negative media attention during this period of right-wing political attack on the whole idea of public housing.) We saw in Chapter 4 how a queer couple was hounded out of Plymouth in 1982 amid homophobic con-demnation by council leaders and press questioning of how they were allocated a council flat.[41] Such stories reflected and contributed to beliefs that same-sex couples and queer individuals were second-class citizens who were not entitled to local state services. Public housing may have been an especially sensitive local issue in Plymouth following its postwar construction of large new housing estates.

By the 1980s, the election of LGBT Labour councillors and the lobbying of local authorities marked the beginning of a shift in a few local areas both in official policies and in on-the-ground housing practice.[42] The succession rights of men whose partners had died of AIDS-related illnesses was a key concern for gay activists; bereaved men could be made instantly homeless with no claim to a continuing tenancy for their own home. The 1985 Homeless Persons Housing Act extended the concept of 'vulnerability' to include other groups of people if local authorities chose to.[43] Using this power some left-leaning councils outside the capital as well as some London boroughs allocated single and LGBT people to specific estates, harder-to-let properties or those not up to the required official standard.[44] Other property might also be distributed to housing co-operatives to run. Many groups of households that were formerly squats were able to convert their occupancy into this more secure type of longer-term tenancy, as we saw above. This policy by councils of giving second-class housing to lesbians and gay men indicates their profoundly lesser claim to citizenship in this period but also the beginnings of greater recognition of their needs.

The heyday of LGBT council housing – such as it was – came in the 1980s, when local authorities still had a reasonably good supply of flats and houses, which was yet to be seriously eroded by the Thatcher government's policy of the 'right to buy'. But the availability of council housing also varied enormously by region, northern cities then as now having less pressure on public housing than those in the south, such as Brighton. It's for Manchester that we have most evidence that queer people's housing needs were addressed by the local council and housing associations. The city began a concerted drive to house lesbians and gay men in the mid-1980s, leading to the delightfully named 'fairy towers' in Hulme.[45] This commitment continued. Rowena said:

> I definitely remember it being totally fine, if not positively good, to be gay when you were trying to get a housing association flat. I had a friend who is a Black lesbian from Cardiff, who arrived in Manchester during the second half of the 1990s, and she didn't have anywhere to live. She turned up at a housing associa-tion place with a bin bag with her clothes in. She joked that being a Black lesbian

who was homeless was the perfect […] – she just walked straight into a housing association flat. I think there was definitely a politics around that. At the same time, it didn't guarantee that you were going to get housed somewhere that was a great place to be gay.[46]

In the 2000s other local authorities followed suit. By 2009, Brighton city council had developed an official strategy which recognized the particular needs of LGBT people in the city, including their greater risk of homelessness and vulnerability to hate crime, as indeed all local authorities were now required to do.[47]

Lesbian and gay gentrification

This chapter began by highlighting the queer bedsits and small flats of central Brighton. By the end of the 1990s the chances of living in such gay-friendly neighbourhoods had shifted in the four cities with urban regeneration, and city centre living became increasingly fashionable. The idea of gay gentrification – the creation of 'gaybourhoods' – is a concept applied mainly to North American cities.[48] Gay men and lesbians move into low cost, often run-down neighbourhoods and improve them by restoring homes and creating a friendly, increasingly chic and more middle-class environment. Property prices then rise, these neighbourhoods become less socially mixed and younger, lower-income gay people can no longer afford to live there. This pattern is less directly applicable to Britain, where urban regeneration has also been state-sponsored as well as commercially led, but it is relevant to central Brighton. Queer people living on benefits or low wages can no longer afford city centre bedsits and flats. As housing in Brighton became increasingly expensive it altered the queer geographies and feel of the city. Some Brighton residents have moved away from the city to find cheaper housing. Sandie started her life in Brighton in the 1960s living in a big double bedsit with her girlfriend on Grand Parade.[49] Over the years she gradually traded up but was only able to buy her 'first small house' after she moved to much cheaper Eastbourne.[50]

Homeowner James became quite angry as he described the degaying of central Brighton over the twenty-five years he lived there:

> Brighton was just much more cosmopolitan [in 1993]. Twenty-five years ago, amazing how run-down it all was. […] And there were lots of antique shops and junk shops and flea markets and it was a great place to live. […] Well, it changed a lot. It got much richer. It became fashionable. […] It's all fashion shops and these sort of candle shops that don't really sell anything. These sort of awful fucking lifestyle shops. […] It's very fake and phoney, a lot of it, I think. And incredibly expensive.[51]

171

By the time that James and his partner sold their house in Brighton, prices had increased enormously and those streets of central Brighton had become a lot less queer. He vividly describes how much more middle-class and heterosexual the central area became in the 2000s:

> Our rather scruffy street, when we left it in 2015, had become smart. It was young, reasonably well-to-do married couples who wanted decent schools for their kids, it was that kind of smart. My local junk shop had become a deli.[52]

The gentrification of Brighton is also confirmed by its pattern of owner occupation. Having followed the broader national trend throughout the period, the proportion of owner-occupiers in the city fell below the national average quite sharply from 1990 as house prices rose.[53] Its increasingly youthful population was less able to afford to buy there.

In many British cities over the past fifteen years, there have been moves to regenerate city centres by encouraging the construction of private housing: by adapting former industrial buildings in cities such as Manchester and Leeds and with new-build blocks of flats. This process can be seen most strongly in Leeds and Manchester, and to a lesser extent in Plymouth where some former dockyard buildings have been converted into flats.

Queer folk such as Kate, as we saw earlier, were pioneers of city centre living at a time when central Manchester had few residents and many dark corners of danger and opportunity alongside its lesbian and gay bars. As Kate said: 'now it's really normal to live in town. [...] The queers might have kick-started that.'[54] Accompanying the branding of the gay village, the conversion of warehouses and similar buildings around Tib Street and Princess St, near Canal St, into private flats began. Just the other side of the city centre, the development of purpose-built student accommodation near the universities on Oxford Road also played a part. The TV drama *Queer as Folk* (1999) incorporated apartment living into an exciting rendition of Manchester's gay sexual scene, as did council promotion of the area for gay tourism and advertising by property developers. In 2000 Caroline moved to Manchester and bought one of the stylish new loft apartments in a converted warehouse in Tib Street, where among her neighbours 'there clearly were a number of gay men'. She found it: 'a very gay-friendly environment. Definitely, it was *Queer as Folk*, that's how it felt. It was all very queer. I'd lived in London before. But Manchester just had that gay vibe, really.'[55] A little later, the Northern Quarter saw further residential development and this area, too, gained a reputation as being more densely queer than elsewhere, aided by party nights in local bars.

With their queer residents, bars and businesses, these areas of central Manchester have clearly become 'gaybourhoods'. However, to focus only on this pattern is to ignore the way that gay gentrification is affected by gender and class.[56] A high proportion of central Manchester's new apartments were bought or rented by affluent gay men and were much less affordable for lower-paid LGBTQ people. As Rowena described:

House prices went up quite quickly. I think it happened [...] around 97, 98 [...] It was all the gay men, because none of the lesbians had any money to do anything like that. The lesbians were all still living in these awful flats, concrete floors [...] and gay guys were living in the city centre, converted flats. That's an overgeneralization, but there weren't many lesbians with any money, so [...][57]

At this point, Salford's new high-rise city centre flats became a cheaper gay-friendly option, especially for less affluent gay men.[58] In earlier years lesbians had contributed to the gentrification of the suburb of Chorlton, which 'was the dream place to live'. However, it is now too expensive for many lesbians, except those on professional salaries, to rent or buy there. 'Whalley Range, which is next to Chorlton [...] was a bit cheaper. A lot of lesbians lived there as well.' As Rowena pointed out, inner suburbs such as Hulme remained key residential districts for lesbians and gay men but in social housing. '[A] lot of gay people I knew lived in housing association flats. Hulme was a big area for that.'[59]

In Leeds the picture is even more mixed. New city centre flats probably have a higher than average population of LGBTQ people (though this is less in evidence than in Manchester) and the increased number of queer bars and clubs in the area has created a sense of a gay village. The inner north-west suburbs of Hyde Park, Woodhouse and Headingley, which were more expensive than other inner-city areas in the 1970s and 1980s, and which were popular with gay men in particular,[60] have all become 'studentified' with the growth of the nearby universities. Other formerly lesbian-favoured residential areas such as Chapeltown and Harehills in the north-east have remained relatively cheap and run down.

LGBTQ people have established specific queer-friendly neighbourhoods in our cities, but these locations have often shifted over time. Class, income and local housing policies have shaped the patterns of queer home-making, as has the type of physical housing stock available. There has been a queer permeation into family housing areas across Plymouth and movements of LGBTQ people in and out of the tight streets of Brighton and the city centres (and inner suburbs) of Leeds and Manchester. More affluent gay men and lesbians have contributed to gentrification in particular suburbs and central areas. But rising property prices and rents have at the same time pushed other LGBTQ people, especially those on lower incomes or who have children, out of central Brighton and Manchester to cheaper suburbs and local towns.

Queer families, queer friends

Queer and 'normal' families

The ease of making queer home in a reasonably open manner by lesbians and gay men and same-sex couples was very different across the four cities and over time. From the 1960s to the 1990s, LGBT people were likely to experience overt discrimination and hostility. During the 1990s and subsequently, there were uneven shifts towards increasing acceptance, especially after the 2004 Civil Partnership Act recognized and normalized same-sex couples, though homophobia remained. Despite this, some LGBT people were able to negotiate tolerance and a degree of acceptance in the family and home city where they grew up. Staying put rather than moving away meant it was much more likely that you would cross paths with former school friends, neighbours or friends of the family as well as relatives in local neighbourhoods and near the gay scene in ways that could by turn be affirming or compromising. Ted enjoyed an extensive social life in the gay venues of early 1960s Plymouth but it was sometimes impossible to avoid neighbours:

> [O]ne night I went and a voice shouted out 'I'm gonna tell your mother, Teddy Whitehead' [laughs] [...] another time she saw me she was in a friend's flat in Union Street and [...] saw me walking down with a group of chaps, late at night, and again I heard this voice from the darkness 'I'm gonna tell your mother, Teddy Whitehead' [laughs]. [...] And she was looking out the upstairs window.

Apparently the threat was never carried out, and this person seems to have noted Ted's gay socializing without drawing it to the attention of his family: perhaps because, as he went on to say, 'Plymouth people, then they were quite accepting'. The potential awkwardness nevertheless meant it remained in Ted's memory fifty years later.[61]

In typical Plymouth style Ted 'never broadcast' his sexuality; 'I just lived my life', he said. And so when he asked his mother if his boyfriend Don could stay she assumed he was a friend:

I can remember saying to my mother [...] I said 'Don's thinking of coming down to Plymouth and can he stay here?' And she said 'Yes, but he'll have to sleep with you [...] – and I know what you're like for sharing your bed'. So I thought 'I'll put up with it mum' [laughs].[62]

Ted was living with his mother in her council house (where he was born) but a few years later he and Don bought a house, to which all three of them moved. This echoes heterosexual family patterns in the postwar years, when the shortage of housing meant many newly wed couples either moved in with one set of parents or had a widowed parent come to live with them. Living with Ted's mother indicates some innocence on her part, or else a deliberate avoidance. Importantly the arrangement provided cover for the couple in a period when male homosexuality was still criminalized and condemned. Don could easily have been perceived as a lodger by neighbours within this family set-up.

Among the four cities it is Plymouth where we found the highest proportion of LGBTQ people who had been raised in the city and continued to live there for most (if not always all) of their adult lives. In a city that prized strong family networks, it is striking to observe the extent to which 'born and bred' Plymouth queers sought to create a comfortable home within conventional parameters – near their families of origin but alongside their same-sex relationships and wider queer lives. This negotiation of birth family, home city and adult queer life can probably be found in many other smaller cities around Britain, where neighbours, family and friends and employers were enmeshed in relatively limited circles adjacent to the lesbian and gay scene.

In a very different way from Plymouth, Manchester's civic politics from the early to mid-1980s created a culture that fostered family acceptance of lesbian and gay young people. There were relatively high-profile support services, beginning in the early 1980s with council-supported youth services at the Gay Centre in Bloom Street. Joyce Leyland's work with young LGBT people and their parents at the Centre led to the formation of the Parents Support Group in 1986. This pioneering group became Family and Friends of Lesbians and Gays (FFLAG) in 1993, a nationwide organization. Barbara's son, born in Bolton, came out in the mid-1990s, and in his late thirties continued to work in neighbouring Manchester. Barbara was an early member of Manchester Parents Group (later FFLAG), supporting other parents as well as her son: 'it is a learning curve for parents. And some people can cope with it, and others can't, so we try to be there for the ones who can't'. In 2014, Barbara talked with pride about 'the variety of people that we have in our parents' group' and the range of good jobs that their lesbian and gay children had found, both in the city and all over the country. 'I've marched down Oxford Road with banners against Section 28, I've been on Radio Manchester telling the story, been interviewed by some of the other gay radios and I'll stand my corner and fight for the freedom that is needed for all of you [LGBTQ people] as long as there's breath in my body.'[63]

But many queer people were unable to be open about their sexual desires as they reached adulthood, especially in the first half of this period, and used various methods of concealing their other lives from the gaze of their families, friends and workmates. Common in Plymouth and elsewhere were stories of men hiding a queer life within a semblance of heterosexuality, probably because of those tight local networks of relatives, colleagues and friends. Many married men pursued brief and anonymous same-sex sexual encounters in cottages or public places, as well as more sustained relationships, without the knowledge of their girlfriends, wives and families. When Dennis's wife found out about his sexual flings with other men, their twenty-year marriage broke down completely.[64] The hurt and betrayal of hidden same-sex relationships coming to light was highly likely to cause considerable distress to the men's female partners and possible estrangement from their children.

Other people pursued same-sex relationships with the tacit knowledge of their heterosexual spouses. Noreen felt familial and social pressure to marry as she was growing up in 1950s Wakefield. She had a brief relationship with another woman in her late teens but then met a man through a marriage bureau and married him in 1961, moving to Leeds. The marriage continued until his death thirty years later, during which time Noreen had a three-year relationship in the mid-1960s with a woman she had met through her church and other later lesbian affairs:

[B]etween my husband and myself it was an open secret, but credit to him he accepted it because he didn't want to lose me [...] the way he saw it – I gave him two sons [...] and as long as I put a good meal on the table and I left him in peace to see the sport on the television, that's all he asked for!

Noreen's decision to remain married nevertheless meant she couldn't live a more openly lesbian life and find a same-sex partner, as she would have preferred. She had few contacts with the lesbian scene and didn't really venture onto it until the early 1980s when her children were grown up.[65]

Noreen's story may be fairly typical. For many women (to a much greater extent than for men), issues of social respectability, lack of an independent income, the prospect of losing custody of children and the difficulty of finding alternative housing were powerful factors against leaving a marriage. We saw in Chapter 3 how Joyce Edwards successfully ran a well-known lesbian club in Ashton-under-Lyne near Manchester in the 1970s. She had married a man who was a war hero, as 'it was a case of "your mother thinks you should be married": that's what you did in those days'. Joyce had a son and saw her girlfriends alongside her marriage. Her husband didn't realize this until a girlfriend told him, but he apparently accepted the situation. Theirs was a marriage of affection and Joyce felt very loyal to him. 'I don't regret it', Joyce said of her marriage, 'he was a really, really good man, my husband'.[66]

Other references to the heterosexual family could act as foils to dissemble same-sex relationships. We saw above how Jeannie's lack of confidence and need for social approval (about which she spoke more explicitly later in the interview) meant she pretended to her Plymouth neighbour that her lover was her sister, even though she would rather not have hidden her lesbianism. Similarly, two men living in a same-sex relationship in a high-rise council flat near Leeds in the 1980s described how the large age difference between them (of 15–20 years) led to their neighbours assuming that they were uncle and nephew. Again their relationship was perceived to be a familial bond.[67] In this way, standard heterosexual family patterns were used, either by same-sex couples themselves or assumed by their neighbours, to explain away queer household types, especially between the 1960s and the 1980s. But looking at this from the other direction, these examples suggest how many supposedly heterosexual households might in fact have been queer.

Moving on just a decade, we can see that, at least in more cosmopolitan cities and neighbourhoods, it became easier to live as an openly same-sex couple.[68] James and his partner moved to Brighton in 1993 fairly soon after starting their relationship:[69]

> [W]e managed to buy our pretty Victorian house with a big garden and got a dog and so on. Completely stereotypical Brighton gay couple. We lived in a rather tatty, rather run-down street. Very pretty houses. We had lots of gay neighbours, which was nice. We had straight neighbours banging on the door, saying hello, we're so-and-so, we are your neighbours, welcome to our street.[70]

Here in central Brighton there was no difference between the friendliness of their straight and gay neighbours. This transparency and confidence in setting up queer home as a couple was, in the early 1990s, perhaps particular to Brighton, Hebden Bridge (in West Yorkshire), some neighbourhoods in London and some in Manchester, such as Chorlton. Ten years further down the road in the 2000s, the equalization of the age of consent, greater concern about homophobia as a hate crime and the legislation for civil partnership would rapidly make lesbian and gay couples more respectable, if not always completely accepted.

Lesbian mothers: building queer families

Like households consisting of same-sex couples, queer families with children can be found in all our cities. Yet the context for raising children (usually, but not only, in a lesbian household) differed between the cities and, as one of the most politically controversial family arrangements, this is one of the most important markers for change over time in LGBTQ experiences of making home and family.[71] In the first decades of this period, children in queer homes were usually born into a previous heterosexual marriage. Raising children in the context of divorce or separation was fraught with danger for lesbian mothers. Laws biased in favour of men and heterosexuality meant that if challenged for custody on the grounds of their lesbianism (or even simply their feminist politics), the children would always be removed from the mother's care and custody awarded to the father. The first case in which a lesbian mother won custody was not until 1980.[72] Married young at seventeen and with two children, Lynne met a woman at work in the Clarks shoe factory in Plymouth in the mid-1970s and came out as a lesbian. She had a traumatic (though probably fairly typical) experience of divorcing her violent husband. Even her own solicitor 'was horrible':

> he made me feel so dirty [...] he had his pen in his hand and he was writing things down and said I've had a letter from your husband's solicitor saying that you are seeing a woman and [...] I didn't know what to do [...] I thought if I omit it I'm going to have my children taken away from me, because it was like a war [...] and he threw the pen down and I was so scared because .... my ex-husband was threatening me as well [...] in the end I actually left the children in the home with him [...] [and] never lived with them again.[73]

Lynne was, however, able to remain in close contact with her teenagers. They were given a difficult time in their neighbourhood but her daughter stood up strongly against the gossip:

> [W]hen it all came out about me, she had a bit of a hard time about it at school, your mum's a lesbian cos it spread all the way through Southway,[74] all my people, all the married women I use to knock around with, their husbands [...] [It was a] close community in each other's houses all the time. [...] I had to go up to the school once about it because she was being accused of it as well because your mum is, so you are. [...] I was very lucky, that my daughter was so open for

her 15 [years] [...] but my poor son [...] took it quite hard, sometimes he didn't want to speak to me because he heard all the horrible stuff about it from my ex-husband.[75]

Ten years later, Sharon had a very different experience of lesbian parenting in Plymouth. Like Lynne, she was a born and bred Plymouthian and known in her neighbourhood. Sharon, a social worker, moved in with her partner and her four children in 1985. Asked about any homophobia shown towards them as 'two mums' or to their children she explained:

[A] lot of the neighbours knew, and their kids played with our kids [...] it actually was fine, they were really good. [...] I don't remember anything – we used to drink in the local pub. [In Ford, in west central Plymouth] Yeah, so we didn't encounter anything much to our face, whatever was said behind our backs, who knows? But [...] I suppose we didn't kind of shove it down people's throats, mainly because we probably were being a bit sensible, just in case, maybe. But we were clearly an item and we were out and about [...][76]

Sharon and her partner exercised typical Plymouth queer caution while being open about their sexuality and family set-up. They carefully thought through the ways their children could negotiate any difficulties:

[W]e always talked to them [to say] – they didn't need to tell anybody if they didn't want to. [...] I certainly wasn't going to make them have to feel like they had to participate in any bloody cause, you know what I mean?[77]

Sharon was very involved with lesbian and gay community initiatives in Plymouth, and so the family did enjoy broader social support. She said: 'I think we've been lucky, I think we've been blessed. I think [...] we have moved in circles where you almost should expect people to have a little bit more understanding, I suppose.'[78] These equivocal stories from Plymouth were typical; many families had a tough time, even in cities with a wider backdrop of alternative politics.

In the 1970s, lesbians began to seek artificial insemination by donor as a way of having babies. Organized initially through the lesbian organization Sappho, which referred lesbians to a sympathetic doctor, this caused a media scandal in 1978.[79] Women soon began to pursue DIY self-insemination using sperm from male friends and supporters, a practice that was well underway in the 1980s in cities beyond London. Indeed, Leeds lesbians claim they were pioneers in organized self-insemination, both within couple relationships and in the more political environment of collective households. 'Leeds was one of the first places to have a really strong and organized movement for lesbians to have babies',

Miriam remembered.[80] Jude described how one of the lesbian self-insemination networks operated:

> The man who donated, would donate, and it would get picked up by a go-between. So basically we would have this lovely woman, she was quite buxom, and at that time the sperm would be secreted into a little film canister, because they were a really good seal. When they click shut. Washable and easy. And of course you've got to keep it at body temperature. So she would basically put it down her cleavage. So then she would arrive at the front door and – here you go![81]

To support their children, the women in Jude's network organized regular events and holidays for their dozen or so children of similar ages. '[T]he kids have grown up together. They're very much like cousins to each other, which is lovely.'[82] Lesbian motherhood was a political and community issue as well as a personal undertaking, and later in the 1980s the women's discos held at the Dock Green pub in Harehills funded the Lesbian Mothers Group on alternate weeks.[83] Expressions of homophobia about gay parenting and the belief that children would be harmed in lesbian and gay families meanwhile reached a crescendo with the debates over Clause 28 and the notion of 'pretended family relationships'.

Bringing up children in lesbian or queer households involved interacting with state authorities such as medical services, nurseries and schools in ways that were much more intense than for gay adults without children. As Al put it earlier: 'when you have children you have to engage with the mainstream rather a lot'.[84] Jess, who brought up a child with her partner in Manchester, explained that some areas of the city were better places to do this:

> We knew that there were a couple of schools in Manchester where it was ok to be gay parents and take your child. … Chorlton had and still has quite a few people who move there because it's easier to bring their kids up there.[85]

Despite being in Chorlton, Jess and her partner still found it wearing to have to repeatedly explain the family relationships:

> [I]f they see you're a parent, they assume you're straight. […] they'll ask you where your husband is, or they'll want to know where his dad is, things like that. […] And it takes them a while. You have to keep saying: no, he has two mothers. […] Having to go over and over again.[86]

Schools and teachers might adhere to an ideal of welcoming diverse sexualities by the 2000s, but in practice they still interacted with parents on the basis of deeply held heterosexist assumptions.

Of course, many lesbian and gay parents did not have the option of moving to a district where others had been pioneers in educating schools and medical services about LGBTQ families, as with Lynne's family in Plymouth. In other places expectations had shifted considerably by the 2000s, and by this period there is more evidence of gay men involved in parenting. Gay men as dads were most extensively – or perhaps just more freely – mentioned in Brighton.[87] Seventeen-year-old Charlie was 'raised in a family that's not even conventional by gay family standards'.[88] He lived with his two mums, a half-sibling and family input from four other women (his mums' former partners), as well as being close to his gay dad. Living in Brighton he had friends with similarly multifaceted families, and although he found it quite confusing to explain, '[a]ctually no one ever really did have a problem with it'.[89] Although the experience of bringing up children in a queer family varied between the four cities, it is the time period that is crucial. It got a lot easier in the 2000s. The establishment of support networks and the migration of lesbian mothers to particular localities was a key element in creating a more relaxed context in which to bring up children.

Socializing at home

Using houses and flats to host lesbian and gay parties and consciousness-raising groups also challenged the idea of the conventional home. The friendship networks formed at these gatherings created queer 'families of choice' for many people.[90] One member of the Leeds Gay Community group described the importance of gay liberation meetings in people's houses to his developing sense of self as a gay man in the 1970s:

> We had awareness group meetings which I found extremely productive where people talked about themselves. [...] I thought it was very good, for me anyway, it really liberated me in many ways. We used to stay in various houses around Hyde Park, particularly on Sunday afternoons.[91]

A little later in the city, Ajamu valued socializing with other queer people of colour in their own homes, the place where they could most comfortably be both gay and Black. In late 1970s working-class Plymouth, Lynne described how, as a newly out lesbian, she did her socializing at the gay bars and clubs but that also 'we used to meet up in peoples' bedsits and flats'.[92] Plymouth CHE organized fancy dress parties in members' houses (Figure 27), as did Kenric for Brighton lesbians. The private home was particularly valuable during times when homosexuality was socially stigmatized and seen as shameful and contaminating.

181

Image 27 A Plymouth CHE fancy dress party, 1976

In 1960s Brighton, invitation-only gay parties were held behind the closed doors of flats and houses often owned by a more affluent theatrical crowd. In the Manchester area, videos made of an all-male sex party at one man's home led to the conviction of the 'Bolton 7' in 1998.[93] A sense of community through queer friendship networks cemented within the home as well as in more public venues comes through many of the interviews. This was not necessarily class-specific, but better-off white-collar and professional LGBTQ people could choose the location of their (often larger) homes and have greater control over their use. James and his partner in Brighton socialized in a way that paralleled heterosexual couples – at least those without children. James said, 'it was very much a kind of dinner party circuit. […] We loved entertaining. We turned the basement of our house into a big dining and entertaining area. And we built an extension out the back. We had loads and loads [of] dinner parties and parties. We had a huge garden. And it was all very, very social.'[94] But in an even queerer way, the room in their home that would have been the nursery was 'devoted entirely to dressing up and jewellery, because that's what we do'.[95]

Socializing at home was particularly important for lesbians, who were more susceptible to gender-based ideas of respectability if they had professional jobs such as teaching. In the 1960s and 1970s, home-based social gatherings were often the only opportunities for closeted middle-class lesbians to meet others. Such parties offered discretion and avoided the potential dangers of meeting publicly in gay pubs and clubs. When Doreen moved to Leeds in 1967 she found other lesbians in the city and West Yorkshire through the national lesbian network, the MRG and its newsletter *Arena Three*, and soon got involved in these parties:

> [W]hether I had an address or what from London I don't know but there was a lass had a farmhouse outside Keighley and once a month we used to have a get-together there [...] we used to put a supper on and we danced, talked, and you just let your hair down and you could relax completely and utterly and that was the whole idea of it. [...] [W]e all became friends type of thing.[96]

These lesbians had the mobility to enjoy a social and sexual life. Doreen made the jaunt from Leeds to Keighley on her scooter: 'I used to take the record player plus records on the back of it [laughs] to this place'.[97] Despite the Keighley farmhouse being off the beaten track: 'everybody turned up from – we had people from Newcastle came down [...] [from] Rochdale there were people, Manchester'. While lesbians did go to gay pubs, class and gender norms generally meant they did so less frequently than gay men. Doreen describes going to the New Penny, the longstanding gay pub in Leeds, in the late 1960s or early 1970s, but she was anxious about seeing colleagues from work there and thought that the people there were 'coarse'.[98]

Socials in private homes remained important for women who sought discretion in the decades that followed. Millie, who worked as a teacher, came out in her mid-fifties in the 1980s in the context of a regular lesbian social hosted by a couple in Brighton's suburbs:

> I had no idea what being gay was like. Not a clue. I went to an open house in Preston Drove. Once a month they had socials. [...] It was just music and some nice food. [...] And gradually it became less scary. It became somewhere you went for a laugh. For women like me, who are not very out in many respects, it was comfortable.[99]

Even in the gay city of Brighton, Jill said that at these parties: 'You never revealed your surname or expected anyone to give theirs, because many women knew they could be sacked for being gay, or lose their children'.[100] The socials were freer in some respects than the gay scene. 'You felt comfortable there wearing whatever you wanted at a time when make up, long hair and skirts were often frowned on in lesbian venues.'[101]

In all of these ways, LGBTQ people and groups queered the structure, dynamics and uses of the home. The politics of home had its most visible, confrontational and elaborate expression in the city centre bedsits in Brighton and the lesbian collective households in Leeds. Only a minority of lesbians and gay men ever lived communally in squats and collective houses, but these models of home were politically important in the 1970s and 1980s. The public commercial scene acted as an additional form of home in a hostile environment during much of this time. Less obvious to non-queers, but fundamental to the lesbian and gay community, was its opposite – the turning inside out of the home through its use as a party space for collective queer pleasures, from lesbian socials in Brighton to CHE parties in 1970s Plymouth. Of course, lesbians and

Image 28 Lesbian poetry evening at home, Brighton, 1990

gay men lived in ordinary suburbs as well and became increasingly confident about their right to be who they were, to social housing and to be safe in everyday neighbourhoods. This may have happened first in parts of Brighton and Manchester, but queer families and households have become increasingly out and evident in Leeds and Plymouth too. Just as powerfully, the supposedly heterosexual private home and idea of family has turned out to be very permeable to queer networks and desires. The normal-seeming household in Plymouth, Leeds, Manchester or Brighton might accommodate and have connections to multiple queer families of choice.

7

Making histories, memories and communities

In Brighton, Leeds, Plymouth and Manchester, many people felt so passionate and enthusiastic about the queer past that they gave up their time to get involved in community history projects and also agreed to be interviewed for Queer Beyond London and take part in our workshops to tell the stories of their city.[1] The people whose memories were recorded offer a huge range of visions and perceptions of the past: the kaleidoscope of 'experiences, opinions, historical anecdotes and arcane facts, the regrets and aspirations of a community, of our kind', in the words of the Queer in Brighton group.[2] All of these memories contributed to the histories of these cities as distinct places, and this chapter takes a step back to compare them and look at this upsurge in individual and community history-making in the 2000s.[3]

First of all I briefly discuss the explicit – perhaps abstract – reasons that people give for believing that LGBTQ history is important: what they think its purpose and significance is. They acknowledge a generation gap between older and younger queer people and conjure up a range of LGBTQ generations: pre- and post-law reform, survivors of the 1980s, veterans of GLF or lesbian feminism and post-equality 'millennials'. This theme of the divisions among LGBTQ 'communities', between different generations and also between the sexes and sexual identities will recur throughout the chapter. Evoking and talking about the past often generates strong emotions, and these are discussed in the main central section of this chapter. Those feelings about the past often rebound into the present-day telling of the story, providing astonishingly diverse interpretations of past time periods. Many contributors seek to weigh up the past dispassionately. But they are telling their stories at different times, from the 1980s to the 2010s, and these contexts make a difference to the way they remember and talk about the past. Among certain generations of LGBTQ people, in particular cities, there are powerful bursts of

Image 29 You Were Known to Us: Transgender Memorial, Sackville Gardens, by Rita Hester, 2013. The inscription reads: 'We remember those who have gone before us and we will fight for those yet to come'

nostalgia – for the warm secret world of 1960s queer bars or for the politicized gay community of the 1980s.

Finally, I move from the people and their stories to the community projects that gathered their voices together. The varying focus and aims of these LGBTQ history projects reflect the cities in which they were based: their gender divisions, their politics and their partying. Their distinctive kinds of history-making help us to understand further the differences between our cities and their queer cultures. We see discussions of community and nostalgia in Plymouth, a valuing of current gains over a darker past in Leeds and a celebration of the city's clubs, campaigns and history-making in Brighton. The interviews I chose to discuss in this chapter lean towards Leeds, Brighton and Plymouth. These cities shared some similarities in that their oral history collections were primarily about people's personal experiences, their sense of identity and how that was lived out in their local areas.

Reflecting on history-making: the importance of the queer past

Two common concerns expressed by the people who took part in the various oral history projects were a lack of knowledge about the queer past among younger LGBTQ people and the political importance of being aware of that past. The idea of a generation gap, of LGBTQ history not being known about and not passed down, was discussed by many people. Older gay men in Leeds, for example, believed there was widespread ignorance: '[I]f you went to the gay bars in Leeds tonight and asked people, very few there would actually know that it used to be illegal to practice homosexuality. It's just totally out of their orbit.'[4] Young LGBTQ people largely agreed. Participants in the Bradford gay youth group said they felt disconnected from the gay past: 'It feels like a long time ago to me.' Another pointed out: 'It's only the age of my parents. It does feel to me like another world.'[5] Alan, from Plymouth's Pride in Our Past project, spoke of the difficulty of engaging younger audiences at a local youth group:

> I could see I was losing them. I was talking about archives and history and it was kind of a bit, 'yeah, that's nice'. And then I said something about knowing I was gay before I knew there was a word for it, and Ty was really taken with that. He's like, 'I don't understand how that can happen'. And, it's like, 'well, you know, I'm not saying it's easier now but there is some representation. The words are out there. Celebrities are out, things happen in soap operas, films. But for me, there wasn't that representation'. And that really struck a chord with him, that things had moved that quickly in that time.[6]

Older and younger contributors agreed on some of the reasons for this lack of knowledge and even of interest in the past. Several made the point that particular age groups focus only on their own era of LGBTQ history. '[H]istory makes sense when you've lived through it, but if it's somebody else's history you don't want to know.'[7] They emphasized that LGBTQ history should be part of the history curriculum in schools, making parallels with the still slow moves towards women's history and Black history. 'Things aren't written about it. There aren't history books written about gay history.'[8] Jill pointed out: 'That's one thing about gay history, that we don't have institutions. We don't have places we can go over many years and we can think, that's us.'[9] Jill and others in these discussions valued finding others like themselves in the past: a form of history that identifies an LGBTQ lineage.[10]

A key factor, as people perceptively noted, was the 'huge generation gap in the gay scene, and so there isn't the opportunity for intergenerational stories and anecdotes to get passed [on]'.[11] One younger man made a comparison with broader social histories. 'There are always stories passed down to you. We all know about the war and stuff because your nan and granddad passed those stories down to you and unless you've got gay relatives nobody's going to know that and these groups are relatively new.'[12] Many of the community LGBTQ history projects in the four cities were designed to bring older and younger generations together.[13] The Manchester project 'This Is How We Got Here' in 2014, on the history of the LGBT centre, trained younger queer people in interviewing skills to gather the stories of older folk. The focus of the LGBT Centre and the city council on youth groups since the 1980s has led to more attention being paid in Manchester to what young queer people might need or want to know. Queer in Brighton similarly fostered moments of real connection and shared feelings. Lesley Woods, the project leader, described how 'David, a young gay man, inspired confidence and trust in his 80 year old interviewee Kenneth, who had been jailed for 3 years [for] importuning as a young man. Kenneth cried as he remembered the kindness of fellow inmates who presented him with bags of sugar for his 21st birthday.'[14] Lesley suggested that the intergenerational disconnect was due to no recent large-scale political activism drawing together the queer community as had been the case in the 1980s and, for gay men in particular, AIDS meant there was a missing generation of mentors.[15]

Keeping the queer past alive and passing it on to younger generations was felt to be important as a political lesson: to teach people to guard against any rolling back of LGBTQ rights. As Melita, a veteran of 1980s Brighton activism, put it:

No one else is going to tell our history for us, we have to tell our own histories. And our own stories. I think lessons from history are really important. So with Brexit and Trump, there is a definite turning of the tide. And to me, it's [that] rights are always fought for and won, rights are never granted. And those rights can easily be taken away.[16]

In other cities too, older narrators especially drew stark historic analogies to warn against forgetting the past, including not only the Thatcherite 1980s but also 1930s Nazi Germany: 'the speed [of it …] you had a city [Berlin] that was so open, and *suddenly* […] they changed a society so quickly'.[17]

As imagined by younger narrators who had not lived through it, the queer past assumes exaggerated features. Earlier periods – indeed any time before the 2000s, let alone before gay liberation – were seen as a kind of sexual dark ages. In some discussions there was a repetition of oppressive forces – religion, medical attitudes, and social stigma. When asked about the past, one member of the Bradford youth group responded: 'Things like aversion therapy spring to my mind, like medical treatments, electric shock treatment.'[18] Those who had not lived through the 1970s or 1980s were more likely to think of these periods as catastrophically awful for queer people. We can see here how younger people's knowledge about the past from LGBTQ popular culture (or lack of it) comes in the form of generalized myths and usually with a narrative of unrelenting repression and difficulty.

In Brighton since the late 1980s, LGBTQ histories have been actively shared at a whole range of events involving younger people who were, Melita said, 'absolutely horrified' by Clause 28 and 'these kinds of things'.[19] A younger woman, Kathrine, referred to the importance of Brighton's community history in her understanding of the gay scene in the 1960s: 'It's only through reading *Daring Hearts* that I saw that lesbians had much of a life back in that era anyway.'[20] As this comment indicates, younger narrators find it difficult to imagine how different the queer past was from the present day. Another Brighton lesbian said, during a discussion of lesbian separatism in the 1970s and 1980s:

And it kind of seems a bit old-fashioned. And I can't imagine a gay man being misogynistic towards me. So it's nice that I don't live back in the 50s. […] I can't imagine a time when everyone would have been at each other's throats.[21]

This contributor confuses the 1980s with the 1950s, as if the 1950s represents a generalized historical era of repression for lesbians and gay men that persisted for decades. And clearly the past history of political differences is deeply unattractive compared to what was felt to be a more relaxed and convivial present day.

Feelings about the past

When people record their oral histories they are organizing their memories into stories – stories of their personal journey through life and stories about the places where they have lived. It is the strong feelings attached to these stories as much as the description of 'what happened where' that has lodged these past events into the interviewee's mind. As people told others about their queer lives, the accompanying emotions reveal not only their experience of historic events but also their feelings about their present-day circumstances. Deliberately or unconsciously, a comparison is being made. So the feelings that collect around visions of each city's history can tell us about that city and also about how its queer citizens are dealing with change at the time that they gave voice to their past experiences.

The most powerfully remembered time periods for people in Brighton, Leeds, Manchester and Plymouth were, first, the years between the 1960s and the early 1970s and, second, the 1980s. These were intense periods for gays and lesbians: the first marked by the partial decriminalization of sex between men followed by the development of lesbian and gay activism; the second by the HIV/AIDS crisis and hostility from the government in the shape of Clause 28. A third period, the 2000s, saw the rapid introduction of equalities legislation, and for most of the oral history projects this was 'the present day' which participants might compare with their pasts.

Particular generations of people who shared similar experiences of being lesbian or gay in the past when they were young often merge these into a group or collective memory of their city.[22] Sometimes stories reinforce each other so that it becomes difficult to challenge agreed narratives and perspectives. The feelings those past experiences evoked, which people might have had few opportunities to express at the time, echo in the present and future for the people in that age group. In creating narratives about their past lives, queer people find themselves standing outside the conventional heterosexual chronologies: of marriage and family, for example.[23] The themes that repeatedly surfaced were the nature of lesbian and gay community, the role of political activism and the experiences of fear or of safety. What was strikingly different about the cities was the extent to which interviewees felt something had been lost. This feeling often depended on the time period in which they were doing their remembering, whether that was in the late 1980s for Brighton Ourstory, in 2008 in West Yorkshire or in 2017 at the Queer Beyond London workshops. The 'present' continuously moves forward, differently refracting the view of the past.

The 1960s remembered in Leeds and Brighton

While there was a gay scene in both Leeds and Brighton in the 1960s, the previous chapters have shown that Brighton's was perceived as already more open and welcoming to lesbians and gay men. When LGBTQ people recall these years – of partial decriminalization of sex between men in 1967, the beginnings of a gay press and in the early 1970s the activism of the GLF and CHE – the contrast in feelings about the two cities is sharp. The 1960s are remembered with warm nostalgia by Brightonians telling their stories at the end of the 1980s in the context of AIDS and Clause 28 but are seen as grim and difficult by people in Leeds, looking back from 2008 with the age of consent now equalized and other equalities legislation in place.

Lesbians and gay men who had lived in Brighton during the 1960s described the effects of social stigma and criminalization on their personal lives. Some were fearful of losing their jobs if they were seen in a gay pub, and some had indeed been sacked. Sheila described her anxiety about being outed if seen in her butch lesbian gear:

> Most of our concern was the fact that you'd be there in your regalia – because when you went out you dressed up in your regalia – that you'd be discovered by someone and that would be it, you'd be branded. My biggest fear was that one of my customers would come into the pub. I think I would have died.[24]

Men described how they were 'terrified of the law'.[25] The police certainly raided and closed down various queer-friendly pubs and clubs in Brighton over the years, as well as arresting men for cottaging. People spoke of their sense of guilt, of loneliness, of having breakdowns because of their sexuality, of trying to go straight and of knowing friends who had committed suicide – stories repeated across the country.

But what was remarkable about LGBTQ memories of Brighton in the 1960s is that alongside these accounts of intolerant attitudes and repression, people also felt very strong nostalgia for the period, a sense that some elements of the queer life they enjoyed then were lacking in their present, the late 1980s. 'It was a wonderful world, this secret world behind closed doors, like Alice going through the Looking Glass into Wonderland', said Pat.[26] The thrill of finding these places and being part of the *cognoscenti* was also bound up with the freedom to be ambiguous about sexual identity. Peter felt that '[i]t was part of the excitement, was the secrecy. [...] The queans these days, they go camping it around quite openly and it's lost something. It's lost a bit of its charm about it, the fact that it's no longer a secret. Now you're gay or you're straight, you're one or the other.'[27]

The contributors to *Daring Hearts* tell tale after tale about the fun they had in the pubs and clubs, the pianists and the sing-alongs, the pub crawls and parties. There are also stories of queer people asserting their presence, of 'wicked' camp queens talking back to and embarrassing straight men in pubs and shops who dared to cross them.[28] This feeling about 1960s Brighton is summed up by Sandie: 'There was a real sense of comradeship then, you know.' She describes how she and her gay friends would run along Brighton's Lanes at two in the morning singing popular songs:

> And other daft things we did. But oh, it was fun. [...] In the sixties, there was more of a sort of family feeling. I don't know how else to express it. Because we used to say, then, 'Oh, he's family or she's family.' That was an expression [...] meaning, 'That's another gay person.' Even if you didn't know them.[29]

Simon, who went to Sussex University in 1967, had more complicated feelings about these years. He described coming out on the cusp of law reform. 'I was very consumed with guilt and anxiety about my sexuality. My knees would knock and I'd go into The Heart and Hand, the old gay bar in the Lanes and sit on a high stool trembling with terror.'[30] However, he also remembered the scene with fondness: '[My boyfriend and I] were two cute bunnies so we were taken up by the older gay scene in Brighton to some extent. There were all these extraordinary people round.'[31] He describes meeting well-known artists and writers while also initiating a gay liberation group, importing the politics from visits to London. Simon, however, was alive to having misplaced feelings about the past: 'I'm not saying it was better – I don't have pink spectacles. I think it's easy to be fanciful about the past. It wasn't better at all. It was an appalling environment. It was a cruel and terrible time as well.'[32]

But nostalgia was the dominant mood for gay men and lesbians remembering the 1960s and 1970s in Brighton. Freddie, whose shop selling gay magazines and sex toys was raided by the police during the 1980s, had a positive, indeed romanticized view of earlier times:

> At the 42nd Club you had to knock on the door and the little old lady upstairs would say, 'Who is it?' And when I said my name she'd let me in. It was good fun. Back then, although life was hard being gay, once you got to know people in Brighton it could be naughty but nice! People looked out for each other and gay men, especially older gentlemen, used to speak Polari. [...] It was much more fun being gay then than it is today.[33]

Freddie particularly pointed to ageism on the contemporary scene, whereas in the past he remembered an idealized, more mixed community: 'Back in the good old days everyone was in the bars, all together, young and old, black and white – it didn't matter. It could be camp as Christmas or rough as a dog's arse, the whole package.'[34] Both Freddie and Simon remember the 1960s as a time when different generations mixed in the Brighton bars and a gay scene that was less exclusive and cliquey than some other accounts suggest.

Nostalgia, a yearning for times past that can no longer be experienced that is tinged with both sadness and pleasure, has a complicated role in making memories of the queer past. Nostalgia is often a way of expressing the loss of what was remembered as a place and time of comfort and safety that no longer feels so available in the present. The nostalgic feelings of some Brightonians for the 1960s centred on the loss of an idealized queer community, aptly recalled as one of 'family' by Sandie, and perhaps standing in for the security associated with birth family.[35] For some Brightonians, belonging to a semi-secret society of other queers was also part of this vanished past. There was an excitement in being an outsider, yet one in the know, so that the knock on the door of the hidden upstairs club was an adventure in itself – enhanced by the sexual possibilities that might lie beyond. Of course, for many people, the nostalgia for a past that was full of fun, sexual freedom and camaraderie was also a lament for their lost youth, when the horizon was expanding.[36] A longing for – and indeed making a history out of – this now-lost world of the bars, with butches and femmes and queens talking back, is also a way of asserting that queer life had value in what had been an era of hostility and exclusion from mainstream society.[37]

Memories of the 1960s in Leeds, recorded mainly from gay men by the West Yorkshire Archive Service (WYAS) LGBT project of 2008, make a sharp contrast to those of Brighton. Many who had been young in 1960s Leeds had dark stories to tell about this time, having experienced interpersonal violence, self-loathing or a sense of hopelessness, actual or anticipated hostility from family, friends and employers, and collectively a fear of the police. Partial decriminalization of sex between men in 1967 was not seen as a turning point, though the beginnings of gay social and political groups in the early 1970s did provide the relief of being 'normal' among other gay men in a context that was not only about sex.

The older men in Leeds described a vivid set of circuits and places in the city where they met other queer men and their friends, both before and after law reform in 1967. But they also recalled the negative side of being socially marginalized. David said:

Yes, there were good times but also there were a lot of bad times. The good times were drinking in the Hope & Anchor in the Calls and then Charlie's [...] It was great, yes, there were places like bars and that sort of thing and that was the sad thing, people knew who they were and what they were, [but] the only way they could do it was in dirty little toilets or 12 o'clock at night in woods and it was sad, but people lived that way because they didn't know what else to do.[38]

David also described his fears, repeated by other men of his generation, of 'the police and entrapment' in public toilets. 'I know friends who got five years' hard labour for doing that', he said.[39]

Although at times there is a frisson of excitement conveyed in the men's accounts, and certainly a remembered camaraderie, there is no regret expressed for that way of life. They dispassionately and in detail weigh up the appalling effects on them of being social outcasts. Law reform in 1967 made little difference to most of them in the short term, as police harassment continued: 'in some ways things got a bit worse in terms of convictions for cottaging and that sort of thing'.[40] The men described 'considerable apprehension' well into the 1970s. One said:

[Even] in the 70s a gay man would not divulge his address to another gay man, and certainly wouldn't give them a phone number because everybody was paranoid about them telling the police where they lived, not only the police but your employers as well.[41]

This fear of being outed stunted many gay men's relationships and their emotional lives. Some of the members of the Leeds Gay Community (LGC) group discussed their internalized homophobia and feelings of disgust about men who picked each other up in cottages while doing the same thing themselves. A common theme was the impossibility of developing a deeper relationship with another man, even if anonymous sexual partners were to be found. As one man said:

[Y]ou had a sexual urge, you went out and somehow you managed to find somebody but on the other hand it's not just the sexual side but the emotional side and I found personally that ok, you went out and [...] got to know how gay people met and all about the steam baths [...] but it didn't stop you from falling for people of a similar age and you had an emotional urge towards them.

Fear had made sustained relationships impossible or very difficult in the 1960s, but he thought 'that these days it is possible to have an emotional relationship with somebody'.[42] For others the effects were long-lasting. Ted, describing the psychic costs of this life, said, 'not to this day have I let go of my emotions and

I would never allow myself to fall in love with anybody, not even now'. He described this as a learned distrust of his own feelings and a distrust of other people. Working as a teacher, he only began to have sexual flings away from Leeds when visiting London in the late 1960s when he himself was in his thirties. It was not until he slowly made contact with other gay men through the LGC in the mid-1970s when he was forty that he found friendship with other gay men. LGC 'contextualized being gay. The first time I met people in partnerships, good heavens! [...] You'd think they were normal people!'[43] Ted treats with ironic humour the painful fact that he had not been able to have a 'normal' gay relationship himself and also signals the importance of community groups like LGC and earlier the GLF and CHE. Another man affirmed the importance of the alternative spaces these groups opened out: 'we used to have picnics in Woodhouse Moor and there was a fair amount of socialising and for me personally [...] it was absolutely wonderful because I met a lot of people like myself'.[44]

The divergence in memories of the 1960s in Brighton and Leeds reflects some real differences between the cities and the people who lived there. Brightonians were positive because for most of them the town offered greater freedom than the places from which they had escaped. As migrants – including Freddie – they relished their good fortune. While both cities had a well-developed queer scene, this was more densely concentrated and unashamed in Brighton. Sociable gay Brightonians had a certain confidence and a feeling of safety in numbers which comes across in many stories. There may also have been less effective policing in Brighton: certainly the police were remembered as just part of the weather there, unless you were unlucky, while in Leeds there were strong memories of being fearful.

But these LGBTQ people are also doing their remembering at different times and that context is important. The Brighton stories in *Daring Hearts* were recorded by Ourstory at the end of the 1980s, only twenty years after the 1960s, but at a time when the gains in social tolerance that appeared to have been made in the 1970s had come under attack from government and the gay community was ravaged by HIV/AIDS. Contributors may have felt that the 1960s were free and easy in comparison: a time when lesbian and gay life was felt to be improving. The continuing – and worsening – riskiness of being out as a gay man or lesbian in the insecure 1980s might have led men like Peter to mourn the loss of 1960s possibilities of living outside a defined sexual identity. In contrast, the Leeds narrators were looking back from 2008, when equalities legislation was beginning to make an impact, the police were starting to liaise with LGBT communities and queer life could be more relaxed. Their recollections of the 1960s were voiced with strong emotions but without nostalgia. Their sense of a safe, indeed normalizing, community was rooted beyond the 1960s, in the beginnings of gay liberation and a sense of group affirmation in the early 1970s.

The 1980s: a difficult reckoning

Strong sentiments were also attached to memories of the 1980s. It is between Leeds and Plymouth that we find the greatest contrasts in how those challenging 1980s years were remembered, years when gay liberation gains were confronted by the AIDS crisis and new homophobic legislation. Participants in our Plymouth workshop in 2017 were markedly nostalgic for the 1980s (and 1990s), seen as the heyday of the city's gay scene. In contrast, interviewees from the 2008 Leeds LGBT project remember the hostility towards them as gay people, which was relieved by the exhilaration of a collective political response. These gay men looked back on their youth in Leeds as a time of antagonism not only from the police but also from the state in the shape of Clause 28. Their sense of self was also deeply affected by the experience of the AIDS epidemic, both in their own fears of contracting the virus and in the homophobia shown by neighbours and workmates. Yet many of the stories of Leeds in the 1980s are infused with an intense sense of camaraderie – indeed euphoria – experienced at times by those who mobilized to demand gay rights. In fact, more extreme feelings were described in these contributors' memories of the 1980s than even the older men's accounts of the 1960s and 1970s.

When Paul came out in his very early twenties in the mid-1980s, he was kicked out of the parental home but quickly found a connection with the Leeds Lesbian and Gay Youth Group, which offered both social and political activities and gave him a circle of friends. Unlike the experiences of the older men in the 1960s, this queer community cushioned Paul against the worst aspects of the 1980s, which he described as 'a horrible time to be gay'.[45] Paul was involved in letter-writing and direct action against Clause 28 in the late 1980s and a little later with Outrage over the campaign to equalize the age of consent for sex between men. 'We organised marches down in London, got arrested a few times for breach of the peace', he said. 'The atmosphere was really electric, everybody was so up for it'.[46] Craig described a similar contrast between a supportive group of queer friends at a time of hate and homophobia in the wider world. Living on the dole in Huddersfield bedsits, he partied on the flamboyant punk and goth scene where he found community: 'We had a nick-name of the screaming queens.'[47] These young people faced many dangers. 'I think the drug scene was beginning to take its toll on a lot of people because slowly but surely one by one people started to have breakdowns. [...] The party stopped as it were.'[48] Craig's memory of this queer community is tinged with loss, of the friends who burned out. There was also the threat of violence out on the scene in both Leeds and Huddersfield. 'I've been in the Gemini [nightclub] when it's been boarded up when there's a gang outside trying to break the door in.'[49]

Several men talked about their visceral fear during the AIDS crisis, but as something now safely in the past. Paul said: 'AIDS and HIV had a big impact on the gay scene. I knew two people who got HIV and they're both dead now. [...] There was a lot of HIV around in the 80s. It scared me and I tried not to have unsafe sex and casual sex with people.'[50] Craig linked the fear of HIV with the wider threat to gay men and lesbians from the state. He was advised to think carefully about going for an AIDS test because his name might be recorded. 'Basically, what was said on the grapevine was that if it went to epidemic proportions then they'd be rounding up the gays and lesbians.'[51] Both men also described the heightening of casual homophobia in their neighbourhoods and workplaces. Craig worked as a gardener for a nursing home, where 'I knew things weren't right, the staff were looking at me like dirt'. After he left, a sympathetic neighbour told him the backstory: 'she said every time you had a drink they were bleaching your cup just in case you'd got AIDS. I couldn't believe it.'[52] But like Paul, Craig's involvement in the political response to Clause 28 gave him a powerful feeling of community resistance. He described marches and rallies in various northern cities which were 'so uplifting... you got a lot of abuse and we did exactly the same back'. He travelled from Leeds to London for an 'absolutely massive' march and rally:

> I remember walking through the streets and being told keep together, keep together, the National Front is out in force, don't go anywhere on your own [...] The atmosphere was euphoric, the feeling was such an enormous high [...] If anybody had tried to stop us, if the police had tried to stop us, we'd have turned and that was that feeling that we had such power.[53]

In his narrative, Craig switches sharply between recalling the fear and abuse they experienced and the exhilaration of collectively defying it. For the most part, the men assess their 1980s emotions powerfully but with a sense of distance, removed from that time. Nevertheless, the memory of local antagonism lingered, and the equality gains made by 2008 were not yet solid; the threat of hate crime remained. Craig noted that 'in Dewsbury Moor or in Huddersfield Town Centre it will still be there and still be rife'.[54] The men tell their stories with a kind of clear-headed hindsight, weighing up the positives and negatives, what has gone and what has endured (including in some places this threat of violence). If there is any nostalgia at all in these 1980s accounts, it is related to their feelings about friends from that time who didn't make it through those turbulent years.

In Plymouth, the dominant feelings about the 1980s (and the 1990s) were of nostalgia, loss and regret. The Queer Beyond London group discussion kept returning to the social scene in the city at this time, recalling the lesbian and gay clubs and pubs and In Other Words bookshop, and the part these venues played in people's coming out and queer lives. People constantly returned to their dismay that these gay-friendly venues had closed or were felt to be less congenial. As Colin said:

> But what we've lost, I think, is that sense of community where we all meet in one place. 'Oh, I'll go down the Swallow tonight because so-and-so might be there. [...]' And it doesn't happen anymore, or not to the same extent anyway.[55]

Some also recalled the less cosy elements of the 1980s and 1990s, especially the threats outside the safety of the gay pubs and back bars: the fears of police raids

Image 30 Gay and Prudence outside In Other Words bookshop, *c.* late 1980s

and of being outed, especially to employers. Kevin said that the police 'were always our enemy. They were always raiding the cruising areas, which were the renowned toilets [...] There were so many all over Plymouth, which have all been closed down now. So [...] [group laughter] sadly.'[56] Here, nostalgia is expressed even for the sites of danger, men's cruising places, which of course were also places for sexual pleasure. What was being mourned was a gay community in its heyday, when Plymouth's queer pubs and clubs were perceived to have supported and embraced LGBT people. 'I think, yes, we have lost spaces where people can go in and nothing needs to be said. You just know that you feel at home', said one. 'There was a real feeling of safety there', said another.[57]

In the Plymouth narratives, the rich communal past of lesbian and gay socializing was contrasted with a deficient present in which sexual identities have less obvious homes. Jo said that the new inclusion of LGBT people was 'wonderful' but described the sense of loss of valued women-only nights and predominantly lesbian spaces. There was, she said, 'a sadness because of the demise of these places, where you really did feel that you could be absolutely yourself'.[58] Jo and other women recalled these lesbian bars and club nights in some detail, and in so doing drew attention to sex differences in queer experience and some feelings of vulnerability for lesbians within the Plymouth gay scene, perhaps indicating flaws in the fantasy of being one big family:

> There was a big, big gay scene. There were all sorts of places to go to. The Penrose was [...] very much for women. We used to go as a group, and it was really huge. [...] And then there was Harry's, of course [...] We were a lot of lesbians and also gay men, and we used to go down and have great fun. I think the thing from a lesbian point of view is that we were actually really looked after there. Harry and the bouncers were very protective of us. [...] So there was this real feeling of welcome.[59]

The nostalgia is rooted in actual loss – there were fewer gay and lesbian venues in Plymouth in the 2010s than there had been earlier. These older lesbians and gay men probably socialized less than they had in their youth. But Jo also evokes an idealized community, as in memories of 1960s Brighton, where people looked out for one another despite their differences. Nostalgia can also in this way have a restorative function, as a means of coming to terms with the hurt and pain of queer experience in the past, as perhaps it does here. For all the fun Jo describes, Plymouth wasn't an easy place to be gay or lesbian.[60] She and her friends had to manage a more complex social exclusion than in other regional cities, many of them still subject to the criminalizing military ban that was not lifted until 2000. When the memory of this otherness, of being an unacceptable minority, can be set alongside a safe space of imagined (or actual) community, of queer family, then the warm feelings of remembered cohesion can override the more difficult histories. In Plymouth there is a weaker feeling of local or political agency in memories of the 1980s. While in Leeds the stories of 1980s political campaigning help to redeem the harshness of that time, the lack of local activism in Plymouth makes the memories of its social scene all the more important and powerfully nostalgic.

Weighing up past and present in the 2000s

It is in accounts of the 2000s, and especially people's views of equality legislation and LGBT integration into the mainstream, that past–present dialogues reveal both disappointments and collective triumphs. Milestones of the 2000s include protection against hate crime, equal treatment in the provision of public and commercial services and, perhaps most visibly, civil partnership (2004) and gay marriage (2014). In thinking aloud about the impact of equality legislation, people often engage in a 'gains and losses' discussion through which they compare present-day protections with the earlier distinctiveness and security of LGBT venues and events such as Pride.

The 2008 West Yorkshire contributors – who were directly asked to assess the present-day situation for LGBT people – were the most clear-cut in welcoming twenty-first-century gains, though not without some qualifications. The older gay men in different ways agreed that there had been considerable political achievements for LGBT people in their lifetimes: one describing progress as 'absolutely incredible'.[61] Christopher believed that Pride 'used to be a march for political rights and stuff but basically you've got all the rights now – I can marry or the equivalent. [...] I mean I can't think of anything else that we could need [...] There are openly gay MPs now which is something that in the 1980s you never would have.'[62]

Most of the LGC group felt that civil partnership was a powerful symbol of progress and only one questioned the desirability of marriage, whether for heterosexual or gay couples, perhaps harking back to the radical GLF principles of the 1970s.[63] The issues that people raised as unfinished business in the 2008 Leeds narratives included the ban on gay men giving blood and the inequalities faced by LGBT people overseas. They were particularly insistent on the importance of challenging bullying in schools, which seems to be linked with their sense that the homophobic violence that they had experienced in the past in and around Leeds was continuing into the present.[64]

There was more ambiguity about whether a tangible lesbian and gay 'community' remained. The mostly male interviewees tended to elide the gay scene with community, saying that it had changed or declined, or that they no longer took much part in it mainly because of their age. These perceptions were geographically specific. Older and younger contributors agreed that 'in Bradford the scene's gone really down', pointing to the much bigger choice of gay bars in Leeds and Manchester.[65] One said: 'It's all about hedonism now rather than trying to bring about change. It's all about wearing the right clothes, drinking the right drinks, going to the right places.' Community, it seemed, had been lost to consumerism.[66] An older Bradford man thought that 'it's far too commercial now, you know, it's like the pink pound is something I disagree with because everything costs so much more on the gay scene'.[67] Nevertheless, Paul felt that the commercial gay scene in Leeds had grown and he welcomed its greater openness:

> We had to fight to get more gay bars, and now it's brilliant, there's Leeds Pride and marches but you couldn't have done that five years ago because society's attitude was 'get away I don't want it on my doorstep'. [...] There's more gay bars now in Leeds [...] they advertise more putting billboard stickers up or posters up around town and you wouldn't have seen that 10 years ago, most were just hidden away.

Significantly, Paul, speaking in 2008, dates this positive change back to between five and ten years previously and the beginnings of LGBT equalities legislation at the turn of the century.

Craig, on the other hand, was ambivalent about gaining social acceptance at the expense of a distinct sense of community.[68] Pink Picnic in Huddersfield, for example, had grown less queer and more family friendly. While in its heyday 'these evil drag queens were really, really funny and cutting [and] used to swear and F and curse', now the event also catered to families with kids and was somewhat sanitized. 'It's good, it's a natural progression', said Craig, and yet he regretted the disappearance of a sharper sense of sexual identity around the event. Now the Pink Picnic 'is just like a carnival for anything, you wouldn't know it was specifically for gay and lesbian people anymore, apart from the dodgy drag acts'. Craig still wants to celebrate a more edgy and authentic queer culture, and though he loyally attends the Pink Picnic each year he is uncomfortable with present-day assimilation and crossover. There was also a sense more broadly in the WYAS interviews that working-class and young gay men had been left behind in this normalization process and were offered a mainly expensive gay scene while still facing hostility and violence.

The loss of queer culture was strongly voiced in Plymouth in 2017, where it infused the whole discussion of the past. If '[s]tories about what is lost speak directly to what is desired', then here the price of equality could be felt as the disappearance of community.[69] Colin, joint landlord of the Swallow in Plymouth for twenty years until 2009, welcomed greater acceptance: 'I saw in the last few months two things I never thought to see. One was two Marines having a full-on snog at the end of the bar, and the other was two sixteen-year-olds walking down the street outside hand in hand.'[70] However, Colin believed that specifically gay spaces like his pub had lost out. Jo, too, felt that 'that feeling of family' had gone. 'The fact that nowadays we can get married, we have law on our side so much, in spite of all of that [...] I think the loss of these places is that no matter how at ease you feel in other things, there's that missing bit of feeling totally at home, totally at ease.'[71]

Despite the new presumption that it was OK to be out in everyday life, there was a lack of trust that it actually was alright, with some trepidation about personal exposure and the potential repercussions. Plymouth contributors did not offer specific reasons for the disappearing gay scene. Commercialization was mentioned only indirectly. But adding to their feelings of dislocation were the changes in the city itself – the loss of some key industries and its military identity and the (welcomed) growth of the university which had created a more open and more ethnically diverse population. In this new context the evolution of Plymouth Pride has created feelings of achievement. Jo spoke about the significance of Pride being in a public place in the city – in recent years they had managed to get it routed through the Hoe. 'I think it's something about ... if you're seen. For me, it's really joyous to see your *community* just joining in with the LGBT without it being a big song and dance.'[72] By 'community' here she means the city-wide population and her comment reflects the still-anxious process of navigating tricky waters as LGBTQ Plymouthians take their place as visible citizens. The deep nostalgia among many in Plymouth acts as a buffer to the more uneasy present, creating a story of the 'mythic playgrounds' of the queer past, a heritage that rallies people as they work through the uncertainties of being newly out and proud.[73]

In contrast to the story of lost LGBT camaraderie in Plymouth, in our 2017 Brighton workshop there was a stronger sense that queer culture was alive and well in the present day. However, the commercialization of the scene was subject to a more thoroughgoing analysis at our workshop here than in the other cities. It was Melita who was most critical of the process of mainstreaming in the 2000s:

I think we have become too […] assimilated and too comfy. We've got marriage, isn't that great. [said with sarcasm] […]. Fantastic, well, ignore the other shitty things that the Tories have done. […] We are part of an eco system of hated people by certain sections of society.[74]

Equality gains such as gay marriage were valued less than a continuing feeling of queer freedom. Increasing market forces had, people felt, detracted from the gay scene and dissipated a sense of queer collectivity. Sue pointed out that community centres and bookshops had closed and that 'now that everything is so much more commercialized […] there's nothing to replace them really. Apart from the internet.'[75] While recognizing the same changes, others argued that Brighton was still special. Belle said: 'Gay people have these clubs and you can spend money in these clubs, and spend money at Pride. But this is also a place where I feel we have more agency than anywhere else in the UK. I really believe it.'[76] Others in the group agreed. 'I think without a doubt, you see people who are much more confidently queer here. […] I think Brighton's definitely much more visibly queer than a lot of other places. […] Individuals and eccentricity, embraced in all its forms.'[77] Yet a consensus of local pride in Brighton's queer singularity did not inhibit strong and divergent views being aired about the impact of commercialization on LGBTQ politics. The intolerance and antagonism experienced in earlier years bequeaths a long afterlife. It has helped generate a sense that life has definitely improved, though for many veterans of the 1980s a concern remains that society could too easily turn on queers again.

This debate played out strongly in the discussion of Brighton Pride. Some workshop participants criticized the way it had become part of the pink pound economy rather than queer solidarity. Steve saw it nowadays as being 'a big money maker, for Brighton' and Melita offered a forceful dissection:

I'm quite cynical about it. I kind of liked the olden days when it was just us in the back of a truck, and about politics. Now, it's become […] a depoliticized party and straight people can bring their family and go: look at the man-ladies, aren't they pretty?[78]

Like Craig in his description of Pink Picnic, Melita resents a straight rereading of queer drag that makes it marketable and innocuous. She feels there is now a loss of authenticity and localism connected with the event.[79]

Other participants were less critical of present-day Pride, which has become a huge event in Brighton, drawing in people from all over the country. Jill emphasized its importance to LGBTQ visibility over many years and saw it as a marker of belonging to the wider city:

Brighton Pride – the streets are lined with people, gay or not. You get families with small children, older people, you get all sorts of different types of people lining the street and cheering and welcoming you. [...] there is a sense that the town is happy that we're here, in general. Not everybody. [...] But broadly, that's the prevailing ethos, I would say.[80]

These sentiments are similar to Jo's in Plymouth, though the Pride events in the two cities were on a very different scale. Kathrine also emphasized the importance of Pride as a public statement of sexual identity:

Seeing even now people coming out while going to Pride. And I had a girlfriend about fourteen years ago who was in the police. [...] I remember her joining the parade in a police uniform. It was incredibly moving, people cheering. I think symbolically, it was quite amazing what Pride meant. The history of Pride.[81]

Belle agreed: 'Even when it's completely commercialized and you feel quite cynical about it, it's gay Christmas, isn't it.'[82] The annual Pride festival here and in other cities is an important touchstone for many LGBTQ people, even if they criticize its present form in comparison to the past (see Image 6).[83] It is a recurring event that marks sexual identity, it shows strength in community and it is often used as a reference point for individuals' life stories, as we have seen in different ways for Kathrine in Brighton, Craig in West Yorkshire and Jo in Plymouth.

The collective and individual memories relating to the four cities exposed very different feelings about the LGBTQ past, in part coloured by the time period in which people were doing their remembering. In the Leeds stories there is a striking sense of realism and thoughtfulness about the costs of pleasure in earlier times alongside vivid recollections of historic dangers and divisions. Plymouthians were inclined to view their city's queer past with emotions of melancholy and loss, while different age groups in Brighton were both more upbeat and more critical. Looking back from 'today', people in most of the cities (though less enthusiastically in Brighton than elsewhere) welcomed equalities legislation and the move to becoming 'ordinary' everyday citizens.[84] A number of contributors pointed out that the new acceptance on offer was for certain kinds of queer people – affluent and married lesbian and gay couples, for example, rather than poly, trans and non-binary people.

Recording queer histories

Recording LGBTQ voices – from Brighton Ourstory to Plymouth's Pride in Our Past – was itself a community venture. We could not have written this book without the amazing range of oral history projects that LGBTQ people have organized in Leeds, Brighton, Plymouth and Manchester.[85] An enthusiasm for exploring and gathering up local queer history has been a very strong feature of the 2000s. These community projects have had different aims, but they have each highlighted the significance of locality in LGBTQ people's lives and have been triggered by ordinary people working in grassroots organizations. In the last fifteen years, public funding has increasingly become available, and the past experiences of LGBTQ people and groups are now more often seen in local museums, in art and theatre and on local queer history websites. But beyond preserving queer histories, the most important outcome has been the rekindling or heightening of a sense of LGBTQ community and new ways of celebrating it.

Queer oral history was initially inspired by political motives. The Brighton Ourstory collective came together in 1988 and announced its work as a strand of direct political activism, declaring:

> In Section 28 Britain [...] [e]mergency oral history work is urgently needed. Every lesbian and every gay man is a walking library of information on our life and times. This information does not exist outside our heads. Our passions and experiences are worth preserving for future generations.[86]

Image 31 Two women on Brighton beach, *c.*1960

In a period of political antagonism when lesbian and gay histories were not just ignored but actively suppressed through Section 28, and when gay men's voices were cut short by their deaths from the AIDS virus, the Ourstory group pointed out that those histories were not to be found in libraries and museums and asked, rhetorically, 'Are we all ghosts then?'[87] Ourstory's book, *Daring Hearts: Lesbian and Gay Lives of 50s and 60s Brighton* (1992), demonstrated Brighton's longstanding history as a vibrant lesbian and gay hub through the voices of its queer residents. Brighton Ourstory was part of a broader drive for lesbian and gay oral history in the 1970s and 1980s, spurred on by the gay and women's liberation movements, that stressed the importance of recording these otherwise hidden life histories.[88] But *Daring Hearts* was the first in Britain to move beyond London-centric and national frameworks to examine the queer past in a particular town or city.[89]

These first community queer history projects were part of a broader movement for 'people's history', to bring to light untold stories 'from below'. They aimed to challenge the traditional themes of history, inform political activity and strengthen the communities that they were part of.[90] In Leeds, the political motivation was to preserve the history of early second-wave feminism in the region, and the first oral history collection, 'The Women's Liberation Movement in Leeds and Bradford 1969–79', was organized by local women in 1995. More than half of the contributors were lesbians who had been involved in local feminism.[91] The next oral history drive, for the Lesbian Identity Project (LIP), was started here in 2001 by members of the Northern Older Lesbian Network. Although it was concerned with recording women's personal and community histories rather than with activism, it was undoubtedly political in its aim of valuing the life stories of older lesbians.[92] We can see already how the cultural and political context meant that these earlier Leeds area history projects were more sex-specific than Brighton Ourstory, which in *Daring Hearts* included equal numbers of lesbians and gay men. None of the earlier community histories explicitly sought out bi or trans histories, however.

These projects not only recorded the queer past but also created friendship networks among the people who participated and shared their skills. By getting LGBTQ histories out there they strengthened local communities. For twenty-five years, the Brighton Ourstory group, completely run by volunteers, was highly successful in publicizing the queer past through books, performances, exhibitions and local guided walks. This sense of belonging together and sharing a heritage was especially important in the early years when lesbians and gay men were battling with AIDS and homophobic legislation. Throughout the

1990s and 2000s, Ourstory created an annual show based on the interviews for *Daring Hearts*. They 'created this huge buzz, people loved it!', said Jill:

> We used to do a show in the Brighton Festival each year, at the Royal Albion Hotel, with actors reading from the interviews, and it would be packed out. [...] And people would be crying and laughing during the readings, they would come up and hug you afterwards, and thank you for doing it. It had such a big impact, particularly the first few times, because it was new. It made people feel valued [...] [They] all felt that their lives were being recognised and included.[93]

Until the 2000s, lesbian and gay history groups were largely, though not entirely, unfunded.[94] But in the new environment of 'social inclusion', equality and diversity, LGBTQ history-making gathered strength, this time often in partnership with public institutions such as archives and museums, and resourced by the Heritage Lottery Fund (HLF).[95] The LIP was in the vanguard in securing HLF funding, and from the mid-2000s many other LGBTQ groups in towns and cities across the country successfully set up funded projects, many based in the arts and most including oral histories. In the period up to the end of 2018, the HLF awarded more than £5.4 million to over 130 projects concerned with LGBTQ heritage.[96] This sounds impressive but is actually a disproportionally tiny fraction of all HLF grant funding in this period.[97]

This newly available funding could be used to pay project leaders, fund training and support the costs of publication and project websites. But external funding, and a shift towards professionalizing LGBTQ community history, could also highlight new issues. Who is included in the LGBTQ 'community', and who has control over the creation and destinations of these new queer histories, especially when mainstream organizations are also involved as partners? The WYAS LGBT project of 2007–2008, one of the first LGBT projects to be initiated by an institution, was conceived as 'celebrating' local LGB heritage through stories about the Pride festival. However, local LGBT community groups felt that Pride was a cliché of LGB life and instead emphasized the importance of the everyday lives of lesbians and gay men.[98] They also successfully challenged the project coordinators to extend its scope to include trans histories.[99] In fact, the project resulted in a preponderance of gay men's accounts, though this was unintended, ironically entrenching the sex-segregated nature of queer histories in the region.[100] The Archive Service was also keen to gather objects and documents about past activism but was only partially successful. The men who held the papers from the 1970s Leeds GLF decided that they preferred to keep control of these sources rather than relinquish them; they 'felt a history of GLF should be written by GLF itself [...] Certainly they felt the WYAS project was an outside body' and did not want to 'let some sociology student get their hands on [the material]'.[101] There is a long history of LGBTQ mistrust of official bodies, and institutions such as archives may seem to be distant from everyday queer life and community.

There is still a danger that once the interviews and other material gathered by particular projects have been deposited in local archives and museums, or on websites, they can become forgotten about or are difficult to access.[102] Despite the archivists' best efforts, it is not easy to find the 2008 LGBT project interviews on the WYAS website, for example, and the same is true elsewhere. Nor has all of the Brighton Ourstory material yet found its way to the Keep, the local archives for East Sussex.

Potential LGBTQ contributors to community projects might also have questions about the allegiances of paid workers, heritage professionals and local organizations.[103] HLF funding for Brighton Trans*formed (2013–2014) was secured by QueenSpark community publishers (who had earlier published *Daring Hearts*) after consultation with some of Brighton's trans groups. However, QueenSpark were accused of appropriation by others, 'who felt that it was an affront [...]: "You're not a trans organisation"'.[104] After the initial hiccup, the project was highly successful in mobilizing the local trans community, but these experiences demonstrate the potential missteps for funded LGBTQ oral history projects, especially if they explore deep-seated political positions or are conducted at politically sensitive moments.

When postgraduate researcher Jeska Rees interviewed revolutionary feminists in Leeds and Bradford between 2004 and 2006 she found continuing division and mistrust: 'an uncertainty as to which "side" I was "on" led two of my interviewees to be very suspicious of what I intended to do with the interviews'.[105] As a heterosexual feminist, Rees was seen as an outsider who might not protect the version of lesbian feminist history preferred by these former activists. In contrast, the successful Pride in our Past LGBT history project (2011–2012) in Plymouth was started by someone who was himself a member of Plymouth's gay community in conjunction with the county archives and university, was funded by the HLF and formed the basis of his PhD thesis.[106]

Imbalances of power remain between LGBTQ communities and the mainstream institutions of history and heritage, but these stories also show that it is possible for LGBTQ groups and local organizations to work together successfully, resulting in better representation of queer history in museums and archives (if sometimes quite fleetingly). In 1998, an exhibition titled 'Lesbian and Gay Campaigns in the Late 80's: Ten Years On' was created by local LGBTQ people in Manchester, using material from the city's activism against Section 28. It was shown in various venues, including Manchester Town Hall. Then, in 2003, a further exhibition at Manchester Central Library, 'Repealed!', also of photographs, memorabilia and people's experiences, celebrated the final overturning of the statute.[107] Brighton Museum has meanwhile been transformed, hosting the Museum of Transology over three years (2017–2020), featuring continuous pop-up exhibitions on queer themes and integrating LGBTQ histories into its permanent displays. This inclusion has reoriented understandings of the city for the wider visiting public, and suggests how queer community history can rewrite other themes in local and national history. This has happened in Manchester too. The online exhibition 'Queer Noise' has, since 2010, 'invite[d] queer people from across the generations to share their memories, pictures, artefacts and stories – with the aim of constructing a fuller history of the city's oft-forgotten queer scenes and their wider influence upon British pop and club culture'.[108] This and further exhibitions on LGBTQ music in the city are part of the Manchester Digital Music Archive, set up in 2003 to promote the heritage of Manchester music and clubbing culture.

Following in the footsteps of Brighton Ourstory, subsequent LGBTQ local history projects have also been a powerful force in building community, bringing in different generations, focusing on previously unrepresented identities (such as trans) and exploring new ways of making history. The chain of people involved in successive projects in Brighton has created a palpable sense of historical continuity in the city and an acknowledgement across the generations of the importance of making queer history. Although they might disagree about aspects of Brighton's LGBTQ past, people who came along to the Queer Beyond London workshop in 2017 were united on the importance of queer history as activism and paid generous homage to earlier generations. Melita described the courage of Brighton Ourstory co-founder Linda Pointing, whose name and photograph were printed in the local newspaper in 1988 to publicize the project: 'we were all so in awe of her, sticking her neck out. She could, at that time, have lost her job at the Council. By being an out lesbian.'[109] Later on in the workshop discussion, a younger woman in turn paid respect to Melita and her generation for organizing Brighton Pride from the 1990s. 'I don't think we can underestimate the courage it took for people like yourself [Melita] setting up events like Pride. The fight. What that must have meant for thousands of gay people.'[110]

In Plymouth, Hannah and Alan had not felt part of Plymouth's LGBT 'family' during the 1990s and 2000s, but it was their involvement in the Pride in our Past project in 2011–2012 that gave them a sense of being part of an evolving gay community in the city. Alan said: 'I got to talk to a lot of people and interview them about being LGBT, and that's the first time in my life I've felt part of that community.' Hannah agreed: 'Young people were involved, and through the generations. It was fantastic. It was absolutely fantastic.'[111]

Despite its rocky start, described above, Brighton Trans*formed helped to knit together and consolidate the city's trans and non-binary communities and increase their visibility. This story is best told by E-J Scott, one of its co-producers:

> Brighton still only had a small, emerging trans scene and this project galvanized us, bringing us together to talk to each other. [...] Central to its success was the fact that we ran training workshops that skilled trans people to record *each other's stories*, so that they didn't have to 'transplain' everything and in turn, felt safe and listened to very closely. [...] [E]veryone who was involved had their photo taken and these were used across the city – we projected the photos 10 foot high onto a church in the centre of town one evening (and hundreds and hundreds of people stopped and watched). So the confidence that was built by telling our stories to each other meant that people really stepped up and made themselves then known to the broader community – it gave us a sense of being 'safe in numbers'. It was really terrifying, I remember us all being really brave and scared, knowing we simply 'had to' do it. It then created a wave through the city and on social media, and the trans community has never looked back.[112]

This trans courage resonates with the earlier strength and resolve shown in the 1980s and 1990s by Linda and Melita in developing lesbian and gay history as activism.

These community history projects have used contemporary identity terms in their titles, moving from 'lesbian and gay' in the 1980s and 1990s, to 'LGBT' by the 2000s, and most recently to 'LGBTQ', 'LGBT+' or 'queer'. There has been an increasing awareness that many people – especially queer people of colour, bisexuals, trans and non-binary people and those who are working class – have been underrepresented in LGBTQ community history-making, often due to the routes through which participants were found.[113] The more frequent appearance of the term 'queer' signals a commitment to greater inclusivity as well as reflecting its increasing use among younger generations questioning fixed gender and sexual identities. The attempt to 'queer' community history, as Queer in Brighton (2012–2013) shows, is a push for diversity and inclusivity across the spectrum of queer identities. This HLF-funded initiative was based in performance and the arts, the longstanding strengths of Brighton's queer culture. It offered workshops on writing and photography and aimed to bring older and younger LGBTQ people together.[114] The resulting book, *Queer in Brighton* (2014), features a queer visual archive as well as short memoirs and interview segments, capturing trans and bisexual experience alongside lesbian and gay histories.[115]

The Queer in Brighton project also forged a new path in queering the *process* of exploring the past, declaring that history 'is not neat or tidy […] because life is messy. It stutters and stumbles, repeats itself and hesitates, changes its mind and reinterprets itself.'[116] As well as the traditional narrative structures of coming out stories and community progress, Queer in Brighton mobilized the idea of the 'delirious museum [in which] histories, myths and reinterpretations are woven together'.[117] This reflects not only Brighton's creative heritage but also a queer turn towards the playful and celebratory, following on from the earlier *Daring Hearts* stories that recorded the collective joys of the past. These histories of change, fun and pleasure reflect communities whose past has also been heavily shadowed by pain and loss, AIDS (which hit Brighton especially hard) and queer bashing. This cutting-edge new approach, a playful turn in queer community history practice, is one that emphasizes the sensual pleasures of people's memories while at the same time acknowledging the painful moments. It brings into view a past that can be enjoyed in the present day and asserted as a springboard for a distinct queer future.[118] Queer delights and collective pleasures have also taken root up north with the recent West Yorkshire Queer Stories project (2018–2020), which has pursued a more gender-integrated and queer-inclusive approach.[119] Led by E-J Scott, who was involved in Brighton Trans*formed and curated the Museum of Transology, it extends queer community histories beyond the urban hubs and into West Yorkshire's villages and rural places, which of course have their own queer histories.

People want to put their cities and towns on the map of the queer past. There is a strong desire to chronicle the special significance of their locality – whether that is a particular politics such as lesbian feminism in Leeds or the civic equalities achieved in Manchester, the queer welcome of Brighton or the play between gay identities and military traditionalism in Plymouth. These community historians are concerned with local events and change. Their histories blossom beyond London, which is either taken for granted in a mundane way or exists barely at the edge of their consciousness. For Brightonians, there is constant contact and overlap with the capital as people travel back and forth to work, to see friends and lovers, to go to exhibitions or to go out on the scene. There has also been traffic to and fro between Plymouth and London, especially for work.

In the early part of our period, the experience of London could be transformative, particularly for men who imported metropolitan conceptions of what it meant to be gay back to the south-west, while for lesbians, migration to London and elsewhere offered employment opportunities not available back home. The northern cities have different relationships to the capital. For Manchester there often appears to be a queer rivalry, while Leeds' LGBTQ communities are more self-contained. It's here in Yorkshire that London is mentioned least often – interviewees seem to have felt little need to measure their city against the capital.

National trajectories of legislative or cultural change for LGBTQ people do matter in regional cities, but these are not necessarily the historical moments that are most remembered locally; other stories are writ larger. Often this is an assertive and electric pride in collective action, such as Brighton's celebration of the political mobilization against Clause 28. In Plymouth and Manchester as well as in Brighton there was successful pushback in the early 1990s against police harassment and the revelation of databases recording the details of hundreds of gay men; in these cities the police were forced to destroy such material and liaise more productively with gay men and lesbians. The very early organization of lesbian self-insemination was a historic triumph claimed for 1980s Leeds with the networks of lesbian families and children that followed, remembered along with the important contribution of lesbians to the feminist arts flourishing in that city. At the same time as its early and sustained civic support for lesbian and gay rights, Mancunians like to remind others of the city's diverse and vibrant alternative queer scene. These are the kinds of local urban achievements which don't always surface in national LGBTQ histories yet are fundamental to building change.

This book, we hope, brings this local impetus for community history-making and the testimonies from these projects into conversation with each other. We have observed and enjoyed the differences between the four cities and their local areas. That distinctiveness and vividness in turn challenges the hierarchies of national, regional and local, queering the national story and assumptions of London's pre-eminence.

Epilogue

Image 32 Mr Harry Club, 1983, by Robert Lenkiewicz (1941–2002). 188 × 305cm. Emulsion on Canvas. Project 16 Sexual Behaviour (courtesy of the Lenkiewicz Foundation)

The people taking part in the various community history groups wanted to share their particular experiences of life in their home cities. There was, as well, a recurring drive to create narratives about a shared queer past – to conjure a story of belonging to a broader LGBTQ heritage. This is a persistent trend towards valuing a coming together, a desire for unity and conviviality among diverse queer people and with other groups and individuals in the local community. This was happening at the same time as new sexual and gender identities were being debated and named, and as more of them were added to the LGBT acronym – with 'Q' (queer), 'Q' (questioning), 'I' (intersex) and the embracing '+'. These extensions point to a desire for inclusivity, a drawing in of everyone who has a sense of sexual difference or gender dissonance. There is a conviviality in this, a way of being which usually suggests the pleasures and possibilities of actual social mixing – drinking and chatting together, forming friendships – in everyday meetings in the pub, café or neighbourhood. Conviviality sidelines more fixed ideas of identity while also suggesting how different facets of ourselves (such as class, race and gender, sometimes clunkily referred to as 'lived intersectionality') can sometimes be suspended while also being instrumental in our human interactions with all kinds of people, whether in specifically queer places or the wider streets, shops and suburbs.[1]

This kind of social mixing highlights openness and friendliness, whether transient or more profound, and thinking about everyday life in this way moves us away from assessing the changes in queer experience on the basis of official or legal rights (which can be granted or taken away) towards a more holistic appraisal, seeing social cohesion being made from the ground up. The feeling of conviviality – that community, in whatever form, is available – is especially important for marginalized people with queer affiliations who need a sense of belonging with others in the face of negative everyday experiences due to their race, class, age, disability and a host of other aspects of identity. The ground-level, everyday experiences of LGBTQ people in the four cities show that common interests and shared camaraderie with others across identity boundaries are valued, but that these opportunities are constantly shifting.

Conviviality is about creating trust as people mix and come together with each other. For that trust to be built, in-person smiles, chats and shared work in real time and actual places are valuable, though not essential. All kinds of places might foster connections. There might be the glances of recognition as we circle around other people on the streets, on the train and in the pubs – an acknowledgement made easier by shared queer styles and dress codes (as recently celebrated in the exhibition 'Queer Looks' at Brighton Museum). Identifying our queer kind – and those who are queerly different yet part of our extended family – might happen at performances, screenings and art shows as well as at dance parties and raves. There were opportunities for this at Brighton poetry readings, at Gay Sweatshop performances in Leeds and at Hacienda and Paradise Factory club nights in Manchester.

There is, too, a conviviality of the imagination, when we visualize our community as reaching internationally, to include, for example, the inspiration and joy created by the new South African constitution from 1993 which was the first to explicitly include equal lesbian and gay rights. Community history groups in our four cities expressed their support for their sisters, brothers, siblings and cousins working against repressive cultures elsewhere across the world, as well as affiliating with local LGBTQ asylum seekers (via the African Rainbow Family in Manchester, for example). And throughout the work of the LGBTQ community history groups there is a conviviality across time, when participants, audiences and readers are brought close to people in the past. This is expressed in the emotions felt when queer history is enjoyed collectively and publicly, in the tears and identification among the audiences for the annual Ourstory oral history events in 1990s Brighton and in the pleasure at the unveiling of the Pride in our Past exhibition in Plymouth. These are feelings of validation which also speak of a profound communion and alliance with the past, the experience of that 'touch across time' to the queer folk in our histories, who seem to be so similar to us even when they are not.[2]

The trustingness of conviviality might involve sharing particular places and venues with people we don't know, and these have changed over time. Back in the era of more overt social exclusion, especially in the 1960s and 1970s, pubs that tolerated gay men and lesbians – like the Lockyer in Plymouth, the New Penny in Leeds or the New Union in Manchester – were often located in liminal areas of the city, near railway stations and docks or in industrial or warehouse districts. These places were often 'home' to an array of outsiders, and spending time there meant meeting others who were different but also similarly marginalized. This was an experience of people being thrown together outside mainstream and more respectable venues, which could result in a sense of fellowship for some and a further feeling of alienation or exclusion for others. Those queer people who wanted or needed to be discreet to sustain jobs or relationships with friends or family could feel distinctly uneasy in these places. Once lesbian and gay groups started to grow from the 1970s onwards, offering alternative ways to meet up, there were wider choices for LGBT people (even though these groups were also often stratified by class and race). This created greater segmentation of both alternative and commercial meeting places (some excluding bi and trans people) but also some new kinds of integration, for example among queer and straight young people involved in student and alternative politics and community activism.

General LGBTQ histories of Britain have tended to highlight a further splitting by sex that started in the early 1970s, with many lesbians identifying with feminist politics and constructing separate spaces from gay men – with separate meeting places, separate music scenes and separate publications. In our research on being queer beyond London we wanted to test this out and we have, we hope, been able to add greater nuance to this theme. Although at times politically necessary, gender division and segregation is clearly the antithesis of conviviality, since it divides queer networks and groupings into smaller shards of politics and identity. In Brighton, while there was some lesbian separatism, queer and feminist women and men still came together to produce music and theatre, in another form of queer family. In Manchester, people like Jess deliberately chose the city specifically for its lack of gender tensions, (relatively) relaxed racial mingling and general party spirit. And while Leeds saw a highly developed lesbian separatist politics, many of those same lesbians enjoyed a convivial mixing in the wider community across class and race boundaries in the African-Caribbean dance clubs they frequented after their single-sex discos. Physical proximity helped – lesbians and Black Caribbean people in Leeds often lived in the same cheap inner-city areas – as did the involvement of lesbians and gay men in contemporary anti-racist campaigns. Such shared politics is a reminder that conviviality can be built by association and by working together, as well as by casual social contact.

While silos resulted from some threads of lesbian and gay politics, other queer practices of the 1970s and 1980s opened up alternative ways of being convivial – in the experiments in collective living or parenting, for example. It is important to remember that 'rainbow coalition' politics started to reshape wider local politics early in the 1980s and raised awareness of people's varying identifications of race and class belonging, health and disability status, age and gender. Local activism to demand rights and make change in the political mainstream is a more organized form of social mixing than spontaneous or organic conviviality. But the process of arguing for political change and rolling it out on the ground in alliance with others was part of a learning to live with difference. We can see Mancunians especially marrying a formal push for equality via the city council with a more informal and inclusive partying. This underpinned their sense of what was particular about the spirit of their queer city from the 1980s onwards. As we've seen for Brighton, lesbians and gay men started to work together again in anti-Clause 28 and AIDS activism in the 1980s and early 1990s. Straight allies also stepped up in wider ripples of support and conviviality to make common cause.

The new treatments for HIV/AIDS and the lowering of the age of consent for sex between men helped to create a more expansive feeling among LGBTQ people from the mid-to-late 1990s – a feeling that improved legal rights were on the horizon and that society was less hostile. A pattern of greater gender mixing in the burgeoning gay pubs and clubs and alternative large-scale forms of socializing, such as the enthusiasm for ballroom and line dancing in the 1990s, meant that queer fun was more publicly and collectively expressed by younger generations of people. In Leeds, this was the time of the Victor-Victoria dances and of mixed gay choirs.

In Manchester, the 1990s saw the birth of the gay village and the often-cited bars with plate glass windows, demonstrating a growing confidence and openness to the straight world. There are conflicting forces at play here, however, in shaping conviviality. Alternative spaces such as radical bookshops, which had been so important for uniting various strands of lesbian, gay, feminist, green, peace movement and anti-racist ideas, as well as providing welcoming meeting places, began a slow decline. The most prominent loss is Plymouth's In Other Words, but there are examples in all four cities. Expressions of overlapping community, for example of lesbian and gay listings pages in local alternative magazines or on those all-important bookshop and café notice boards, became less cheek-by-jowl as the gay press itself expanded and diversified. In parallel, the shiny new gay bars and clubs – providing a more explicit gay quarter in Leeds, for example – seemed to some to enforce a new separation among LGBTQ people. They welcomed the more affluent, the young and fashionable, and appeared to provide less of a home for older queer people and those with disabilities. Of course, the older, less upmarket venues also had enforced codes, often excluding bisexuals, people of colour and those who didn't look sufficiently gay or lesbian. The new gay quarters in Manchester and Leeds led to different social mixes – of gays, lesbians and straight women primarily. This was certainly a form of conviviality but one that, for some in Manchester, seemed to go too far in the wrong direction, as heterosexuals began to find the gay village a congenial place to party at weekends, dissolving the sense of belonging and safety it was supposed to provide for the LGBTQ population.

So conviviality is something to be welcomed in as much as it promotes acceptance, a pleasure in rubbing along together with people of other queer identities or none. But in a context of (assumed) greater equality there is a worry that further assimilation simply leads to queer people losing particular identities and places of their own. We saw this in the history groups, when people expressed nostalgia for an LGBT community life that they felt no longer existed. Here, a feeling of conviviality with the past can be reassuring in a more fragmented present. Now that queer people were more widely accepted, the sense of identity that went alongside the lesbian and gay venues had been lost. The venues themselves were perceived to be disappearing, and in some cities they actually were as opportunities to meet up with other people moved onto smartphones. Furthermore, the welcome offered by mainstream places often seemed to involve a policing of queer identities into more conventional forms – established same-sex couples especially being the accepted face of LGBTQ presence.

In the current moment there are also real rifts that cannot be papered over with rosy aspirations of community. The personally and acutely felt differences about the meanings of sex and gender, and how the interests of some feminists and some trans people do not easily mesh together and indeed conflict, has led to entrenched positions, hostility and crisis, undermining notions of a family of LGBTQ people and our allies. At the same time, and again at the grassroots, people immersed in their own distinct identities – lesbian, trans, bi, non-binary and gay – have found ways to work queerly together and the allegiance signalled by the LGBTQ umbrella has been a cue for solidarity and compassion even in the face of internal disagreement.

We see the drive for conviviality in the widespread adoption of the term LGBT from the 1990s onwards as a sign of welcome for bisexual and trans people. Nevertheless, while LGBT centres (in Manchester) and community projects elsewhere actively promote inclusivity, this sometimes runs in a shallow vein. In both Plymouth and Leeds, oral history projects in the 2000s tried to recruit trans contributors, but in each case they found only one trans participant, each of whom gave accounts of feeling marginalized, of everyday life being difficult, and certainly not feeling part of the LGBT community and its spaces in either city. In Manchester and Brighton there was more of a sense that it was easier to be trans or gender subversive and that people identifying in these ways had laboured to create their own now flourishing subcultures. Most of the trans voices deployed in this book have been those of younger contributors. It is only in the 2010s, with Queer in Brighton, Brighton Trans*formed and (now) West Yorkshire Queer Stories that better representation of non-binary and trans people began to happen.

Community is a word that has been overworked, not least in this book. But a desire for community and conviviality has burned throughout the stories contained here. And as we finish this book in lockdown, with the chance of an in-person drink at a queer-friendly bar seemingly a vanished dream (hopefully to have been resuscitated by the time you read this), such an aspiration feels ever more important. Queer conviviality, the almost accidental living alongside or thrown togetherness in urban spaces with people like, yet also unlike, ourselves, has happened at times when LGBTQ people have been obliged to occupy marginal areas and venues. But it has also been more strongly sustained through deliberate efforts – from the radical politics of the 1980s which sought to unite lesbians and gays in common cause with wider political activism to the recent moves to build community through history-making. Local neighbourhoods and local venues are the places where conviviality starts, and our journey around these four cities has revealed the vitality of their diverse queer communities.

Note on sources

The challenge we faced in writing this book was not one of finding needles in haystacks.[1] Instead we struggled to know how to navigate the sheer volume of oral histories, letters, clippings from local and national newspapers, photographs and community and activist ephemera that has been amassed by LGBTQ history projects, groups and individuals. Librarians and archivists in our cities have meanwhile curated much of this material alongside masses of other relevant resources. Leeds University library hosts the Feminist Archive North, with its records of a range of feminist and lesbian feminist groups. The Keep Archive in Brighton brings together parts of the Ourstory collection, the papers and interviews of more recent LGBTQ projects, local surveys of gay and lesbian life, and council records. The Plymouth and West Devon Archive (now part of The Box, Plymouth) has been proactive in making visible the materials from Pride in our Past and the subsequent Lesbian Voices of Plymouth project. Manchester has the largest and most varied LGBTQ archive outside London, including the records of early law reform and equality groups from the 1960s, oral histories of the festival 'queerupnorth' and the records of gay councillors and of FFLAG,[2] a group for the friends and family of lesbians and gays that became a national organization.

Though we had similar types of material to draw on for Brighton, Leeds, Manchester and Plymouth, it was often hard to compare it directly. Surveys and interviews took place at different times, as part of distinct projects, with different aims and methodologies. Newspaper editorial policies meant there was an unevenness in the way queer lives were reported from place to place. As a result, different times, sites and themes come into focus in relation to the different cities. The sense we could get of Brighton in the early part of our period was fuller because of the reach of the Brighton Ourstory interviews. We get glimpses of a Manchester scene that was also lively then, but later oral history projects and resulting walks, publications and exhibitions drew us to map out later years in more detail there. We discuss AIDS and HIV mostly in relation to Brighton; in Leeds the significance of different strands of feminism to lesbian identity and community come into sharpest relief. The Manchester chapter has the most substantial discussion of race and ethnicity. The occupational profile of Plymouth is writ large in our discussion of that city. Of course, AIDS was not only an issue in Brighton, feminism went beyond Leeds' city limits, and Plymouth and Manchester were not the only cities where class and race (including concepts of whiteness) were significant to the histories we explore. We thus try to be self-conscious about our sources and where they take us in painting and comparing our queer city portraits.[3] By drawing newspaper and oral history accounts of cottaging in Brighton into conversation, for example, Matt shows how public sex was woven into everyday queer experience in Brighton and in ways that qualify the confected outrage of the local newspaper, *The Evening Argus*. The 'hotbed lavatory' 'exposed' by the paper in 1959 was also the one recalled fondly by Harry as the place where he met his lifelong partner.[4]

Oral history testimonies like Harry's are central to the book. Some we gathered ourselves, but most are the legacy of the community history projects to which we are so indebted. We drew on archived oral histories made by twelve local community history projects (listed below). They sought interviewees largely through local LGBTQ life – through lesbian and gay bars and social and political groups. Gathering such testimonies was seen in the 1980s and 1990s especially as a deliberate form of activism, as Alison showed in Chapter 7.

The testimonies from these projects are rich and absorbing, but using them also presents some challenges because they do not provide a clear window on the past. In the 2008 WYAS LGBT project, for example, lesbian and gay council networks were key routes to interviewees.[5] As the project worker noted, 'it was soon clear that the project was often recording a particular type of voice: one that was out, proud, currently politically active through employer networks and/ or enjoying the gay scene'.[6] The focus (and in many ways success) of this and other oral history projects is that they capture stories that relate to an owned and current sense of being lesbian, gay, bisexual or transgender.[7] Recruiting such narrators in these ways can nevertheless exclude others and obscure the crossover between queer and 'normal'. Gay men often dominate; the voices of bisexuals, trans people and queer people of colour tend to be underrepresented (though some more recent projects partially redress the balance).[8] Often missing from LGBTQ oral history collections are those who didn't align themselves with a particular identity or whose desires and self-perception shifted across their lives.[9]

LGBTQ oral history projects are sometimes framed in ways which underpin a strong story of progress and emphasize pride and positivity. This might well be appropriate but can shade out more complex feelings and histories and also shameful 'bad gays'.[10] Moreover, one-on-one interviews almost of necessity focus on the individual and individual 'truths' at the expense of the wider social, cultural and economic structures and changes which shape a person's experiences and perceptions.[11] In our analysis we seek to identify these tendencies. We interpret them for the social and cultural contexts which direct a person's account of themselves and their milieu, for example. We think too about the way in which interviewees remembered places and times, often nostalgically, from the vantage point of the present, and at how the gap of time and collective community perceptions (of Brighton as a 'gay mecca' or Plymouth having a discreet gay culture, for example) affected their accounts.[12]

In addition to using interviews from these other projects,[13] we also carried out some of our own to explore themes that were only touched on tangentially elsewhere. These included people's reasons for moving to their city, their sense of regional belonging and their experience of mixed or same-sex socializing or of home and family. In addition, we conducted workshops in each city in the spring of 2017 in which participants shared their stories, prompted by each others' memories and by displays of photos, newspaper clippings and activist and scene ephemera from LGBTQ scenes. These workshops allowed us to test out our developing understandings of Brighton, Leeds, Manchester and Plymouth and to identify some of the collective stories and mythologies associated with each place.

Table 1 *Key oral history archives*

City	Project	Date	No. of interviews	Available as/at
Brighton	Ourstory	1988–c.2013	40+	Published book and the Keep archive
Brighton	Queer in Brighton	2012–2014	21	Published book
Brighton	Brighton Trans*formed	2014		Published book and website
Plymouth	Pride in our Past	2012	c.20	Plymouth and West Devon Record Office (now the Box)
Leeds/Bradford	Women in the WLM in Leeds and Bradford 1969–1979	1995–2001	20	Feminist Archive North, University of Leeds
Leeds/Bradford	Lesbian Identity Project		32	Feminist Archive North, University of Leeds, Leeds Beckett University Archive
Leeds	Revolutionary Feminism (Jeska Rees)	2004–2006	14	Feminist Archive North, University of Leeds
Leeds	WYAS LGBT Project	2008	30	West Yorkshire Archives Service (WYAS)
Manchester	This is how we got here (LGBT Centre)	2014	44	Manchester Central Libraries
Manchester	Queerupnorth	2007	11	Manchester Central Library
Manchester	MDMA Manchester Digital Music Archive	c.2010 ongoing		www.mdmarchive.co.uk/
Manchester	The Modern Lesbian Project	c.2010?		https://soundcloud.com/themodernlesbian

Notes

Introduction

1 Brighton Ourstory, *Daring Hearts: Lesbian and Gay Lives in 50s and 60s Brighton* (Brighton: QueenSpark Books, 1992), pp. 7 and 59.
2 Rowena (pseudonym), interviewed by Alison Oram for QBL, 26 June 2018.
3 London is writ large in, for example: Richard Davenport-Hines, *Sex, Death and Punishment: Attitudes to Sex and Sexuality in Britain since the Renaissance* (London: Collins, 1990); Rictor Norton, *Mother Clap's Molly House: Gay Subculture in England 1700–1830* (London: GMP, 1992); Patrick Higgins, *Heterosexual Dictatorship: Male Homosexuality in Postwar Britain* (London: Fourth Estate, 1996); Matt Cook (ed.), *A Gay History of Britain: Love and Sex between Men since the Middle Ages* (Oxford, CT: Greenwood World, 2007); and Rebecca Jennings, *A Lesbian History of Britain: Love and Sex between Women since 1500* (Oxford, CT: Greenwood World, 2007).
4 Especially those at the London Metropolitan Archive each December since 2002 and at the international Archives, Libraries, Museums and Special Collections LGBTQ (ALMS) conferences (from 2006).
5 Ourstory Project, *Daring Hearts*. Robert Howes, *Gay West: Civil Society, Community and LGBT History in Bristol and Bath 1970 to 2010* (Bristol: SilverWood, 2011).
6 Paul Flynn, *Good as You* (London: Ebury Press, 2017). Sociologist Mike Homfray compared Manchester's scene with that of nearby Liverpool in the 1990s: Mike Homfray, *Provincial Queens: The Gay and Lesbian Community in the North-West of England* (Oxford: Peter Lang, 2007).
7 Helen Smith, 'Working Class Ideas and Experiences of Sexuality in Twentieth Century Britain: Regionalism as a Category of Analysis', *Twentieth Century British History* 29, no. 1 (2018): 58–78; see also: Helen Smith, *Masculinity, Class and Same-Sex Desire in Industrial England, 1895–1957* (London: Palgrave Macmillan, 2015).
8 See, for example: John Howard, *Men Like That: A Southern Queer History* (Chicago: University of Chicago Press, 1999); E. Patrick Johnson, *Sweet Tea: Black Gay Men of the South* (Chapel Hill, UNC Press, 2008); Japonica Brown-Saracino, *How Places Make Us: Novel LBQ Identities in Four Small Cities* (Chicago: University of Chicago Press, 2017); Valerie J. Korinek, *Prairie Fairies: A History of Queer Communities and People in Western Canada, 1930–1985* (Toronto; Buffalo; London: University of Toronto Press, 2018).

9 See: Hall Carpenter Archives. Gay Men's Oral History Group, *Walking after Midnight: Gay Men's Life Stories* (London: Routledge, 1989); Hall Carpenter Archives. Lesbian Oral History Group, *Inventing Ourselves: Lesbian Life Stories* (London: Routledge, 1989); Kevin Porter and Jeffrey Weeks, *Between the Acts: Lives of Homosexual Men, 1885–1967* (London: Routledge, 1990); Ourstory, *Daring Hearts*.

10 See: John Vincent, *LGBT People and the UK Cultural Sector: The Response of Libraries, Museums, Archives and Heritage since 1950* (London: Routledge, 2016).

11 *This Week*, ITV, 22 October 1964 (on male homosexuals); 7 January 1965 (on lesbians).

12 Measures introduced by the New Labour government (1997–2010) included: the lifting of the ban on gays and lesbians in the military and the equalisation of the age of consent (2000), the right for same-sex couples to adopt (2002), the repeal of Clause 28 and the Gender Recognition Act (2003), same-sex civil partnerships (2004) and later the Equality Act (2010). The ensuing Conservative-led coalition government introduced marriage equality (2014).

13 Jeff Meek, *Queer Voices in Post-War Scotland: Male Homosexuality, Religion and Society* (Basingstoke: Palgrave Macmillan, 2015); Daryl Leeworthy, *A Little Gay History of Wales* (Cardiff: University of Wales Press, 2019); Marian Duggan, *Queering Conflict: Examining Lesbian and Gay Experiences of Homophobia in Northern Ireland* (London: Routledge, 2016).

14 On queer London see: Matt Cook, *London and the Culture of Homosexuality, 1885–1914* (Cambridge: Cambridge University Press, 2003); Matt Houlbrook, *Queer London: Perils and Pleasures in the Sexual Metropolis, 1918–1957* (Chicago: University of Chicago Press, 2005); Morris B. Kaplan, *Sodom on the Thames: Sex, Love, and Scandal in Wilde Times* (Ithaca, NY: Cornell University Press, 2005); Frank Mort, *Capital Affairs: London and the Making of the Permissive Society* (New Haven: Yale University Press, 2010).

15 'Boy (12) Handed "Gay" Leaflet', *Yorkshire Evening Post*, 1 November 1971.

16 For more on queer theory and history see: Laura Doan, *Disturbing Practices: History, Sexuality, and Women's Experience of Modern War* (Chicago: University of Chicago Press, 2013); Matt Cook, *Writing Queer History* (London: Bloomsbury, forthcoming).

17 For more on the shifts in the meanings and associations of 'trans' see: Susan Stryker, *Transgender History: The Roots of Today's Revolution* (New York: Seal Press, 2017).

18 On the complexities of community see especially: Kathryn Bond Stockton, *Beautiful Bottom, Beautiful Shame: Where 'Black' Meets 'Queer'* (Durham, NC: Duke University Press, 2006); Eleanor Formby, *Exploring LGBT Spaces and Communities* (London: Routledge, 2017); Kath Browne and Leela Bakshi, *Ordinary in Brighton? LGBT, Activisms and the City* (London: Routledge, 2016).

19 *Come Together* was the newspaper that emerged from the GLF in the early 1970s.

Chapter 1

1 'Four Fined in Whipping Case', *Brighton Gazette*, 24 July 1964.

2 Ted and Aileen in: Brighton Ourstory, *Daring Hearts: Lesbian and Gay Lives in 50s and 60s Brighton* (Brighton: QueenSpark, 1992), p. 14 (Ted) and (Aileen).

3 The council estimated that 2,760 trans people lived in Brighton and Hove in 2009 – about 1.2 per cent of the population. The Office for National Statistics's upper estimate of the UK's trans population was 300,000 (or 0.45 per cent of the population) in 2009. See: *Brighton and Hove City Snapshot: Report of Statistics 2014* (Brighton and Hove City Council, 2014), p. 20; *Trans Data Position Paper* (Office for National Statistics, 2009), p. 13.

4 *Brighton and Hove City Snapshot*, p. 20. For an estimate of the UK's lesbian and gay population see: 'Sexual Identity UK: 2016' (Office for National Statistics, 2016), www.ons.gov.uk/peoplepopulationandcommunity/culturalidentity/sexuality/bulletins/sexualidentityuk/2016 (accessed 2 March 2020).

5 'Homosexual Groups', in Liz Stanley, *Sex Surveyed, 1949–1994* (London: Routledge, 2014), appendix 2, pp. 199–205; Southern Report, 'Coming Out' (1976), www.youtube.com/watch?v=VKIA8Udsi00 (accessed 1 April 2021); Channel 4, *My Transexual Summer* (2011).

6 GB Historical GIS/University of Portsmouth, 'Brighton and Hove UA through Time', www.visionofbritain.org.uk/unit/10056410 (accessed 17 June 2018).

7 'Brighton and Hove', www.visionofbritain.org.uk/unit/10056410/rate/IND_MAN (accessed 12 August 2017).

8 See: Matthew Williams and Tony Wilson, 'IES at 50', www.employment-studies.co.uk/news/ies-50-half-century-brighton-hove-our-local-labour-market (accessed 18 June 1918); Alison Oram, 'Arena 3 and Lesbian Politics in the 1960s', in Marcus Collins (ed.), *The Permissive Society and Its Enemies: Sixties British Culture* (London: Rivers Oram, 2007), p. 63.

9 Brighton's student population rose from 2,990 to 11,340 between 1961 and 1971. Registrar General for England and Wales; General Register Office Scotland (2002): 1961 and 1971, census aggregate data. UK Data Service.

10 'The Beachniks Who Sleep on Brighton Front', *The Times*, 29 August 1962.

11 Dick Hebdige, *Subculture: The Meaning of Style* (London: Methuen, 1979), pp. 46–62; and Jonathan Green, *All Dressed Up: The Sixties Counterculture* (London: Jonathan Cape, 1998), pp. 5–13.

12 Jim Stanford, cited in Maria Jastrzebska and Anthony Luvera (eds), *Queer in Brighton* (Brighton: New Writing South, 2015), p. 188.

13 Colin Campbell, 'Beatniks, Moral Crusaders, Delinquent Teenagers and Hippies: Accounting for the Counterculture', in Collins (ed.), *The Permissive Society*, p. 97; Jeffrey Weeks, *Sex, Politics and Society: The Regulation of Sexuality since 1800*, 4th ed. (London: Routledge, 2018), p. 274.

14 On this developing reputation see: 'The System of Pleasure': Liminality and the Carnivalesque at Brighton', *Theory, Culture and Society* 7, no. 1 (1990): 39–72.

15 Ourstory, *Daring Hearts*, pp. 62–63.

16 Ourstory, *Daring Hearts*, p. 74.

17 Dave Haslam, *Life after Dark: A history of British Nightclubs and Music Venues* (London: Simon and Schuster, 2015), p. 295; Ourstory, *Daring Hearts*, p. 77.

18 Ourstory, *Daring Hearts*, pp. 66, 73, 106.

19 Ourstory, *Daring Hearts*, p. 65.

20 Ourstory, *Daring Hearts*, pp. 70, 73–74.

21 Ourstory, *Daring Hearts*, p. 66.

22 Ourstory, *Daring Hearts*, p. 71.

23 Ourstory, *Daring Hearts*, p. 115.

24 Stanley, *Sex Surveyed*, p. 203.

25 Ourstory, *Daring Hearts*, pp. 103–104.

26 Ourstory, *Daring Hearts*, pp. 109 and 51.

27 Ourstory, *Daring Hearts*, p. 52.

28 Ourstory, *Daring Hearts*, p. 38.

29 Ourstory, *Daring Hearts*, p. 30.

30 Ourstory, *Daring Hearts*, p. 14.

31 Geoff Roberts, 'Last Exit to Brighton', [likely *Brighton Gazette*, *c*.1968], Lesbian and Gay Newsmedia Collection, Bishopsgate Institute Library (East Sussex folder).

32 Ourstory, *Daring Hearts*, p. 100.

33 Ourstory, *Daring Hearts*, pp. 59–60.

34 Ourstory, *Daring Hearts*, p. 58.

35 Ourstory, *Daring Hearts*, p. 59.

36 'Hotbed Lavatory to Close', *Brighton Gazette*, 23 April 1965; 'Sent for Trial', *Evening Argus*, 2 March 1965.

37 Ourstory, *Daring Hearts*, p. 103.

38 'Four Fined in Whipping Case'.

39 'Court Hears of Queer Rolling', *Brighton Gazette*, 23 September 1966; 'Detention for Two Teenage "Rollers"', *Evening Argus*, 12 October 1966.

40 'Four Fined in Whipping Case'.

41 Ourstory, *Daring Hearts*, p. 85.

42 GB Historical GIS/University of Portsmouth, 'Brighton and Hove UA through Time'.

43 Ourstory, *Daring Hearts*, p. 52.

44 Ourstory, *Daring Hearts*, p. 112.

45 Ourstory, *Daring Hearts*, p. 112.

46 Ourstory, *Daring Hearts*, pp. 56, 116.

47 Ourstory, *Daring Hearts*, p. 116.

48 Ourstory, *Daring Hearts*, pp. 85–86.

49 Ourstory, *Daring Hearts*, p. 87.

50 Ourstory, *Daring Hearts*, pp. 28–29.

51 Ourstory, *Daring Hearts*, p. 50.

52 'Dirty Books Case Ends in Uproar', *Evening Argus*, 28 August 1968. See also: www.ballardian.com/a-dirty-and-diseased-mind-the-unicorn-bookshop-trial (accessed 7 April 2019).

53 Chris Moores, *Civil Liberties and Human Rights in Twentieth Century Britain* (Cambridge: Cambridge University Press, 2017), p. 120.

54 Ourstory, *Daring Hearts*, p. 95. *Spartacus Monthly*, issue 1.

55 Justin Bengry, 'The Queer History of Films and Filming', *Little Joe: A Magazine about Queers and Cinema, Mostly* 2 (2011): pp. 31–41.

56 Ourstory, *Daring Hearts*, p. 97.

57 'Francos Bully Boys Beat Me Up', *Evening Argus*, 10 August 1969. On the reputation of Morocca see: Robert Alrdich, 'Homosexuality in the French Colonies', *Journal of Homosexuality* 41, no. 3–4 (2002): 201–218.

58 'Jail Would Make You a Greater Menace', *Evening Argus*, 1 March 1967.

59 Ourstory, *Daring Hearts*, p. 14.

60 Roberts, 'Last Exit'.

61 Ourstory, *Daring Hearts*, p. 72.

62 'Church Hall with Startling New Image', *Evening Argus*, 20 October 1977.

63 Jude, in Jastrzebska and Luvera, *Queer in Brighton*, p. 94.

64 See Lauren Fried, 'A Material History of Trans Identities in UK Performance (1967–1990)', PhD thesis (September 2019), p. 123. *Gemini*, 1 [*c*.1975], p. 4; Wellcome PP/KIN/C/5, 'Subcultural groups'.

65 On the significance of wider counterculture to gay liberation see: Lucy Robinson, 'Three Revolutionary Years: The Impact of the Counter Culture on the Development of the Gay Liberation Movement in Britain', *Cultural and Social History* 3, no. 4 (2006): 445–471.

66 Jim, in Jastrzebska and Luvera, *Queer in Brighton*, p. 189.

67 Angela, who we meet in Chapter 3, describes identifying as bisexual when she first went to university and how this was an important stepping stone for her. Angela, interviewed by Sarah Feinstein, 28 September 2016, for 'Queer Noise', Manchester Digital Music Archive at www.mdmarchive.co.uk/exhibition/id/77/QUEER_NOISE.html.

68 Jim, in Jastrzebska and Luvera, *Queer in Brighton*, p. 95.

69 'Driven Underground', *Brighton Gazette*, 12 March 1965.

70 'Sussex Undergrads Lobby MPs', *Hastings Evening Post*, 10 February 1966.

71 'And a Gay Time Was Had by All', *Evening Argus*, 1 June 1971.

72 'It Looks Grim for the Gay Front', *Evening Argus*, 9 September 1971.

73 See: www.electionscentre.co.uk/wp-content/uploads/2016/03/composition_calc.html (accessed 4 June 2020).

74 See: David Glass, *Small Business and Society* (London: Routledge, 1991).

75 'Coming Out', Southern TV, 30 January 1976. See: 'Gay: Angry in Worthing', *Streetlife*, 6 March 1976.

76 'John Inman: Brighton Dome', *Streatham Observer*, 16 October 1977; 'He's Free but Is He Funny?', *Shropshire Star*, 14 October 1977.

77 'Gang in Black Attacks Gays', *Evening Argus*, 24 January 1979; 'Opinion Sparks a Gay Protest: 100 in Rights Demonstration Outside Argus House', *Evening Argus*, 26 January 1979. See also: Brighton Ourstory, 'Out of the Closet: 1967–1987', *A History of Lesbian and Gay Brighton* at: www.brightonourstory.co.uk/brighton-s-history/a-history-of-lesbian-and-gay-brighton-chapter-3-out-of-the-closet-1967–87/ (accessed 17 November 2018).

78 Sue, QBL workshop Brighton, February 2017.

79 Sue Bruley, 'Women's Liberation at the Grass Roots: A View from Some English Towns, c.1968–1990', *Women's History Review* 25, no. 5 (2016): 723–740.

80 Jude, in Jastrzebska and Luvera, *Queer in Brighton*, p. 90.

81 Melita, QBL workshop Brighton.

82 Belle (pseudonym), QBL workshop Brighton.

83 Melita, QBL workshop Brighton.

84 Williams and Wilson, 'IES at 50'.

85 Melita, interviewed by Justin Bengry for QBL, June 2017.

86 Melita, QBL workshop Brighton.

87 Alf, in Jastrzebska and Luvera, *Queer in Brighton*, p. 89.

88 See: Brighton Ourstory, 'A History of Lesbian and Gay Brighton' (2001) www.bright onourstory.co.uk/brighton-s-history/a-history-of-lesbian-and-gay-brighton-chapter-3-out-of-the-closet-1967-87/ (accessed 24 June 2018).

89 'Why Suspicion Stalks Brighton's Pink Zone', *The Standard*, 19 August 1983.

90 On rising homophobia in this decade, see: British Social Attitudes Survey: www.bsa. natcen.ac.uk/latest-report/british-social-attitudes-34/moral-issues.aspx.

91 'Go Gay Quietly', *Evening Argus*, 20 April 1978; 'Family Life Is at Stake', *Brighton Gazette*, 30 July 1978; *Evening Argus*, 20 April 1978; *Brighton Gazette*, 30 June 1978.

92 'Gay Love Lessons: Give Children the Facts about Homosexuality Say Teachers', *Evening Argus*, 20 January 1978; 'National Front to Fight Those Gay Love Lessons', *Evening Argus*, 24 January 1978.

93 On these rising fears in the 1980s see especially: Nick Basannavar, *Sexual Violence against Children in Britain since 1965* (London: Palgrave, 2021).

94 'Police Scour Gay Scene for Child Sex Attacker', *Capital Gay*, 19 August 1983.

95 'Brighton: The Town without Innocence', *The Daily Express*, 22 August 1983; see also: 'The Secret Side of Brighton', *Daily Mail*, 19 August 1983.

96 'Gays in Fear: They Dread Revenge after Attack on Boy', *The Sun*, 20 August 1983. 'Why Suspicion Stalks Brighton's Pink Zone'.

97 'Friends Rowed after Drinks', *Evening Argus*, 28 August 1985, p. 11; 'Navy Killer Is Jailed', *Evening Argus*, 28 July 1985, p. 3; 'My Bloody Knife Fight', *Evening Argus*, 25 February 1986; 'Man Who Flipped in Pub Attack', *Evening Argus*, 20 June 1984.

98 'Sailor in Death Trial Saw Red', *Evening Argus*, 20 June 1985; 'My Bloody Knife Fight', *Evening Argus*, 20 June 1985.

99 '"Queer Bashers" Sent to Jail', *Evening Argus*, 3 March 1971.

100 Melita, QBL workshop Brighton.

101 See for example: 'Terror Drive Noose Ordeal, *Evening Argus*, 30 April 1981; 'Man's Ordeal in Gay Terror Attack: Knifepoint Nightmare in Seafront Home', *Evening Argus*, 4 May 1982; 'Queer Scarer Fined £550', *Evening Argus*, 19 July 1985; 'Attacks on Gays on the Increase', *Evening Argus*, 23 April 1988, 'Gay Alert after Series of Attacks', *Evening Argus*, 18 August 1988.

102 Jill Gardiner, note to Matt Cook, 4 September 2018.

103 'Raid Club Owner Has Quit', *Evening Argus*, 30 January 1981.

104 See: Weeks, *Sex*, pp. 317–322.

105 'Deputy Mayor in Gay Rights Row', *Evening Argus*, 22 May 1985; 'Gay Lessons Get Education Elbow', *Evening Argus*, 19 November 1986.

106 'Brewer Fights for Mums and Dads: No Gay Sex Lessons in E.Sussex Classrooms', *Eastbourne Herald*, 22 November 1986.

107 'I Believe in Live and Let Live', *Brighton and Hove Leader*, 4 August 1988.

108 'Council Attack on "Distortion"', *Evening Argus*, 24 August 1983; 'Gays "Hit by Unfair Publicity"', *Evening Argus*, 29 November 1983; '10 Crimes and Misdemeanors that Shocked Brighton and Hove', www.brightonandhovenews.org, posted 13 March 2016 (accessed 15 July 2019).

109 For criticism of Councilor Blackman: 'Councilor Censured', *West Sussex Gazette*, 11 August 1988.

110 'AIDS Seaside Shocker', *Sunday Mirror*, 15 December 1985.

111 'Town of Terrror', *The Sun*, 4 November 1986; see also: 'AIDS Crisis Hits Gay Capital of Britain', *The People*, 12 June 1988.

112 Source: HIV and AIDS reporting section of Public Health England in 2017 (in response to a freedom of information request from Matt Cook, QBL).

113 See: Matt Cook, 'Archives of Feeling': The AIDS Crisis in Britain 1987', *History Workshop Journal* 83, no. 1 (2017): 51–78.

114 The rate rose from 0.19 of Brighton and Hove's population in 1991 to 0.9 in 2011. By comparison: Manchester – 0.12 of the population in 1991 rising to 0.86 by 2011; Leeds – 0.04 rising to 0.3; and Plymouth – 0.02 rising to 0.13.

115 J. A. Walsh, in Jastrzebska and Luvera, *Queer in Brighton*, p. 72.

116 Melita, QBL interview.

117 Melita, QBL interview.

118 Linda Pointing, 'Obituary: Barbara Bell', *Guardian*, 20 April 2005.

119 'Anne's Battle with Prejudice', *Evening Argus*, 21 July 1988.

120 Ken's testimony in: Stephen Mayes and Lyndall Stein (eds), *Positive Lives: Responses to HIV – A Photodocumentary* (London: Cassel, 1993), p. 77.
121 Melita, QBL interview.
122 Allie Rogers, in Jastrzebska and Luvera, *Queer in Brighton*, 179.
123 Melita, QBL interview.
124 Melita, QBL interview.
125 For a flavour of reporting on BAAAC28 activism in *Capital Gay* see: 'Brighton Equality Plan Comes under Fire', *Capital Gay*, 13 September 91; 'Labour Sticks at "Free Vote" on 16', *Capital Gay*, 15 October 1991; 'Kiss-in', *Capital Gay*, 11 January 1991.
126 Findings by BAAAC28 were echoed in London by GALOP and signalled by the British Social Attitudes Survey. See: *Brighton Action against Section 28 Newsletter*, 28 December 1990; on GALOP (Gay London Policing Group) see: 'Annual Report' 5 (1988/9) and 6 (1990) at: www.galop.org.uk/annual-reports/ (accessed 18 April 2018). For the BSAS data see: www www.bsa.natcen.ac.uk/latest-report/british-social-attitudes-34/moral-issues.aspx (accessed 18 April 2018). See also: Weeks, *Sex*, 321.
127 'Challenge to Brighton and Plymouth: Police Face Data Complaint', *Capital Gay*, 30 November 1990.
128 'Police Shred the Gay Files', *Brighton and Hove Advertiser*, 24 September 1992.
129 Jill, QBL workshop Brighton.
130 Melita, QBL interview.
131 Judith Barrington, in Jastrzebska and Luvera, *Queer in Brighton*, 30.
132 Queer in Brighton (2013) and Brighton Trans*formed (2014).
133 'Brighton Guide', *Queer Tribe*, January–February 1990, 17–19.
134 *Gay Times*, October 1990.
135 Sean, QBL workshop Brighton, June 2017.
136 https://youtu.be/SlCI_RQrzk8 (accessed 17 February 2021).
137 Alf Le Flohic, email to Matt Cook, 16 February 2021.
138 Marion Prince, in Jastrzebska and Luvera, *Queer in Brighton*, 78.
139 Jim Stanford, in Jastrzebska and Luvera, *Queer in Brighton*, p. 188.
140 'What a Way to Die: Reserved for the Last Days of AIDS Patients', *Evening Argus*, 17 October 1986.
141 Cited in: Mayes, *Positive*, p. 77.
142 On this point see: Cook, 'Archives of Feeling'.
143 See: Peter Scott, *Zorro Report: An Assessment of the HIV Prevention Needs of Gay Men in Brighton* (Essex: Project SIGMA, 1998), p. 5; 'Gay Protest in AIDS Capital', *Guardian*, 1997 (reference incomplete: LAGNA folder East Sussex IV 085); 'Gay Men Ignoring Advice on AIDS Avoidance', *Independent*, 30 March 1998.
144 Rose Collis, *Death and the City: The Nation's Experience Told through Brighton's History* (Brighton: Hanover Press, 2013), p. 77; Scott, *Zorro*, p. 9.
145 Martin Fisher was employed in this year and was instrumental in transforming AIDS care in the town. See: 'Obituaries: Martin Fisher', *British Medical Journal* (1 August 2015).
146 'Gay Protest in AIDS Capital', *Guardian*.
147 The research material and all the forms were deposited with the Brighton Ourstory Project archive and are now held at the Keep archive centre.
148 Scott, *Zorro*, 52.
149 For more on the Zorro approach see: Peter Scott and Les Wood, *Critical Tolerance: A Gay Community Led Modelling Needs Assessment* (Brighton: Critical Tolerance, 1997). Zorro's steering committee ultimately decided not to publish the report directly because it was

seen as too critical of the local authority, too negative in its portrayal of gay community and too partial. Project SIGMA ultimately undertook publication and distribution.

150 Scott, *Zorro*, 45.

151 Sean, QBL workshop Brighton.

152 Dennis, interviewed by Matt Cook for QBL, September 2017, QBL.

153 Brighton and Hove City Council, '2011 Census Briefing' (2001): www.bhconnected.org.uk/sites/bhconnected/files/2011%20Census%20Briefing%20-%20City%20Profile.pdf (accessed 10 August 2021).

154 Williams and Wilson, 'IES at 50'.

155 Scott, *Zorro*, 137.

156 Kath Browne, *Count Me in Too: LGBTQ Lives in Brighton and Hove: Initial Findings – Academic Report* (Brighton: University of Brighton, 2007), pp. 31–32.

157 'Council Most Gay Friendly', *The Argus*, 9 January 2009; *Brighton and Hove City Snapshot* (2014), 19.

158 Melita and 'Belle', QBL workshop Brighton. For more on Cowley see: QueenSpark authors, *Who Was Harry Cowley?* (Brighton: QueenSpark, 1984).

159 E.-J. Scott (ed.), *Brighton Trans*formed* (Brighton: QueenSpark, 2014), p. 106.

160 Jess, interviewed by Matt Cook for QBL, October 2017. See also: Alf Le Flohec, 'Justin Fashanu Brighton Memories', *G-Scene*, October 2020, https://issuu.com/gscene/docs/10_gscene_oct2020/s/11057319 (accessed 16 February 2021). In 2001, 94.3 per cent of people living in Brighton and Hove described themselves as white; by 2011 the figure was 89.1 per cent – still higher than the national average of 85.4. *Brighton and Hove Snapshot*, p. 22.

161 Ourstory, *Daring Hearts*, p. 85.

162 Kate, interviewed by Matt Cook for QBL, October 2017.

163 Browne, *Count Me in Too*, pp. 29–32.

164 See: Scott, *Brighton Trans*formed*, pp. 99, 77, 123 and 87.

165 See, for example, testimonies in Scott, *Brighton Trans*formed*, pp. 23, 54, 58, 146 and 148.

166 Brighton Museum, 'Interim Report on Visitor Feedback on the Museum of Transology', July 2017–September 2018.

167 As Kath Browne and Leela Bakshi argue in: Browne and Bakshi, *Ordinary in Brighton*.

168 See: www.visitbrighton.com/blog/blog-post/2020/07/never-normal-b246 (accessed 1 August 2021).

169 www.visitbrighton.com/blog/blog-post/2020/07/never-normal-b246, p. 80.

170 www.visitbrighton.com/blog/blog-post/2020/07/never-normal-b246, p. 80; Ourstory, *Daring Hearts*, pp. 7, 59 and 13.

171 Melita, QBL workshop Brighton.

172 Jill Gardiner, email to Matt Cook, 6 September 2018.

Chapter 2

1 Al Garthwaite, interviewed by Jeska Rees, May 2004. Feminist Archive North (henceforth FAN), Brotherton Library, University of Leeds, Gen/AV09.

2 Ajamu X, interviewed by Matt Cook, QBL, June 2017.

3 Katrina Honeyman, *Well-suited: A History of Leeds' Clothing Industry, 1850–1990* (Oxford: Oxford University Press, 2000); Paul Dulton, 'Leeds Calling: The Influence of London on the Gentrification of Regional Cities', *Urban Studies* 40, no. 12 (2003): 2557–2572.

4 See especially: Louise Wattis, 'Exploring Gender and Fear Retrospectively: Stories of Women's Fear during the Yorkshire Ripper Murders', *Gender, Place and Culture* 24, no. 8 (2017): 1071–1089.

5 Freya Johnson Ross, 'From Municipal Feminism to the Equality Act: Legislation and Gender Equality Work in UK Local Government 1980–2010', *Women's Studies International Forum* 66 (January–February 2018): 1–8.

6 Though Labour was in control of the council for most of our period, the Conservatives were in charge for the latter half of the 1970s and the council was under no overall control between 2004 and 2011.

7 David Green, interviewed for West Yorkshire Archive Service LGBT Project, 2008 (henceforth WYAS LGBT).

8 See, for example: 'Blackmail May Have Driven Mr X Insane', *News of the World*, 8 December 57; 'The Repentant Photographer', *News of the World*, 13 April 1958.

9 Ross McCusker, 'Long Lost Gay Bars and Pubs in Leeds', November 2017, www.gayyorkshire.com/2017/scene/LGBTQ-venues/long-lost-gay-bars (accessed 19 August 2019).

10 Pete Wood, 'The Great Disappearing Pubs of Old Central Leeds', *East Leeds Memories*, https://eastleedsmemories.wordpress.com/2012/08/01/the-great-disappeared-pubs-of-old-central-leeds/ (accessed 19 August 2019).

11 'The One in Twenty', *Union News*, 8 March 1968.

12 'Even in These Permissive Times, Do We Want Pubs Like This?', *The People*, 24 March 1968.

13 'The One in Twenty', *Union News*, 8 March 1968.

14 'Even in These Permissive Times'.

15 Gary Edwards, *Paint it White: Following Leeds Everywhere* (Edinburgh: Mainstream, 2003).

16 Roy, QBL workshop Leeds.

17 This is novelist Steve Alcock's take on Charlie's, cited by: Andrew Hirst, 'Remembering the 1970s Heyday of Huddersfield Gay Nightclub Gemini', *Huddersfield Daily Examiner*, 27 February 2016.

18 Robert Salt, interviewed by Robin Kiteley, West Yorkshire Queer Stories (WYQS), 5 March 2019.

19 Gerry Millar, interviewed by Ray Larman, WYQS, 5 March 2019.

20 'Homosexuals a Dirty Minded Bunch', *Yorkshire Post*, 27 January 1971.

21 Historic England, Pride of Place, www.historypin.org/en/prideofplace/geo/53.791593,-1.542752,18/bounds/53.790582,-1.545903,53.792604,-1.5396/paging/1/pin/1036758 (accessed 19 August 2019).

22 Gerry, WYQS.

23 Roy Blanchard, QBL workshop Leeds.

24 Ted Donovan, WYAS LGBT.

25 John Gravett, QBL workshop Leeds.

26 Ruth Middleton, QBL workshop Leeds.

27 'Lesbians Banned in Leeds?', *Gay News*, 18–31, March 1982, p. 13.

28 Lou, interview with Al and Lou, by Jeska Rees, 28 February 2006, FAN.

29 Julie Bindel, interviewed by Rees.

30 Group interview, WYAS LGBT, 27 February 2008; speaker unassigned.

31 Lesley Pattenson, QBL workshop Leeds.

32 Jude Woods, QBL workshop Leeds.

33 Lesley, QBL workshop Leeds.

34 Rex Wockner, 'Worldwide Bulletin', *Outrage* [Australia], April 1991: 11. Archives of Human Sexuality and Identity, http://tinyurl.galegroup.com/tinyurl3U6VD7 (accessed 6 June 2020).

35 Cerydwen Evans, QBL workshop Leeds.

36 Cerydwen, QBL workshop Leeds.

37 John Gravett, QBL workshop Leeds.

38 Cited by Hirst, 'Remembering'.

39 Letter from Kees van der Merwt to the *Huddersfield Daily Examiner*, 18 February 1981.

40 Hirst, 'Remembering'.

41 Roy, QBL workshop Leeds.

42 Patrick Hall, QBL workshop Leeds.

43 'Gross Indecency at Local "Gay" Club', *Huddersfield Daily Examiner*, 19 February 1981; 'Gay Club a "Cess Pit of Sexual Filth"', *Huddersfield Daily Examiner*, 12 March 1981.

44 'Police Undercover Vice Ring', *Huddersfield Daily Examiner*, 6 February 1981.

45 '"Police Harass Us" Say Huddersfield Gay Group', *Huddersfield Daily Examiner*, 12 February 1981.

46 'Gay March Attracts 1,500 and No Trouble', *YEP*, 4 July 1981; see also: Paul Ward, Graham Hellawell and Sally Lloyd 'Witness Seminar: Anti-fascism in 1970s Huddersfield', *Contemporary British History* 20, no. 1 (2006): 119–133.

47 Ajamu, QBL interview.

48 Roy, QBL workshop Leeds.

49 Ajamu, QBL interview.

50 Roy, QBL workshop Leeds.

51 Paul Greystock, WYAS LGBT.

52 'Franco', contributing to the Secret Leeds site, 8 January 2012, www.secretleeds.com/viewtopic.php?t=3618&start=30 (accessed 30 August 2018).

53 Memory recorded for: Historic England, 'Pride of Place'. See: www.historypin.org/en/prideofplace/geo/53.795246,-1.542488,19/bounds/53.79474,-1.544064,53.795751,-1.540913/paging/1/pin/1036375 (accessed 30 August 2018).

54 Paul Greystock, WYAS LGBT.

55 Memory recorded for 'Pride of Place'. See: www.historypin.org/en/prideofplace/geo/53.764832,-1.551627,14/bounds/53.748823,-1.59383,53.780836,-1.509424/paging/1/pin/1036731 (accessed 20 August 2018).

56 Extract from a memory card completed at a workshop for the WYAS LGBT.

57 David Green, WYAS LGBT project.

58 'Men at Baths Complaints', *News of the World*, 7 August 1955. See also: Helen Smith, *Masculinity, Class and Same-sex Desire in Industrial England, 1895–1957* (London: Palgrave, 2015), p. 142.

59 'Shame of Sex Case Official', *Bradford Telegraph and Argos*, 11 December 1987 (Stanningley); 'Case Dismissed', *Wharfdale and Airdale Observers*, 11 December 1981 (Guiseley); 'Park Man Stole from Homosexual', *YEP*, 19 July 86 (Seaford); 'Suicide Threat', *Morley Observer*, 13 November 1980, and 'Shame of a Morley Visitor', *Morley Observer*, 29 April 1982; 'Homosexuals "Dirty Minded Bunch"', *YEP*, 27 January 1971.

60 David Green, WYAS LGBT.

61 "Man Heard Poet Being Beaten to Death – QC', *Yorkshire Post*, 16 June 1979.

62 'Leeds Police', *Gay News*, 24 June–7 July 1982, p. 16. See also David Green, WYAS LGBT.

63 'Blackmail Youth Sent to Borstall', *Leeds Evening Post*, 7 June 1974; 'Man Jailed for Blackmail Bid', 27 June 1984, *Telegraph and Argos*; 'Blackmail Threats Haunted Gay Man', *Telegraph and Argos*, 8 May 1985.

64 David Green, WYAS LGBT.

65 'Boys Decided to Become Prostitutes, Court Is Told', *Huddersfield Daily Examiner*, 14 July 1981. 'Shocked Parents Took Their Son to the Police', *Morley Observer*, 20 May 1982; 'Menace to Young Gets Four Years', *YEP*, 25 March 1982; 'Vice Ring among Boys: MPs Urge Inquiry', 15 February 1977. See also: Patricia Hudson and Ian Rowes, *Men and Boys Selling Sex in the Bradford District* (Yorkshire: MESMAC, 2002).

66 'Gays Are Quizzed in Hunt for Killer', *Bradford Telegraph and Argus*, 20 August 1992.

67 Paul Greystock, WYAS LGBT.

68 Dave King and Richard Ekins, 'The First UK Transgender Conferences', *Gendys Journal* 39 (2007), www.gender.org.uk/gendys/2007/39ekins.htm (accessed 14 December 2019).

69 See: Philip Snaith, 'Gender Reassignment Today', *BMJ* 295 (12 December 1987): 1561.

70 'Burglar Sammy Is Really a Girl', *Daily Mail*, 22 July 1981; 'Sex Change Ordeal of a Thief', *YEP*, 10 October 1980; 'A Strange Marriage indeed', *Fanfare Magazine*, July 1986; see also: 'Man What a Weird Wedding', *Metamorphosis Magazine*, June–September 1986.

71 'All Set then Op Called Off', *YEP*, 29 January 1982.

72 Jude, QBL workshop Leeds.

73 Lynn, QBL workshop Leeds.

74 Jasmine Woolley, interviewed by Fiona Cosson, WYAS LGBT.

75 Leeds City Council Licensing Sub-committee, public document pack, 29 October 2007.

76 Discussion between Matt Cook and MESMAC project worker (unrecorded).

77 See: Peter Keogh, Catherine Dodds and Laurie Henderson, *Ethnic Minority Gay Men: Redefining Community, Restoring Identity – Research Report* (London: Sigma Research, 2004); Elijah Ward, 'Homophobia, Hypermasculinity and the US Black Church', *Culture Health and Sexuality* 7, no.5 (2005): 493–504.

78 For more on the project see: www.forumcentral.org.uk/new-mesmac-project-sholay-love/ (accessed 19 August 2019).

79 'Liberating the Gay', *YEP*, 23 March 1971.

80 Patrick, QBL workshop Leeds.

81 'Boy (12) Handed "Gay" Leaflet', *YEP*, 1 November 1971.

82 Patrick, QBL workshop Leeds.

83 Patrick, QBL workshop Leeds.

84 'Arrests and Violence in Leeds', *Gay News* 7–21 July 1973 (issue 28), p. 4.

85 'A Pledge to Gay Libbers', *Guardian*, 14 September 1974. Milligan was author of *The Politics of Sexuality* (1973).

86 'Radical Objects: General Will, Radical Theatre Group Memoirs', *History Workshop*, 28 July 2013, www.historyworkshop.org.uk/general-will-radical-theatre-company-memoirs/ (accessed 20 September 2019).

87 Yvonne Stringfellow, interviewed by Elizabeth Alridge Ross for the oral history project: Women in the Women's Liberation Movement in Leeds and Bradford, 1969–1979, 14 March 1995; FAN.

88 'Gay Liberals View', *YEP*, 23 April 1974.

89 'Free School View, *YEP*, 17 May 1974.

90 See: Jonathan Kozol, *Free Schools* (Boston: Haughton Mifflin, 1972); Tom de Castella, 'The Anarchic Experimental Schools of the Seventies', *BBC News*, 21 October 2014, www.bbc.co.uk/news/magazine-29518319 (accessed 19 August 2019); David

Buckingham, 'Children of the Revolution? Counter-culture, the Idea of Childhood and the Case of *Schoolkids Oz*', *Strenae: researches sur les livres et objets culturels de l'enfance* 13 (2018), https://journals.openedition.org/strenae/1808 (accessed 20 August 2019).

91 Daniel Chapman, 'Yet Nothing Changes Does It? Leeds, 1990, and the British Art Scene', *The City Talking: Leeds* 20, 13 April 2015.

92 Remembrances from Ray, Jude and Patrick, QBL workshop Leeds.

93 Yvonne, interview, interviewed for Women in the WLF.

94 'Gay Lib HQ Ransacked', *Leeds Evening Post*, 17 December 1973; 'Fascist Violence Increases: Gay Driven Out by Ultra Right', *Leeds Students*, 6 October 1977.

95 'Gays against Fascism Resource Manual' (1978), p. 21, in LAGNA Yorkshire West, folder I 079.

96 Lesley Patterson, QBL workshop Leeds.

97 Ted Donovan, WYAS LGBT.

98 Julie Bindel, interviewed by Jeska Rees, 25 February 2006, FAN.

99 Patrick, QBL workshop Leeds.

100 Lesley, QBL workshop Leeds.

101 Anna Rogers, 'Feminist Consciousness Raising in the 1970s and 1980s: West Yorkshire Women's Groups and Their Impact on Women's Lives', PhD thesis, University of Leeds, 2010.

102 Al Garthwaite, interview with Rees.

103 On the WLM in Leeds see: Jeska Rees, 'A Look Back at Anger: The Women's Liberation Movement in 1973', *Women's History Review* 19, no. 3 (2010): 337–354; Sue Bruley, 'Women's Liberation at the Grassroots: A View from Some English Towns, c.1968–1990', *Women's History Review* 25, no. 5 (2016): 723–740. Also see: Rogers, 'Feminist Consciousness Raising'.

104 Lesley, QBL workshop Leeds.

105 Leeds Revolutionary Feminism Group, *Love Your Enemy? The Debate Between Heterosexual Feminism and Political Lesbianism* (London: Onlywomen Press, 1981), pp. 5–6.

106 Tina Crockett, interviewed by Jeska Rees, 7 June 2004.

107 Lou Lavender, interviewed by Rees, 11 May 2004, FAN.

108 See: Finn Mackay, *Radical Feminism: Feminist Activism in Movement* (Basingstoke: Palgrave, 2015), ch. 4; Louise Wattis, *Revisiting the Yorkshire Ripper Murders* (London: Springer, 2018), ch. 3.

109 Al, interviewed by Rees.

110 John A. Walker, *Art and Outrage* (London: Pluto, 1999), p. 134.

111 'Hot Lesbian Put in Cooler', *Womannews*, June 1983; see also: "British Pigs Hassle Politically Active Angry Women', *Big Mama Rag* (San Francisco), June 1983.

112 Ruth, QBL workshop Leeds.

113 Jane Storr, interviewed by Jeska Rees, 6 July 2004, FAN.

114 *Leeds Women's Centre Newsletter*, no. 7, June 1987, p. 9, Ruth Ingram Collection, FAN.

115 See: Antonia Lant, 'Women's Independent Cinema: The case of Leeds Animation Workshop', in Lester D. Friedman (ed.), *Fires Were Started: British Cinema and Thatcherism* (1993; London: Wallflower, 2006). See also: www.screenonline.org.uk/film/id/824000/index.html (accessed 19 August 2019).

116 Jude, QBL workshop Leeds.

117 Ruth, QBL workshop Leeds.

118 Miriam Zukas, interviewed by Jeska Rees, 27 February 2006, FAN.

119 Miriam, FAN.

120 'Babes for Gays', *Bradford Star*, 18 August 1983; 'Doctors Attack Lesbian Aid Scheme', *Yorkshire Post*, 20 August 1983; 'Lesbians Bizarre Baby Bid Slammed', *YEP*, 20 August 1983; 'Crossing the Line, *YEP*, 2 May 1983. See also: Angela Douglas, interviewed by Miriam Bearse for Women in the WLM, 18 April 1996, FAN.

121 Jude Wood correspondence with Matt Cook, November 2018. See also: Jeffrey Weeks, Brian Heaphy and Catherine Donovan, *Same Sex Intimacies: Families of Choice and Other Life Experiments* (London: Routledge, 2001), ch. 7.

122 Al Garthwaite, FAN.

123 Julie Bindel, FAN.

124 Julia, FAN.

125 Caroline, Rachel and Gilda, group interview by Jeska Rees, 28 February 2006, FAN.

126 Sarah Lockyear, interviewed by Miriam Bearse for Women in the WLM, 14 February 1996, FAN.

127 Sarah, FAN.

128 Bruley, 'Women's Liberation'; Yvonne interviewed by Ross.

129 Roy and Patrick, QBL workshop Leeds.

130 David, WYAS LGBT.

131 Jude, QBL workshop Leeds.

132 Cerydwen, QBL workshop Leeds.

133 Miriam, interviewed by Rees.

134 Julie Bindel, interviewed by Rees.

135 Sandra McNeill, interviewed by Jeska Rees, 11 May 2004.

136 'Pin-ups', *YEP*, 14 March 1984.

137 'Granny's War on "Gay Girls"', *The Mirror*, 25 February 1985; 'Snogging Lesbians Get the Raspberry from Iris', *The Sun*, 25 February 1985; and then in relation to her opposition to the introduction of 'sexual orientation' in to the council equal opportunities statement – 'Grandmother Iris Slams "Gay's Charter', *YEP*, 29 March 1985.

138 'Backing for Gay Centre', *Yorkshire Post*, 4 August 1985; '"Yes" to Gay Centre but Not on Rates', *YEP*, 6 March 1985.

139 Patrick, QBL workshop Leeds.

140 'College Gay Club Ban "Pack of Lies"', *Yorkshire Post*, 19 March 1988; 'College Chief to Sue Gays', *YEP*, 13 May 1988.

141 'Victory for Gay Teacher', *Bradford Telegraph and Argus*, 22 March 1988; Ted, QBL workshop Leeds.

142 'A Lukewarm Kiss', *Bradford Telegraph and Argus*, 10 February 1988.

143 'Switchboard Role', *Bradford Telegraph and Argus*, 11 April 1988.

144 Jude, QBL workshop Leeds.

145 'Leeds Gets Gay Grant Call', *YEP*, 30 July 1988.

146 Ted, WYAS LGBT.

147 Cerydwen, QBL workshop Leeds.

148 Jude, QBL workshop Leeds.

149 Cerydwen, QBL workshop Leeds.

150 Dulton, 'Leeds Calling'.

151 Flyer, Matt Cook's collection.

152 'Gender Identity Clinic Services Under Strain as Referral Rates Soar', *Guardian*, 10 July 2016. The new gender identity clinic saw 131 patients in 2009/10 rising to 414 in 2015/16, indicating escalating demand and the strain now on the service.

153 Colin, QBL workshop Plymouth.

Chapter 3

1 'Reporter Barbara Mcdonald Talks to Homosexual Man', 1966, British Library Sound Archive, call: 1lp0195811.
2 Luchia Fitzgerald, interviewed by Sarah Feinstein for Manchester Digital Music Archive (hereafter MDMA), 28 September 2016.
3 'Homosexuality and the Law', *Leigh Reporter*, 4 February 1965.
4 Paul Fairweather, interviewed by Matt Cook for QBL, 4 September 2017.
5 For an analysis of Mancunian character see: Ian Taylor, Karen Evans and Penny Fraser, *A Tale of Two Cities: Global Change, Local Feeling and Everyday Life in the North of England* (London: Routledge, 1996), ch. 1; Mancunian Pride is epitomised in Tony Walsh's poem 'This Is the Place' (2012): www.youtube.com/watch?v=josaDi9ZBvE (accessed 12 June 2019).
6 Katie Milestone, 'Regional Variation: Northernness and New Urban Economics of Hedonism', in Justin O'Connor and Derek Wynne (eds), *From the Margins to the Centre: Cultural Production and Consumption in the Post-industrial City* (Aldershot: Arena, 1996).
7 Kate O'Donnell, interviewed by Matt Cook for QBL, 4 September 2017; Greg Thorpe, interviewed by Matt Cook for QBL, 5 September 2017; Paul, QBL interview.
8 On the 'flight' from Manchester see: Taylor, *A Tale of Two Cities*, p. 12 and p. 17; for stats see: GB Historical GIS/University of Portsmouth, Greater Manchester through time see: www.visionofbritain.org.uk/unit/10056925/rate/IND_MAN (accessed 20 April 2018).
9 'Teenage Clubs', *Bolton Evening News*, 31 October 1964.
10 'Vice Between Men – and a City's Police', *Manchester Evening News* (hereafter *MEN*), 30 August 1963.
11 Jenny-Anne Bishop, QBL workshop Manchester, 18 March 2017; 'Our Manchester', http://manchesterhistory.net/manchester/gone/gaumont.html (accessed 6 June 2020).
12 'Pubs of Manchester', http://pubs-of-manchester.blogspot.com/2010/02/long-bar-trafford-bar-oxford-street.html (accessed 6 June 2020).
13 'Hotel Outraged Public Decency', *MEN*, 15 October 1965, p. 5.
14 'Why a Policeman Had to Dance', *MEN*, 9 September 1968.
15 'Magazines Not Corrupt: Court', *MEN*, 1 January 1968.
16 Luchia, MDMA.
17 David Smith and Carol Ann Lee, *Witness* (Edinburgh: Mainstream, 2011), p. 54. Smith was implicated in one of Brady and Hindley's murders and subsequently wrote about his experience, here parroting language he claimed Brady used.
18 John Potter, *The Monster of the Moors* (London: Elek, 1966), p. 117.
19 Luchia, MDMA.
20 For details, see Luchia's interview with Alkarim Jivani. Alkarim Jivani, *It's Not Unusual: A History of Lesbian and Gay Britain in the Twentieth Century* (London: Michael O'Mara, 1997).
21 '£6,000 Gift for Research into Homosexuality', *Guardian*, 25 November 1964; see also: Tommy Dickinson, *Curing Queer: Mental Nurses and Their Patients, 1935–1974* (Manchester: Manchester University Press, 2015).
22 'Two Men Sent for Trial', *MEN*, 23 March 1960.
23 Carol Ainscow, interviewed by Rachel Adams for the Modern Lesbian Project (henceforth MLP), 4 August 2010, https://soundcloud.com/themodernlesbian (accessed 10 June 2020).

24 Liz Naylor cited in: John Robb, *Manchester Music City, 1976–1996* (London: Aurum, 2009), p. 157.

25 Judith, interviewed for Lesbian Identity Project (henceforth LIP), 2008.

26 Comment on a 1962 image of the Rembrandt posted on Flickr by Manchester Archives, www.flickr.com/photos/manchesterarchiveplus/5335375310 (accessed 7 May 2017).

27 Judith, LIP.

28 Joyce Edwards, interviewed by Rachel Adams, MLP, 4 August 2010, https://soundcloud.com/themodernlesbian (accessed 6 June 2020).

29 Carole Ainscow, MLP.

30 'Men on Sex Charges Are Sent to Trail', *Bolton Evening News*, 26 June 1963; 'Tempter is Jailed for 18 Months', *Bolton Evening News*, 25 June 1963; 'The Witch Hunt Is Horrifying', *Bolton Evening News*, 12 July 1963.

31 'Homosexuality and the Law', *Leigh Reporter*.

32 'Arran's Wrong, *MEN*, 19 September 1968; 'North to Have Centre for Homosexuals', *MEN*, 1 May 1968.

33 'Churchmen Don't Oppose Homosexual Discotheques', *Oldham Chronicle*, 25 September 1976.

34 'Protests over Ban on Gay Discos', *Manchester Evening News*, 7 August 1978; 'Education Chiefs Rebuff on Homosexuality', *Oldham Chronicle*, 19 February 1975; 'Group Wants Change to the Law', *Bolton Evening News*, 26 November 1980.

35 Angela Cooper, interviewed by Sarah Feinstein, 28 September 2016, MDMA.

36 Luchia, MDMA.

37 Angela, MDMA.

38 Taylor, *A Tale of Two Cities*, ch. 1.

39 Jeffrey Weeks, *Sex, Politics and Society: The Regulation of Sexuality since 1800*, 4th ed. (London: Routledge, 2018), p. 274.

40 'Help for the Troubled Thousands', *MEN*, 28 June 1988.

41 Jenny-Anne Bishop, QBL workshop Manchester.

42 Numbers doubled between 1961 and 1971, from *c*.11,500 to *c*.24,000. See: Manchester, 'A Vision of Britain'.

43 'Gays Disrupt Christian Crusade', *MEN*, 3 June 1976.

44 Unidentified speaker in the small group discussion chaired by Amelia Lee for the This Is How We Got Here project, 1 March 2014 (hereafter TIHWGH).

45 Gay Jones, interviewed for the Before Stonewall project, British Library Sound Archive; call: BL C1159/104.

46 Angela, MDMA.

47 Luchia, MDMA.

48 Rosie Lagosi, interviewed by Rachel Adams, MLP, 4 August 2010.

49 Jess Zadik, interviewed by Matt Cook for QBL, September 2017.

50 Angela, MDMA; 'Biography: Stephen Whittle', Press for Change, https://archive.li/VtrkM#selection-959.0–959.629; 'Stephen Whittle: Body of Work', *Guardian*, 17 April 2007.

51 'Police Hunt Gay Terrorist over Pink Bricks', *MEN*, 4 October 1979.

52 Robb, *Manchester Music City*, p. 70.

53 Paul, QBL interview.

54 Jenny-Anne Bishop, QBL workshop Manchester.

55 Josie Pickering, interviewed by Rachel Adams for MLP, 19 July 2010, https://soundcloud.com/themodernlesbian/josie-pickering-interview-1 (accessed 6 June 2020).

56   Paul, QBL interview.

57   Judith, LIP. See also: Lois, 'Remembering Pride and Celebrating Place: Finding, Mapping and Commemorating Queer Heritage in Manchester', MA thesis 2015, Manchester University, p. 39.

58   'An Evening of Ecstasy for Two Quid on the Door', *Guardian*, 1 May 1981; www.facebook.com/BBCArchive/videos/310087204185535/ (accessed 6 July 2021).

59   Paul, QBL interview.

60   'Farewell Foo Foo', *MEN*, 12 August 2004.

61   Rosie Lagosi, interviewed by Rachel Adams, MLP, 4 August 2010. https://soundcloud.com/themodernlesbian (accessed 6 June 2020).

62   Peter Cookson, interviewed by Alex Cookson for TIHWGH, 1 March 2014.

63   Peter Cookson, TIHWGH.

64   'Gay Support for City Gay Lib demo', *MEN*, 28 February 1981.

65   'Gay Demo', *Peace News*, 6 March 1981.

66   'Police Chief Denies Drive against Gays', *Guardian*, 23 March 1978; 'No War, Says Police Chief', *Stockport Advertiser*, 15 January 1981.

67   'Sex Peril Loos to be Shut', *MEN*, 19 October 1978; 'Police Chief Hits at Gay Groups Criticism', *Oldham Chronicle*, 13 January 1981; 'What Police Saw at a Gay Sauna', *MEN*, 16 May 1979. 'Anderton Cleared Over "Human Cesspit" Speech', *Daily Telegraph*, 16 May 1984.

68   'Shame of Town's Sex Case Figures', *MEN*, 23 August 1980.

69   Peter Cookson, TIHWGH.

70   'Gays Must Stick to the Law', *Halifax Evening Courier*, 11 December 1980; 'Harassment of Gays Deplored', *Guardian*, 18 November 1980; 'When a Catch All Law Wastes Time, Money and Resources', *Guardian*, 28 November 1980.

71   For Jack Straw's advocacy of the Police Authorities (Powers) Bill in parliament on 14 November 1979, see: www.theyworkforyou.com/debates/?id=1979-11-14a.1361.0 (accessed 9 October 2018).

72   Paul, QBL interview.

73   'Gay Groups Challenge Accepted', *Oldham Evening News*, 6 April 1978; 'Attack on Gay Posters in Libraries', *Stockport Advertiser*, 4 May 1978; 'Gay Advert Triggers a Storm', *MEN*, 3 April 1979.

74   Paul, QBL interview.

75   'Police "Waste Time Trapping Homosexual"', *Daily Telegraph*, 2 December 1986; 'Police Methods Offensive, Say Councillors', *Stockport Express*, 9 October 1980.

76   Paul, QBL interview and Paul, interviewed for Lets Talk About Sex project, LGBTQ Foundation, 2017, http://ltas-exhibition.LGBTQ.foundation/ (accessed 12 September 2018). See also: 'AIDS Victim Ordered Confined under New Law, *United Press International*, 15 September 1985, www.upi.com/Archives/1985/09/15/AIDS-victim-ordered-confined-under-new-law/4382495604800/ (accessed 12 September 2018).

77   On this point see: Virginia Berridge, *AIDS in the UK: The Making of a Policy, 1981–1994* (Oxford: Oxford University Press, 1996).

78   Paul, QBL interview. For the *MEN*'s outraged report on housing policy in the city see: 'Alarm over City Havens for Gay', *MEN*, 22 February 1985.

79   Jenny White, interview with Matt Cook for QBL, 4 April 2017.

80   Unidentified speaker in the small group discussion chaired by Amelia Lee for TIHWGH project, 1 March 2014.

81 'Plea for Friends Poster', *Rochdale Observer*, 30 August 1980; 'Ban Those Posters Bid Fails', *Stretford and Urmston Journal*, 9 April 1981.
82 'Convicted Leisure Chief Gets the Sack', *MEN*, 11 April 1980.
83 'Bullet in Head Storm over Gays', *MEN*, 1 April 1981; 'Gay Demo Stops Council Meeting', *MEN*, 10 April 1981.
84 'Gay Rights Woman Is the Mayor', *The Star*, 14 November 1985; 'Lesbian Rights Leftist to Be Lord Mayor', *Daily Telegraph*, 14 November 1985; 'Gay Rights Girl Mayor', *The Sun*, 14 November 1985; 'Lord Mayor Bid Dropped', *MEN*, 28 December 1985.
85 Paul, QBL interview.
86 Ruth Middleton, QBL workshop Leeds.
87 'Never Going Underground' programme, Manchester Central library, GB127.M775, 1 March 2014.
88 'Unusual Spate of Queer Bashing Attacks', *Gay Times*, November 1988.
89 'Gay Festival May Be Illegal', *MEN*, 26 June 1989.
90 '"Gay Day" Flower Tribute Sparks a Blooming Rumpus', *MEN*, 28 June 1989; 'Flower Bed Degrades the City', *MEN*, 30 June 1989; 'Backlash to Gays Written in Weed Killer', *MEN*, 30 June 1989.
91 'Gay "Orgy" Row at Charity Show', *MEN*, 1 June 1988.
92 For discussion of industrial decline in Manchester see especially: Taylor, *A Tale of Two Cities*, p. 8.
93 'The Gay Village', *Independent on Sunday*, 9 June 1996.
94 '"Gaychester": Remembering Manchester's Early 1990s Gay Scene', *Guardian*, 7 February 2013.
95 'Naked City: Flesh – Birthday Jamboree at the Hacienda Manchester', *Select*, January 1994.
96 '"Gaychester"', *Guardian*.
97 Kate, QBL interview.
98 Paul Flynn, *Good as You: From Prejudice to Pride – 30 years of Gay Britain* (London: Ebury Press, 2017).
99 Carol Ainscow interview, MLP.
100 Taylor, *A Tale of Two Cities*, pp. 184–185.
101 'In the Pink', *City Life* (1983), http://pubs-of-manchester.blogspot.com/2011/09/arch way-brickhouse-whitworth-street.html (accessed 11 July 2019).
102 Jen, QBL interview.
103 Mike Homfray, *Provincial Queens: The Gay and Lesbian Community in the North-West of England* (Oxford: Peter Lang, 2007), pp. 153–154.
104 Kate, QBL interview.
105 Greg, QBL interview; Jenny, QBL interview.
106 Taylor, *A Tale of Two Cities*, pp. 194, 182, 193 and 197.
107 Taylor, *A Tale of Two Cities*, pp. 197.
108 'The Village Bobby Trying to Sort Things Out', *MEN*, 5 May 1993; Taylor, *A Tale of Two Cities*.
109 'Honeymoon with Police over Says Gays', *The Observer*, 8 May 1994.
110 'Police Gay Computer Fury', *MEN*, 1 February 1995; 'Police Apologise over Gay Files', *Independent*, 2 February 1995; 'Police Lift Data Threat to Gays', *Guardian*, 2 February 1995.
111 'Police Pioneers Leading the Way for City's Gays', *MEN*, 23 October 1995; 'Building Trust', *Police Review*, 9 May 1997; Chris Fox, *Invisible Minority: Securing the Participation and*

Engagement of Salford's Lesbian and Gay Community' (Manchester: Salford CVS, 2002), p. 14. For discussion of the 'sympathetic' new police chief by an officer forced out of the closet in 1996, see: 'A Cop's Gay Secret', *MEN*, 31 January 1996.

112 Greg, QBL interview.

113 From its 1991 low of 379,529 the population grew to 503,127 in 2011 (still short of the 1951 high of 703,082); the Greater Manchester region meanwhile reached 2.68 million. Source: census.

114 Ian Deas, Jamie Peck, Adam Tickell and Kevin Ward, 'Rescripting Urban Regeneration the Mancunian Way', in Rob Imri and Huw Thomas (eds), *British Urban Policy and the Urban Development Corporations* (London: Sage, 1999).

115 Collection descriptor of the 'queerupnorth' collection at Manchester Central Library, ref: M800.

116 'Manchester Retailers Back Gay Mall Concept', *Property Week*, 29 February 1996.

117 'Manchester Retailers Back Gay Mall Concept'; 'What Happened to Manchester's First and Only Gay Shopping Centre?', *MEN*, 30 April 2016.

118 'Manchester Transgender Businesswoman Stephanie Booth Killed in Tractor Crash', *MEN*, 19 September 2016.

119 Jenny-Anne Bishop, QBL workshop Manchester.

120 Lois Stone, 'Remembering Pride and Celebrating Place', MA thesis, University of Manchester, 2015, pp. 25–26.

121 Jen, QBL interview.

122 Paul Greystock, interviewed for the WYAS LGBT project in 2008.

123 Cerydwen Evans, QBL workshop Leeds.

124 Jo Lewis, QBL workshop Plymouth, 4 March 2017.

125 Alan Butler, QBL workshop Plymouth.

126 Jenny-Anne Bishop, QBL workshop Manchester. See also: 'I'm Sorry, Sir, You Don't Pass the Gayness Test', *Independent on Sunday*, 19 March 2006.

127 Nina Held, 'Comfortable and Safe Spaces? Gender, Sexuality, and "Race" in Night-time Leisure Spaces', *Emotion, Space and Society*, 14 (2015): 33–42, p. 37.

128 Held, 'Comfortable and Safe Spaces', p. 37.

129 Jen Yockney, QBL workshop Manchester.

130 'Drug Gangs Take the Gay Out of Gaychester', *Independent on Sunday*, 22 October 1995; 'All Change in Gay Village', *MEN*, 11 November 1995. 'Wealthy Gays Are Target of Drug dealers', *MEN*, 12 November 1995.

131 'Straights to the Point', *Daily Express*, 30 August 1999; Philip Hensher, 'Please Keep Out of Gay Bars and Clubs', *Independent*, 5 June 2002.

132 'Well, Would You Let Them in Your Club?' *Mail on Sunday*, 7 July 2002.

133 Bev Skeggs and Jon Binnie, 'Cosmopolitan Knowledge and the Production and Consumption of Sexualized Space: Manchester's Gay Village', in *Sociological Review* 52, no. 1 (2004): 39–61; Taylor, *A Tale of Two Cities*, p. 190.

134 In 2011, 83.8 per cent of people in Greater Manchester saw themselves as white, which is slightly less than the UK average of 86 per cent. Source: census.

135 Cover, *Mancunian Gay*, March 1986; 'Black and Gay', *Mancunian Gay*, January 1985.

136 Claud Cunningham, MLP, 4 August 2010, https://soundcloud.com/themodernlesbian (accessed 18 September 2019).

137 Greg, QBL interview.

138 Held, 'Comfortable and Safe Spaces', p. 39.

139 Claud Cunningham, MLP.

140 Skeggs and Binnie, 'Cosmopolitan Knowledge', p. 57.

141 Paul, QBL interview.

142 Cited by Homfray, *Provincial*, p. 153.

143 Greg, QBL interview.

144 'Club Brenda at Urbis', in *Aesthetica* (1 December 2009). See: www.aestheticamagazine. com/club-brenda-at-urbis/ (accessed 20 September 2018).

145 Greg, QBL interview.

146 Project participants cited in: Stone, 'Remembering', p. 37.

147 'Birthday Time for Bollox', *MEN*, 18 April 2010.

148 Greg, QBL interview.

149 On the recourse to the local and the past in the face of economic shifts and globalization see: Taylor, *A Tale of Two Cities*, p. 11.

150 Jen, QBL interview.

151 DJ Wolfy, 'Shake the Foundations' (short documentary, 2017) www.youtube.com/ watch?v=j9FMOunCHGc 20 October 2020.

152 Kate, QBL interview.

153 'We Exist! Manchester LGBTQ Charity Aims to End Erasure of BAME', *Mancunian Matters*, 7 May 2019, www.mancunianmatters.co.uk/content/311074857-we-exist-manchester-LGBTQ-charity-aim-end-erasure-identities-bame-people (accessed 20 August 2020).

154 Kate, QBL interview.

155 Greg Thorpe, QBL interview.

156 On the Turing memorial and the anachronistic seizure of 'gay' icons see: Laura Doan, 'Queer History, Queer Memory: The Case of Alan Turing', in *GLQ* 23, no. 1 (2017): 113–136.

157 Ian Allan, interviewed by Matt Cook, 7 September 2017, QBL.

158 Ian, QBL interview.

Chapter 4

1 Keith Howes, 'Plymouth', *Gay News*, 7–10 October 1976, p. 13.

2 Jo Pine, interviewed by Alan Butler for PioP, 16 December 2011.

3 Howes, 'Plymouth'.

4 Alan Butler, QBL workshop Plymouth.

5 'Cry for Help Brings Line of Hope', *Western Evening Herald*, 21 September 1984.

6 Howes, 'Plymouth'.

7 See: Alan Butler, 'Performing LGBTQ Pride in Plymouth, 1950–2012', PhD thesis submitted to University of Plymouth, 2015.

8 Howes, 'Plymouth'.

9 The population in 2011 was 256,384. Registrar General for England and Wales; General Register Office Scotland (2002): 1961, 1971 and 2011. Census aggregate data. UK Data Service.

10 Jeremy Gould, *Plymouth: Vision of a Modern City* (Swindon: English Heritage, 2010).

11 S. Lloyd Jones, 'Working to a Plan — Committee Structure in Plymouth During Reconstruction and Subsequently', *Local Government Studies* 6, no. 5 (1980): 29–36.

12 Gould, *Plymouth*.

13 'Plymouth', *A Vision of Britain Through Time*, University of Portsmouth: www. visionofbritain.org.uk/unit/10168259 (accessed 13 August 2018).

14 'Sorry to See So Many of these Cases', *Western Gazette*, 14 October 1959.

15 Michael, interviewed by Justin Bengry, QBL, 26 November 2016.

16 Howes, 'Plymouth'.

17 Jeannie, interviewed by Helen Philips, Pride in our Past project (henceforth PioP), Plymouth, 2012. Plymouth and West Devon Records Office.

18 Ted, interviewed by Alan Butler, 2011, PioP.

19 See: www.navy-net.co.uk/community/threads/the-real-diamond-lils.31298/ (accessed 10 September 2018).

20 Kevin Kelland, interviewed by Alan Butler for PioP, 29 February 2012.

21 Michael, QBL interview.

22 Ted, PioP.

23 Ted, PioP.

24 Michael, QBL interview.

25 Howes, 'Plymouth'.

26 Ted, PioP. For more discussion of Ted's testimony and of Lion's Den Cove see: Butler, 'Performing', para. 342.

27 Michael, QBL interview.

28 Post-workshop conversation with Matt Cook.

29 Lesbian line volunteer cited in: 'Cry for Help Brings Line of Hope', *Western Evening Herald*, 21 April 1984.

30 Michael, QBL interview.

31 Michael, QBL interview.

32 Steve Pearce, interviewed by Helen Philips for PioP, 6 December 2011.

33 Kevin, PioP.

34 'Police Are Accused of Witch-hunt After Homosexual Arrests', *Western Independent*, 13 March 1977.

35 'Gays Allege "Witch-hunt"', *Western Independent*, 2 April 1978; 'Police "Help" for Gays', *Western Independent*, 12 March 1978.

36 'Plot by Youths Sordid', *Western Morning News*, 17 November 1971; 'Plymouth "Queer Basher" Given Three Years', *Western Morning News*, 6 September 73. The cases continued; see for example: 'These Attackers Must Be Caught', *Plymouth Evening Herald*, 20 November 1981; 'Assault Case Man's Inborn Disgust' (newspaper and date not clear, *c.*1980), see: LAGNA, Devon and Cornwall folder pp. 6–7.

37 'Medical Clash in Plymouth Stabbing Case', *Western Evening Herald*, 3 April 1977; 'Ratings "Baited Gays"', *Western Morning News*, 8 October 1977. See also: 'Soldier Goes to Jail for Robbery', *Western Evening Herald*, 15 December 1982; 'City Man Jailed for "Appalling" Assault in Flat', *Western Evening Herald*, 26 August 1984. Still one of the best discussions of the slippage from homosocial to homoerotic is: Eve Kosovsky Sedgwick, *Between Men: English Literature and Male Homosocial Desire* (New York: Columbia University Press, 1985).

38 'City Gay Row Cost £510 for 6 Ratings', *Western Evening Herald*, 7 October 1977.

39 Michael, QBL interview.

40 'Wallace Goes West', *CHE Bulletin*, August 1975.

41 Peter Buckley, interviewed by Helen Philips for PioP, 30 January 2012.

42 Jo, PioP.

43 Kevin, PioP.

44 Tony Hall, cited in: Howes, 'Plymouth'.

45 Lynne Roberts, interviewed for PioP, 24 February 2012.

46 'Lesbian Group Warfare Denied', *Western Morning News*, 23 May 1979; '20 Women "Fought Outside Pub"', *Western Morning News*, 24 May 1979.

47 Prudence De Villiers, interview by Mike Upton for Before Stonewall, 7 August 2003, British Library Sound Archive re: 235/PL4; Gay Jones, interviewed by Lorna for PioP, 20 November 2011.

48 'Cry for Help Brings Line of Hope', *Western Evening Herald*, 21 April 1984; 'Plymouth's Invisible People', *Cornish Times*, 18 May 1984.

49 Gay, PioP.

50 'Cash for Gay Groups Storm', *Plymouth Evening Herald*, 26 June 1991.

51 Sharon, interviewed by Lorna for PioP, 25 November 2011.

52 Michael, QBL interview.

53 Lynne, PioP.

54 Hannah Jordan, QBL workshop Plymouth, 4 March 2017.

55 Kerry, interviewed by Lorna for PioP, 17 February 2012.

56 Colin Damp, QBL workshop Plymouth.

57 Dennis, interviewed by Matt Cook for QBL, 21 March 2017.

58 Dennis, QBL interview.

59 For more on reticence in interviews with gay members of the forces see: Steve Estes, 'Ask and Tell: Gay Veterans, Identity and Oral History', *The Oral History Review* 32, no. 2 (2005): 21–47.

60 Jono Madeley, interviewed by Alan Butler for PioP, 13 December 2011.

61 Colin, QBL workshop Plymouth.

62 Michael, QBL interview.

63 Jeannie Crook, interviewed by Helen Philips for PioP, 29 February 2012.

64 'Navy Dubbed Anti-gay after Discovery of "Hello Sailor" Handbook', *Western Evening Herald*, 18 June 1993.

65 'Gay Chef May Sue', *Plymouth Evening News*, 27 September 1999.

66 'Gay Sailor Told to Go', *Western Evening Herald*, 27 August 1999; 'Gay Chef May Sue'; 'Gay Sailor Beaten', *The Star*, 5 September 2000.

67 'Petty Officer Admits Sex Offences', *Daily Telegraph*, 7 May 1982; 'Frigate Officer Guilty of Indecency', *Plymouth Daily Press*, *c.*1982, Plymouth and Devon folder, LAGNA [precise date missing].

68 In response to the statement 'Homosexual relations are always or mostly wrong', 62 per cent of 3,000 people surveyed nationally agreed in 1983; 74 per cent in 1987; 55 per cent in 1995; 46 per cent in 2000; 39 per cent in 2005. "Homosexuality," British Social Attitudes Survey, www.bsa.natcen.ac.uk/latest-report/british-social-attitudes-30/personal-relationships/homosexuality.aspx (accessed 14 July 2020).

69 Dennis, QBL interview.

70 'Plymouth's Invisible People', *Cornish Times*, 18 May 1984; 'Cry for Help Brings Line of Hope', *Western Evening Herald*, 21 March 1984.

71 'Fear Drove Gays in from the Cold', *Plymouth Evening Herald*, 6 March 1997. For more on family life in our cities, see Chapter 6.

72 'Navy Wife Inquiry Still Going On', *Plymouth Sunday Independent*, 14 December 1980.

73 'Husband and Wife Are Both Women: Stranger Chosen to Father Child', *Western Morning News*, 18 October 1982, 'Two Women Flee Love Nest Storm', *Western Morning News*, 26 October 1982; 'Baby Tragedy', *Daily Star*, 16 November 1982.

74 Lynne, PioP.

75 '"Find Moral Cure for AIDS" Plea', *Western Morning News*, 24 February 1987.

76 Mass Observer B1215, Mass Observation Collection, the Keep record Office, East Sussex.

77 Kevin, PioP; Peter, PioP. HIV infection rates in Plymouth rose from 0.25 in 1991 to 0.13 in 2011. In 1991, 58 per cent were thought to have contracted HIV through sex with another man; in 2011 the figure was 48 per cent. By comparison: Brighton, 0.19 (1991) rising to 0.9 (2011); Leeds, 0.04 rising to 0.3; and Manchester, 0.12 (1991) rising to 0.86 (2011). Source: HIV and AIDS reporting section of Public Health England in 2017 (in response to a freedom of information request from QBL).

78 Michael, QBL interview.

79 Ted, PioP.

80 Dennis, QBL interview.

81 David Ross (unrecorded) conversation with Matt Cook.

82 Dennis, QBL interview.

83 Kerry, PioP.

84 Jo Pine, QBL workshop Plymouth.

85 Jo and Alan, QBL workshop Plymouth.

86 '55 Year and Ted and Paul Are as Happy as the First Day They Met', *Plymouth Herald*, 16 September 2015.

87 Gay, PioP.

88 Prudence, After Stonewall.

89 Hannah, QBL workshop Plymouth.

90 Circular letter from Gay to around twenty other west country feminists, 3 February 1984, PioP collection, Plymouth and West Devon Records Office.

91 Butler, 'Performing', para. 560.

92 Sharon, PioP.

93 'Young Tories to Hold Demo at Bookshop', *Western Evening News*, 2 February 1985.

94 Gay, PioP.

95 'Gay Teachers Leads to Policy Row', *Express and Echo*, 24 April 1986; 'Ban These Gay Lesson Plea to Candidates', *Western Evening Herald*, 2 June 1987; 'The Age for Sexual Choice', *Sunday Independent*, Plymouth, 19 April 1987.

96 Sharon, PioP.

97 'Morality Rivals in Secret Sex Debate', *Western Morning News*, 1 December 1992.

98 Jono Madeley, PioP.

99 'Murders in Park: Parents Fear Notorious Haunt', *Plymouth Evening Herald*, 7 November 1995.

100 'They Could Kill Again', *Plymouth Evening Herald*, 8 November 1995; for an image of the graffiti see: 'Brutal Murder that Changed Plymouth', *Plymouth Evening Herald*, 23 November 2015.

101 'Brutal Murder that Changed Plymouth'.

102 'Ex-wife Tells of Her Life with Gay Victim', *Plymouth Evening Herald*, 10 November 1995.

103 'Victim's Brother Speaks Out', *Plymouth Evening Herald*, 10 November 1995.

104 'The Living Hell of Bernie Hawken', *Plymouth Evening Herald*, 6 March 1997.

105 'Challenge to Brighton and Plymouth: Police Face Data Complaint', *Capital Gay*, 30 November 1990.

106 'Stigma Creates Fear of Reporting Attacks', *The Independent*, 9 November 1995.

107 '24-hour Hotline Set Up on Killing', *Plymouth Evening Herald*, 8 November 1995.

108 Steve Pearce, interviewed by Helen Philips for PioP, 6 December 2011; 'Gays Praise Police for Action on Park Killing', *Plymouth Evening Herald*, 18 November 1995.

109 'How Drug Abuse Set Them on the Path to Murder', *Plymouth Evening Herald*, 6 March 1997.

110 Jono, PioP.

111 Steve Pearce, PioP.

112 Cited in: 'Fear Drove Gays in from the Cold', *Plymouth Evening Herald*, 6 March 1997.

113 'Programme: Pink Saturday – What Will the Neighbours Think', 31 March 2001, PioP collection Plymouth and West Devon Record Office, ref: 3901.18.

114 Pride programmes and flyers in the 'Council' folder, Plymouth and West Devon Record Office, ref: 3901:18.

115 'Stigma Creates Fear in Reporting Attacks', *Independent*, 9 November 1995.

116 Gay, PioP.

117 Hannah, QBL workshop Plymouth.

118 Alan, QBL workshop Plymouth.

119 Colin, QBL workshop Plymouth.

120 The number of students over sixteen grew from 8,468 to 16,060 between 1991 and 2011; source: census.

121 Mavis, PioP.

122 Between 1971 and 2011 the number of service personnel stationed in the city fell from 10,870 to 7,580; source: Defence Statistics – Tri-service. On the retraction of the docks from the 1970s see: Peter Brimacombe, *Drake's Drum: A History of the Devonport Naval Base and Dockyard* (Plymouth: Mor, 1999), ch. 9.

123 Kevin Kelland, QBL workshop Plymouth; Dennis, QBL interview.

124 '55 Years on and Ted and Paul Are as Happy as the First Day They Met'.

125 Jo, PioP.

126 Kevin, PioP.

127 Dennis, QBL interview.

128 Jo, QBL workshop Plymouth.

129 Martyn Hammond, interviewed for PioP, 21 February 2012; Alan Butler commented on the more recent success of coffee group in his comments on an earlier draft of this chapter.

130 Kevin, QBL workshop Plymouth.

131 'Peter Was Ginger to My Fred Astaire', *Plymouth Evening Herald*, 17 February 2006; '55 Years on and Ted and Paul Are as Happy as the First Day They Met'.

Chapter 5

1 Jenny-Anne Bishop, Queer Beyond London (QBL) workshop Manchester, 18 March 2017.

2 Jenny-Anne Bishop interview, TIHWGH project, Manchester, 1 March 2014.

3 Andrew Gorman-Murray, 'Intimate Mobilities: Emotional Embodiment and Queer Migration', *Social and Cultural Geography* 10, no. 4 (2009): 441–460.

4 Larry Knopp, 'Ontologies of Place, Placelessness, and Movement: Queer Quests for Identity and Their Impacts on Contemporary Geographic Thought', *Gender, Place and Culture* 11, no. 1 (2004): 121–134; Mark W. Turner, *Backward Glances: Cruising the Queer Streets of New York and London* (London: Reaktion Books, 2003).

5 For the lesbian flâneur, see Sally Munt, *Heroic Desire: Lesbian Identity and Cultural Space* (London: Cassell, 1998).

6 Rebecca Jennings, '"It Was a Hot Climate and It Was a Hot Time": Lesbian Migration and Transnational Networks in the Mid-twentieth Century', *Australian Feminist Studies* 25, no. 63 (2010): 31–45; Carol Dyhouse, *Students: A Gendered History* (London: Routledge, 2006), especially ch. 5.

7 Various contributors, QBL workshop Plymouth, 4 March 2017.

8 Carole Truman and Lynn Keenaghan, *Men Who Have Sex with Men in the North West: A Peer-led Regional Study* (Lancaster: Lancaster University, 1996), summary and see pp. 37–38.

9 Peter Cookson, interviewed for TIHWGH, 1 March 2014.

10 'Caroline' [pseudonym], interviewed by Alison Oram for QBL, 22 February 2019. Note that this is a different Caroline from the Brighton story elsewhere.

11 Jenny-Anne Bishop, QBL workshop Manchester. Northern Concord and the Beaumont Society are trans social organisations.

12 Jenny-Anne Bishop, QBL workshop Manchester.

13 Sheila Jeffreys, interviewed by Jeska Rees, 17 November 2004. GEN-AV09, FAN.

14 Lou Lavender, group interview by Elizabeth Ross for 'WLM in Leeds and Bradford 1969–79', 17 February 1995, FAN.

15 Lesley Pattenson, QBL workshop Leeds, 19 March 2017.

16 Melita Dennett, interviewed by Justin Bengry for QBL, 23 June 2017.

17 Gay Jones, interviewed by Mike Upton for Before Stonewall, 7 August 2003. British Library Sound Archive, C1159/104. GLAM ref no 234/ PL4.

18 Dennis, interviewed by Matt Cook for QBL, 3 April 2017.

19 Deb Ley, QBL workshop Plymouth, 4 March 2017.

20 Bob Cant (ed.), *Invented Identities? Lesbians and Gays Talk about Migration* (London: Cassell, 1997), p. 92.

21 Brighton Ourstory Project, *Daring Hearts: Lesbian and Gay Lives of 50s and 60s Brighton* (Brighton: QueenSpark Books, 1992), p. 24.

22 Cant, *Invented Identities?*, p. 96. Also see Ourstory, *Daring Hearts*, pp. 20–24. Sandie was interviewed by the Daring Hearts Ourstory project in the late 1980s and a few years later by Bob Cant for his book on lesbian and gay migration. (Sandie preferred the term 'gay' to 'lesbian'.) For pull factors in lesbian and gay migration see: Gorman-Murray, 'Intimate Mobilities'; Alva Träbert, 'Great Expectations: Migrating to Edinburgh', in Justin Bengry, Matt Cook and Alison Oram (eds), *Locating Queer Histories: Places and Traces across the UK* (London: Bloomsbury, 2022).

23 Kath Weston, 'Get Thee to a Big City: Sexual Imaginary and the Great Gay Migration', *GLQ: A Journal of Lesbian and Gay Studies* 2, no. 3 (1995): 253–277; Knopp, 'Queer Quests'.

24 Ourstory, *Daring Hearts*.

25 Ourstory, *Daring Hearts*, p. 13.

26 Keith, in Maria Jastrzebska and Anthony Luvera (eds), *Queer in Brighton* (Brighton: New Writing South, 2014), p. 22.

27 Jastrzebska and Luvera, *Queer in Brighton*, p. 57.

28 Jenny, in Jastrzebska and Luvera, *Queer in Brighton*, p. 109.

29 Freddie, in Jastrzebska and Luvera, *Queer in Brighton*, p. 183. Also see p. 101.

30 James Gardiner, interviewed by Justin Bengry for QBL, 21 June 2017.

31 James, QBL interview.

32 Peter Scott, *The Zorro Report* (University of Essex, 1998), pp. 42–43, and see Chapter 1.

33 Sarah, in E-J Scott (ed.), *Brighton Trans*formed* (Brighton: QueenSpark, 2014) and at https://brightontransformed.com/.

34 Sarah, *Brighton Trans*formed*.

35 Transformers group interview, *Brighton Trans*formed*.

36 The Brighton survey *Count Me In* found that queer people in general regarded Brighton as a safe space.

37 Rob Berkeley, 'The Brotherhood Dilemma', in John Gordon and Rikki Beadle-Blair (eds), *Black and Gay in the UK: An Anthology* (London: Team Angelica, 2014), pp. 324–325.

38 Sabah, *Brighton Trans*formed*.

39 Sabah, in Jastrzebska and Luvera, *Queer in Brighton*, pp. 79–80.

40 Sabah, *Brighton Trans*formed*.

41 Caroline in Jastrzebska and Luvera, *Queer in Brighton*, p. 63. Also see J. A. Walsh, pp. 72–74.

42 Cant, *Invented Identities?*, pp. 95–96. (She was speaking in the mid-1990s.) Sandie also socialised in Hastings via the lesbian network Kenric. Also see Jastrzebska and Luvera, *Queer in Brighton*, pp. 43–45 for Millie's story of moving around Worthing, Brighton and Eastbourne.

43 Sue George, QBL workshop Brighton, 22 March 2017.

44 This percentage is of 18–19-year-olds entering higher education. It would be a little higher if mature students were included. HEFCE, 'Young Participation in Higher Education' (2005).

45 There are few studies of queer university choices and those mostly deal with gay male students. See David Telford in Debbie Epstein, Sarah O'Flynn and David Telford, *Silenced Sexualities in Schools and Universities* (Stoke-on-Trent: Trentham Books, 2003), chs 6 and 7; Richard Taulke-Johnson, 'Queer Decisions? Gay Male Students' University Choices', *Studies in Higher Education* 35, no. 3 (May 2010): 247–261.

46 Telford, *Silenced Sexualities*; Taulke-Johnson, 'Queer Decisions?'.

47 Rowena [pseudonym], interviewed by Alison Oram for QBL, 26 June 2018. Rowena also observed that a lot of the students who partied hard in fact dropped out of their courses.

48 Taulke-Johnson, 'Queer Decisions?', p. 260.

49 Caroline M. Hoefferle, *British Student Activism in the Long Sixties* (London: Routledge, 2013), p. 195.

50 Hoefferle, *Student Activism*, pp. 193–196, 208; David Malcolm, 'A Curious Courage: The Origins of Gay Rights Campaigning in the National Union of Students', *History of Education* 47, no. 1 (2018): 73–86.

51 Hoefferle, *Student Activism*, pp. 62–67, 161–162.

52 Nick Thomas, 'Challenging Myths of the 1960s: The Case of Student Protest in Britain', *Twentieth Century British History* 13, no. 3 (2002): 277–297; Hoefferle, *Student Activism*, pp. 114, 116–117.

53 Hoefferle, *Student Activism*, pp. 162–167, 190–196.

54 Patrick Hall, QBL workshop Leeds, 19 March 2017. Patrick stayed on in Leeds, contributing to the city's lesbian and gay energy as well as to its left-wing and Labour politics, becoming a city councillor. With Leeds GLF he leafleted council estates and was a key member of its successor organisation, Leeds Gay Community.

55 Lou Lavender, group interview by Elizabeth Ross for 'WLM in Leeds and Bradford 1969–79', 17 February 1995, FAN. Lou Lavender, interviewed by Jeska Rees, 11 May 2004. GEN-AV09, FAN.

56 Jude Woods, interviewed by Alison Oram for QBL, 5 June 2019.

57 Jude, QBL interview.

58 City-wide protests followed the banning of Gaysoc at Leeds College of Music in 1988, as discussed in Chapter 2, a reminder that not all institutions of higher education were liberal places.

59 See Chapter 3 for a discussion of the contribution of Manchester's universities to the city's gay scene in the 1960s and 1970s.

60 Figures calculated from national census statistics.

61 Nigel Leach, interviewed for TIHWGH, 1 March 2014.

62 *London Evening Standard*, 27 February 1991; *Gay Times*, April 1991; *The Times*, 16 January 2018, p. 53.

63 Nigel Leach, TIHWGH.

64 Paul Cons, interviewed by John Benson for the Queerupnorth Archive, 23 August 2007. GB127.M800, Manchester Central Library.

65 Tanja Farman, interviewed by John Benson for the Queerupnorth Archive, 13 March 2007. GB127.M800, Manchester Central Library.

66 Jess Zadik, interviewed by Matt Cook for QBL, September 2017.

67 The Summer of Lesbian Love was a women-only event hosted at the Hacienda in 1990, directly leading to the setting up of queer club night Flesh there from 1991.

68 Jess, QBL interview.

69 Cant, *Invented Identities?*, pp. 103–104.

70 Jeffrey Weeks, *The World We Have Won: The Remaking of Erotic and Intimate Life* (London: Routledge, 2007), pp. 120, 147–149.

71 Dan Barnett, interviewed for LGBT Project, WYAS, 2008 (no precise date).

72 Dan, LGBT project, WYAS.

73 The proportion of Plymouth's population who were students, according to census figures, was about half that of the city of Manchester between the 1980s and the 2000s.

74 Jono Madeley, interviewed by Alan Butler for PioP, 13 December 2011; Hannah, QBL workshop Plymouth.

75 Judith [pseudonym], interviewed for the LIP, n.d., *c*.2008.

76 Rebecca Jennings, '"The Most Uninhibited Party They'd Ever Been to": The Postwar Encounter between Psychiatry and the British Lesbian, 1945–1971', *Journal of British Studies* 47, no. 4 (2008): 883–904; Tommy Dickinson, *'Curing Queers': Mental Nurses and Their Patients, 1935–74* (Manchester: Manchester University Press, 2016).

77 Judith, LIP. And see Chapter 3.

78 Thomas Wimark, 'Migration Motives of Gay Men in the New Acceptance Era: A Cohort Study from Malmö, Sweden', *Social & Cultural Geography* 17, no. 5 (2016): 605–622.

79 Ted Whitehead, interviewed by Alan Butler for PioP, n.d., *c*.2012.

80 Jeannie Crook, interviewed by Helen Philips for PioP, 29 February 2012. Jeannie was born in 1938.

81 Alison [pseudonym], interviewed by Sean Plume for PioP, 4 November 2011.

82 Ted, PioP.

83 Jennings, 'Hot Climate'. Katherine Holden, *The Shadow of Marriage: Singleness in England, 1914–60* (Manchester: Manchester University Press, 2007).

84 Joanna Pine, interviewed by Alan Butler for PioP, 16 December 2011. Joanna was born in 1951.

85 Joanna, PioP.

86 Paul Greystock, interviewed for LGBT Project, WYAS. 2008 (n.d.).

87 Dan Barnett, WYAS LGBT.
88 Jo Lewis, QBL workshop Plymouth.
89 Jono, PioP.

Chapter 6

1   Robert, in Maria Jastrzebska and Anthony Luvera (eds), *Queer in Brighton* (Brighton: New Writing South, 2015), p. 65.
2   Armistead Maupin, *Tales of the City* series, published between 1978 and 2014.
3   See: *A Vision of Britain through Time*, University of Portsmouth, www.visionofbritain. org.uk/unit/10056410/rate/HOUS_RENT_COUNCIL. The other three cities had rates of owner occupation and council housing that followed the national pattern quite closely.
4   Craig Limbert, interviewed for LGBT Project, WYAS, 2008.
5   Craig, LGBT project, WYAS.
6   Kate O'Donnell, interviewed by Matt Cook for QBL, 4 September 2017. See Chapter 3 for more on Kate's city centre living.
7   This story was told by Rowena (pseudonym), interviewed by Alison Oram for Queer Beyond London, 26 June 2018.
8   Robert, in Jastrzebska and Luvera, *Queer in Brighton*, p. 65.
9   Alf le Flohic, Queer in Brighton oral history transcript. N.d. but c. 2012. The Keep.
10 Rebecca, in Jastrzebska and Luvera, *Queer in Brighton*, p. 41.
11 Freddie, in Jastrzebska and Luvera, *Queer in Brighton*, p. 183.
12 Brighton Ourstory, *Daring Hearts: Lesbian and Gay Lives in 50s and 60s Brighton* (Brighton: QueenSpark Books, 1992), p. 37. Matt Cook, *Queer Domesticities: Homosexuality and Home Life in Twentieth Century London* (Basingstoke: Palgrave, 2014), ch. 5.
13 Mark Armstrong, 'The Bedsit', in Andrew Gorman-Murray and Matt Cook (eds), *Queering the Interior* (London: Bloomsbury Academic, 2017). pp. 108–116.
14 Ourstory, *Daring Hearts*, p. 29.
15 Robert, in Jastrzebska and Luvera, *Queer in Brighton*, p. 65.
16 Christine Wall, 'Sisterhood and Squatting in the 1970s: Feminism, Housing and Urban Change in Hackney', *History Workshop Journal* 83 (Spring 2017): 79–97; Matt Cook, '"Gay Times": Identity, Locality, Memory, and the Brixton Squats in 1970's London', *Twentieth Century British History* 24, no. 1 (2013): 84–109, pp. 87–88.
17 Debs, in Jastrzebska and Luvera, *Queer in Brighton*, pp. 89–91.
18 James Gardiner, interviewed by Justin Bengry for QBL, 21 June 2017.
19 Miriam Zukas, interviewed by Jeska Rees, 27 February 2006. GEN-AV09, FAN.
20 Lynn Daniel, QBL workshop Leeds, 19 March 2017.
21 Lynn, QBL workshop Leeds.
22 Lou Lavender, interviewed by Jeska Rees, 11 May 2004. GEN-AV09, FAN.
23 Debs, in Jastrzebska and Luvera, *Queer in Brighton*, p. 89.
24 Jude, in Jastrzebska and Luvera, *Queer in Brighton*, p. 91.
25 Debs, in Jastrzebska and Luvera, *Queer in Brighton*, p. 91.
26 Al Garthwaite, interviewed by Jeska Rees, 18 May 2004. GEN-AV09, FAN. Women's Land was a real place in North Wales, settled by lesbian feminists.
27 Tina Crockett, interviewed by Jeska Rees, 7 June 2004. GEN-AV09, FAN. Miriam, interviewed by Jeska Rees.

28 Julie Bindel, interviewed by Jeska Rees, 25 February 2006. GEN-AV09, FAN.

29 For more detail about the women's refuge see Chapter 3.

30 Tina, interviewed by Jeska Rees.

31 Lou, Tina, interviewed by Jeska Rees.

32 www.edwardcarpentercommunity.org.uk/about-us/history (accessed 2 May 2018).

33 Lynn, QBL workshop Leeds.

34 These included Tangram, 301, New Arby and Sholebrook Avenue. QBL workshop Leeds.

35 Contemporary research in Scotland shows that LGBTQ people are disproportionately likely to live in the most deprived neighbourhoods, characterised by social housing and by a higher prevalence of homophobia, making these districts less comfortable and sometimes threatening for their queer residents. Peter Matthews and Kirsten Besemer, 'The "Pink Pound" in the "Gaybourhood"? Neighbourhood Deprivation and Sexual Orientation in Scotland', *Housing, Theory and Society* 32, no. 1 (2015): 94–111; Peter Matthews and Christopher Poyner, 'The Experience of Living in Deprived Neighbourhoods for LGBT+ People: Making Home in Difficult Circumstances', *EPA: Economy and Space* 51, no. 7 (2019): 1499–1515, pp. 1502–1503, 1508–1511. (There is no equivalent research into LGBTQ people and social housing in England and Wales.)

36 Jeannie Crook, interviewed by Helen Philips for Pride in our Past, 29 February 2012.

37 Jeannie, PioP.

38 Jeannie, PioP.

39 LGBTQ people have historically been discriminated against in council housing allocation because they do not fit the heteronormative stereotype. Matthews and Poyner, 'Deprived Neighbourhoods', p. 1508.

40 Cook, *Queer Domesticities*, pp. 196–197.

41 *Western Daily Press*, 18 October 1982. See Chapter 4.

42 Davina Cooper, *Sexing the City: Lesbian and Gay Politics within the Activist State* (London: Rivers Oram, 1994), pp. 31, 53–54.

43 Cook, *Queer Domesticities*, pp. 196–197.

44 There is very little literature on this, but see Paul Watt, 'Housing Histories and Fragmented Middle-class Careers: The Case of Marginal Professionals in London Council Housing', *Housing Studies* 20, no. 3 (2005): 359–381, p. 372; Matt Cook, '"Gay Times": Identity, Locality, Memory, and the Brixton Squats in 1970's London', *Twentieth Century British History* 24, no. 1 (2013): 84–109, pp. 101–102.

45 In Leeds, which also had a high proportion of council housing, gay liberationists had leafleted estates in the 1970s. Later, a group of lesbians and gay men who had acquired council homes organised themselves into the group Rainbow Roofs to liaise with the council.

46 Rowena, QBL interview.

47 Count Me In Too, 'Community Summary: Housing and LGBT Lives' (Brighton: University of Brighton, 2009).

48 Catherine J. Nash and Andrew Gorman-Murray, 'LGBT Neighbourhoods and "New Mobilities": Towards Understanding Transformations in Sexual and Gendered Urban Landscapes', *International Journal of Urban and Regional Research* 38, no. 3 (2014): 756–772; Amin Ghaziani, *There Goes the Gayborhood?* (Princeton, New Jersey: Princeton University Press, 2014).

49 Bob Cant (ed.), *Invented Identities? Lesbians and Gays Talk about Migration* (London: Cassell, 1997), p. 94. See Sandie's story earlier in this chapter and also in Chapter 5.

50 Cant, *Invented Identities?*, pp. 95–96. And see Chapter 5 for discussion of LGBTQ people moving between places on the south coast around Brighton, partly due to higher prices in Brighton.

51 James, QBL interview.

52 James, QBL interview.

53 See *A Vision of Britain through Time*, University of Portsmouth, www.visionofbritain.org. uk/unit/10056410/rate/HOUS_OWNEROCC (accessed 20 March 2021).

54 Kate, QBL interview.

55 Caroline [pseudonym], interviewed by Alison Oram for QBL, 22 February 2019.

56 For an interesting critique of the model of gaybourhoods, in a Scottish context, see Matthews and Besemer, 'Neighbourhood Deprivation'. There is a huge academic literature on gay gentrification and gaybourhoods and much less research on other aspects of queer people's housing.

57 Rowena, QBL interview.

58 Rowena, QBL interview.

59 Rowena, QBL interview.

60 QBL workshop Leeds.

61 Ted Whitehead, interviewed by Alan Butler for PioP, n.d., *c.*2012.

62 Ted, PioP.

63 Barbara Spence interview, Manchester Parents Group, for TIHWGH, 1 March 2014.

64 For Dennis's story, see Chapter 4. Also see Chapter 2 (Ajamu) and Chapter 5 (Jenny-Anne).

65 Noreen [pseudonym], interviewed for Lesbian Identity Project, n.d., *c.*2008.

66 Joyce Edwards, interviewed by Rachel Adams for the MLP, 4 August 2010, https:// soundcloud.com/themodernlesbian (accessed 20 March 2021). For the complexities of lesbians' relationship to marriage and domesticity in the postwar years see: Amy Tooth Murphy, '"I Conformed; I Got Married. It Seemed Like a Good Idea at the Time": Domesticity in Postwar Lesbian Oral History', in Brian Lewis (ed.), *British Queer History: New Approaches and Perspectives* (Manchester: Manchester University Press, 2013), pp. 165–187.

67 Information shared by the younger man during the discussion after a public talk at the Equity Centre, Bradford, 16 February 2012.

68 Jeffrey Weeks, *Coming Out: The Emergence of LGBT Identities in Britain from the Nineteenth Century to the Present* (London: Quartet, 2016), pp. 249–263.

69 See Chapter 5 for discussion of the couple's decision to move to Brighton. For the queer home-making of this couple also see: Cook, *Queer Domesticities*, pp. 81–85.

70 James, QBL interview.

71 Jeffrey Weeks, Brian Heaphy and Catherine Donovan, *Same Sex Intimacies: Families of Choice and Other Life Experiments* (London: Routledge, 2001), ch. 7.

72 Rebecca Jennings, 'Lesbian Motherhood and the Artificial Insemination by Donor Scandal of 1978', *Twentieth Century British History* 28, no. 4 (2017): 570–594.

73 Lynne Roberts, interviewed for PioP, 24 February 2012.

74 Southway is a large postwar council housing estate on the northern outskirts of Plymouth.

75 Lynne, PioP.

76 Sharon [pseudonym], interviewed by Helen Philips for PioP, 25 November 2011.

77 Sharon, PioP.

78 Sharon, PioP.

79 Jennings, 'Lesbian Motherhood'.

80 Miriam, interviewed by Jeska Rees.

81 Jude Woods, interviewed for QBL by Alison Oram, 5 June 2019.

82 Jude, QBL interview.

83 Lesley Pattenson, QBL workshop Leeds.

84 Al, interviewed by Jeska Rees.

85 Jess Zadik, interviewed by Matt Cook for QBL, September 2017.

86 Jess, QBL interview.

87 Jastrzebska and Luvera, *Queer in Brighton*, pp. 209–212, 215–217.

88 Charlie, in Jastrzebska and Luvera, *Queer in Brighton*, p. 211.

89 Charlie, in Jastrzebska and Luvera, *Queer in Brighton*, p. 212.

90 The phrase is from Weeks, Heaphy and Donovan, *Same Sex Intimacies*.

91 Participant in Leeds Gay Community (LGC) group interview for LGBT Project, WYAS, 2008.

92 Lynne, PioP.

93 'MP Labels Bolton 7 Gay Sex Trial "Silly"', *Lancashire Telegraph*, 18 February 1998; 'Gays Hail Bolton 7 Victory', *Guardian*, 21 February 1998.

94 James, QBL interview.

95 Quoted in Matt Cook, 'The Nursery', in Andrew Gorman-Murray and Matt Cook (eds), *Queering the Interior* (London: Bloomsbury, 2018), p. 145.

96 Doreen [pseudonym], interviewed for the Lesbian Identity Project (LIP), *c.*2008.

97 Doreen, LIP.

98 Doreen, LIP.

99 Millie, in Jastrzebska and Luvera, *Queer in Brighton*, p. 45.

100 Jill, in Jastrzebska and Luvera, *Queer in Brighton*, p. 186.

101 Jill, in Jastrzebska and Luvera, *Queer in Brighton*, p. 185.

Chapter 7

1 For a list of the oral history projects used in this book see 'Note on Sources'.

2 Lesley Woods, notes for Brighton and Sussex Sexualities Network (BSSN) Conference Keynote 2013, pp. 4–5. www.queerinbrighton.co.uk/wp-content/uploads/2013/09/BSSN-Conference-Keynote.pdf (accessed 17 April 2019).

3 Shelley Trower (ed.), *Place, Writing and Voice in Oral History* (New York: Palgrave Macmillan, 2011).

4 Participant in LGC group interview, LGBT Project, West Yorkshire Archive Service, 2008.

5 Bradford Lesbian and Gay Youth (BLAGY) group interview, 27 February 2008, LGBT Project, WYAS.

6 Alan Butler, Queer Beyond London (QBL) workshop, Plymouth, 4 March 2017.

7 Participant in LGC group interview, LGBT Project, WYAS.

8 Interview with Dan Barnett, LGBT Project, WYAS, *c.*2008. Also see BLAGY interview, LGBT Project, WYAS.

9 Jill Gardiner, QBL workshop Brighton, 22 March 2017.

10 Laura Doan, *Disturbing Practices: History, Sexuality, and Women's Experience of Modern War* (Chicago: University of Chicago Press, 2013).

11 Participant in LGC group interview, LGBT Project, WYAS.

12 BLAGY, LGBT Project, WYAS.

13 The sharing of stories between older and younger community members is encouraged in HLF-funded projects.

14 Woods, notes for BSSN Conference, p. 4.

15 Woods, notes for BSSN Conference, pp. 7–8.

16 Melita Dennett, QBL workshop Brighton.

17 Jo Pine, QBL workshop Plymouth.

18 BLAGY, LGBT Project, WYAS.

19 Melita, QBL workshop Brighton.

20 Kathrine [no surname given], QBL workshop Brighton.

21 'Belle' [pseudonym], QBL workshop Brighton.

22 Ken Plummer, 'Generational Sexualities, Subterranean Traditions and the Hauntings of the Sexual World: Some Preliminary Remarks, *Symbolic Interaction* 33, no. 2 (2010): 163–190; Robert Reynolds and Shirleene Robinson, 'Australian Lesbian and Gay Life Stories: A National Oral History Project', *Australian Feminist Studies* 31, no. 89 (2016): 363–376.

23 For discussion of conventional ways of accounting for time, or chrononormativity, see: Elizabeth Freeman, *Time Binds: Queer Temporalities, Queer Histories* (Durham, NC: Duke University Press, 2010); Judith Halberstam, *In a Queer Time and Place: Transgender Bodies, Subcultural Lives* (New York: New York University Press, 2005); Amy Tooth-Murphy, '"The Continuous Thread of Revelation": Chrononormativity and the Challenge of Queer Oral History', History of Sexuality seminar paper, Institute of Historical Research, 6 January 2015; http://podcast.ulcc.ac.uk/accounts/SAScasts/historyofsexuality/IHR_06_1_15_History_of_Sex_and_Oral_History.mp3 (accessed 29 July 2021).

24 Brighton Ourstory Project, *Daring Hearts: Lesbian and Gay Lives of 50s and 60s Brighton* (Brighton: QueenSpark Books, 1992), p. 63.

25 Ourstory, *Daring Hearts*, p. 38.

26 Ourstory, *Daring Hearts*, p. 13.

27 Ourstory, *Daring Hearts*, p. 37. Quean, as an alternative spelling of queen, was adopted throughout the quotes in *Daring Hearts*.

28 Ourstory, *Daring Hearts*, p. 108.

29 Ourstory, *Daring Hearts*, p. 75.

30 Maria Jastrzebska and Anthony Luvera (eds), *Queer in Brighton* (Brighton: New Writing South, 2014), p. 123.

31 Jastrzebska and Luvera, *Queer in Brighton*, p. 124.

32 Jastrzebska and Luvera, *Queer in Brighton*, p. 124.

33 Jastrzebska and Luvera, *Queer in Brighton*, p. 184. Polari was a semi-secret slang language used in the theatre, circus and by many gay men until the 1950s and 1960s.

34 Jastrzebska and Luvera, *Queer in Brighton*, p. 184.

35 Gilad Padva, *Queer Nostalgia in Cinema and Pop Culture* (New York: Palgrave Macmillan, 2014), introduction; Matt Cook, 'Local Matters: Queer Scenes in 1960s Manchester, Plymouth and Brighton', *Journal of British Studies* 59 (2020): 32–56.

36 Some historians suggest that queer nostalgia is a yearning for a more radical past, but this was a muted theme in our four cities. Kevin P. Murphy, 'Gay Was Good: Progress, Homonormativity and Oral History', in Twin Cities GLBT Oral History Project, Kevin P. Murphy, Jennifer L. Pierce and Larry Knopp (eds), *Queer Twin Cities* (Minneapolis: University of Minnesota Press, 2010), 305–318.

37 Padva, *Queer Nostalgia*. For nostalgia as a means of valuing denigrated past cultures see: Ben Jones, 'The Uses of Nostalgia: Autobiography, Community Publishing and Working Class Neighbourhoods in Post-War England', *Cultural and Social History* 7, no. 3 (2010): 355–374.

38 David Green, interviewed for LGBT Project, WYAS, *c*.2008.

39 David, LGBT Project, WYAS.

40 Participant in LGC group interview, LGBT Project, WYAS.

41 Participant in LGC group interview, LGBT Project, WYAS.

42 Participant in LGC group interview, LGBT Project, WYAS.

43 Ted Donovan, interviewed for LGBT Project, WYAS, *c*.2008.

44 Participant in LGC group interview, LGBT Project, WYAS.

45 Paul Greystock, interviewed for LGBT Project, WYAS, *c*.2008.

46 Paul, LGBT Project, WYAS.

47 Craig Limbert, interviewed for LGBT Project, WYAS. For more on Craig's queer bedsit life see Chapter 6.

48 Craig, LGBT Project, WYAS.

49 Craig, LGBT Project, WYAS.

50 Paul, LGBT Project, WYAS. For the emotional landscape of men remembering the HIV/AIDS crisis see: Matt Cook, '"Archives of Feeling": The AIDS Crisis in Britain 1987', *History Workshop Journal* 83 (Spring 2017): 51–78.

51 Craig, LGBT Project, WYAS.

52 Craig, LGBT Project, WYAS.

53 Craig, LGBT Project, WYAS. See Cook, 'Archives of Feeling' for how men translated their grief during the AIDS crisis into political expression, the renewed homophobia in the workplace and increased anxiety among gay people about how the wider public might respond to their sexuality.

54 Craig, LGBT Project, WYAS.

55 Colin, QBL workshop Plymouth.

56 Colin, QBL workshop Plymouth.

57 Hannah and Jo, QBL workshop Plymouth.

58 Jo Pine, QBL workshop Plymouth.

59 Jo, QBL workshop Plymouth.

60 Nishant Shahani, '"Between Light and Nowhere": The Queer Politics of Nostalgia', *The Journal of Popular Culture* 46, no. 6 (2013), 1217–1230; Padva, *Queer Nostalgia*.

61 Ted, LGBT Project, WYAS.

62 Christopher Woodruff, interviewed for LGBT Project, WYAS, n.d., 2008.

63 Murphy, 'Gay Was Good'.

64 LGC group interview and several individual interviews, LGBT Project, WYAS.

65 Christopher, LGBT Project, WYAS.

66 BLAGY youth group member, LGBT Project, WYAS.

67 Christopher, LGBT Project, WYAS.

68 Craig, LGBT Project, WYAS.

69 Murphy, 'Gay Was Good', p. 314.

70 Colin, QBL workshop Plymouth.

71 Jo, QBL workshop Plymouth.

72 Jo, QBL workshop Plymouth.

73 Padva, *Queer Nostalgia*, introduction.

74 Melita, QBL workshop Brighton.

75 QBL workshop Brighton.

76 'Belle' [pseudonym], QBL workshop Brighton.

77 Melita, QBL workshop Brighton.

78 Melita, QBL workshop Brighton.

79 See Melita's more favourable assessment of Brighton Trans Pride as a smaller, more authentic and neighbourly Pride, discussed in Chapter 4.

80 Jill Gardiner, QBL workshop Brighton.

81 Kathrine, QBL workshop Brighton.

82 Belle, QBL workshop Brighton.

83 As McKinnon et al have pointed out for Sydney Mardi Gras. Scott McKinnon, Robert Reynolds and Shirleene Robinson, 'Negotiating Difference Across Time: The Temporal Meanings of the Sydney Mardi Gras in Lesbian and Gay Life Narratives', *Journal of Australian Studies* 42, no. 3 (2018), 314–327.

84 Jeffrey Weeks, *The World We Have Won: The Remaking of Erotic and Intimate Life* (London: Routledge, 2007), pp. 9, 197–198; Gavin Brown (2012) 'Homonormativity: A Metropolitan Concept that Denigrates "Ordinary" Gay Lives', *Journal of Homosexuality* 59, no. 7 (2012): 1065–1072; Kath Browne and Leela Bakshi, *Ordinary in Brighton? LGBT, Activisms and the City* (Farnham: Ashgate, 2013).

85 See the table in the 'Note on Sources' listing the main LGBTQ oral history projects we drew on.

86 Ourstory, *Daring Hearts*, pp. 9–10.

87 Ourstory, *Daring Hearts*, p. 9.

88 For example, the Hall-Carpenter Archives oral history project (1985–1989).

89 This development parallels the growth and direction of LGBTQ oral history in the USA. See especially: Elizabeth Kennedy and Madeline Davis, *Boots of Leather, Slippers of Gold: The History of a Lesbian Community* (New York: Routledge, 1993); Nan A. Boyd, 'Who Is the Subject? Queer Theory Meets Oral History', *Journal of the History of Sexuality* 17, no. 2 (2008): 177–189.

90 Paul Thompson, *The Voice of the Past: Oral History* (Oxford: Oxford University Press, 1978); Alison Twells, 'Community History' (London: Institute of Historical Research, 2008), www.history.ac.uk/makinghistory/resources/articles/community_history.html (accessed 8 March 2019); Alistair Thomson, 'Oral History and Community History in Britain: Personal and Critical Reflections on Twenty-five Years of Continuity and Change', *Oral History* 36, no. 1 (2008): 95–104.

91 'Women in the WLM in Leeds and Bradford 1969–1979', Feminist Archive North, University of Leeds. Also see Bridget Lockyer, 'An Irregular Period? Participation in the Bradford Women's Liberation Movement', *Women's History Review* 22, no. 4 (2013): 643–657.

92 Copies of the LIP oral histories and the booklets produced by the project are held in several public and university libraries in West Yorkshire. Also see: https://wyqs.co.uk/stories/the-lesbian-identity-project/. For further work on older lesbians and their histories see Jane Traies, *The Lives of Older Lesbians: Sexuality, Identity and the Life Course* (London: Palgrave Macmillan, 2016).

93 Jill, in Jastrzebska and Luvera, *Queer in Brighton*, p. 116. For Brighton Ourstory (1989–2013) see www.brightonourstory.co.uk/ (accessed 30 March 2019).

94 John Vincent, *LGBT People and the UK Cultural Sector* (London: Ashgate, 2014), ch. 5; Angela Vanegas, 'Representing Lesbians and Gay Men in British Social History

Museums', in Richard Sandell (ed.), *Museums, Society, Inequality* (London: Routledge, 2002), p. 105.

95 Vincent, *LGBT People and the UK Cultural Sector*, chs 5 and 6. For a more detailed account of these LGBTQ history projects and their role in queer communities see: Alison Oram, 'Making Place and Community: Contrasting Lesbian and Gay, Feminist and Queer Oral History Projects in Brighton and Leeds', *Oral History Review* (forthcoming, 2022).

96 I am grateful to Liz Kelly, a policy advisor at the HLF, for supplying this statistic. My thanks to Rachel Hasted for accessing this information.

97 This point was made by Rachel Hasted at the Queer Beyond London Panel Discussion, British Library, 14 November 2018.

98 Fiona Cosson, 'Voice of the Community? Reflections on Accessing, Working with and Representing Communities', *Oral History* 38, no. 2 (2010): 95–101, pp. 96–97.

99 Cosson, 'Voice of the Community?', p. 97.

100 The project collected around thirty interviews with forty people (two were group interviews).

101 Cosson, 'Voice of the Community?', p. 98.

102 For further discussion of this see Oram, 'Making Place'.

103 Thomson, 'Oral History', pp. 101–104.

104 Brighton Trans*formed, 'About'.

105 Jeska Rees, '"Are you a Lesbian?" Challenges in Recording and Analysing the Women's Liberation Movement in England', *History Workshop Journal* 69 (Spring 2010): 177–187, p. 184. She carried out fourteen oral history interviews, almost all with lesbians, in 2004 and 2006.

106 Alan Butler, 'Performing LGBT Pride in Plymouth 1950–2012', PhD thesis, Plymouth University, 2015. Alan Butler, 'Creating Space in the Community Archive for Queer Life Stories to Be (Re)performed and Captured', *Oral History* 48, no. 1 (Spring 2020): 57–65.

107 Manchester Central Library: GB127.M775/1/1/1. GB127.M775/1/2.

108 Abigail Ward, 'Queer Noise', www.mdmarchive.co.uk/exhibition/id/77/QUEER_NOISE.html (accessed 20 March 2021).

109 Melita, QBL workshop Brighton.

110 Kathrine, QBL workshop Brighton.

111 QBL workshop Plymouth.

112 E-J Scott, personal correspondence, 28 November 2018. Also see Brighton Trans*Formed, 'About'; *Brighton Trans*formed* (Brighton: QueenSpark Books, 2014).

113 See our discussion of the representativeness of LGBT and queer oral history in the 'Note on Sources'.

114 New Writing South, application for HLF funding for Queer in Brighton, April 24 2012, p. 5.

115 Jastrzebska and Luvera, *Queer in Brighton*.

116 Woods, notes for BSSN Conference, pp. 4–5.

117 Woods, notes for BSSN Conference, pp. 4–5.

118 Elizabeth Freeman, 'Time Binds, or, Erotohistoriography', *Social Text* 23, no. 3–4 (2005): 57–68; Nan Alamilla Boyd and Horacio N Roque Ramírez, *Bodies of Evidence: The Practice of Queer Oral History* (New York: Oxford University Press, 2012); Freeman, *Time Binds*; Ben Walters, 'Dr Duckie: Homemade Mutant Hope Machines', PhD thesis,

Queen Mary, University of London, 2020, especially ch. 5, www.duckie.co.uk/dr-duckie/read-the-phd (accessed 3 August 2020).

119 For West Yorkshire Queer Stories see: https://wyqs.co.uk/ (accessed 10 June 2020).

Epilogue

1 Paul Gilroy, *After Empire: Melancholia or Convivial Culture?* (Abingdon: Routledge, 2004); Doreen Massey, *For Space* (London: Sage, 2005); Jeffrey Weeks, *The World We Have Won: The Remaking of Erotic and Intimate Life* (London: Routledge, 2007), pp. 118–119.

2 Carolyn Dinshaw coined the phrase 'touches across time' in relation to the similarities and queerness of the past. Carolyn Dinshaw, *Getting Medieval: Sexualities and Communities, Pre- and Postmodern* (Durham, NC: Duke University Press, 1999); Laura Doan, *Disturbing Practices: History, Sexuality, and Women's Experience of Modern War* (Chicago: University of Chicago Press, 2013).

Note on sources

1 Barry Reay observed something similar; archives are 'drenched in sex', he wrote. Barry Reay, *Sex in the Archives: Writing American Sexual Histories* (Manchester: Manchester University Press, 2018).

2 FFLAG: Families and Friends of Lesbians and Gays.

3 On this point see: Zeb Tortorici, *Sins against Nature: Sex and Archives in Colonial New Spain* (Durham, NC: Duke University Press, 2018); Jen Jack Gieseking, 'Useful In/stability: The Dialectical Production of the Social and Spatial Lesbian Herstory Archives', *Radical History Review* 122 (2015): 25–37.

4 'Hotbed Lavatory to Close', *Brighton Gazette*, 23 April 1965; Ourstory, *Daring Hearts*, pp. 40–41.

5 Fiona Cosson, 'Voice of the Community? Practical Reflections on Accessing, Working with and Representing Communities in Oral History', *Oral History* 38, no. 2 (2010): 97; see also: Nan Alamilla Boyd and Horacio N. Roque Ramírez, *Bodies of Evidence: The Practice of Queer Oral History* (New York: Oxford University Press, 2012).

6 Cosson, 'Voice of the Community?', 99; Alison Oram, 'Making Place and Community: Contrasting Lesbian and Gay, Feminist and Queer Oral History Projects in Brighton and Leeds', *Oral History Review* (forthcoming, 2022).

7 Nan Alamilla Boyd, 'Who Is the Subject?: Queer Theory Meets Oral History', *Journal of the History of Sexuality* 17, no. 2 (2008): 177–189.

8 For example, the oral histories conducted by rukus! Black LGBT archive, Brighton Trans*formed, and Rainbow Jews.

9 Cosson, 'Voice of the Community?', 100.

10 See Ben Miller's podcast, https://badgayspod.podbean.com; and also: M. M. Umphrey, 'The Trouble with Harry Thaw', *Radical History Review* 62 (1995): 9.

11 J. W. Scott, 'The Evidence of Experience', *Critical Inquiry* 17, no. 4 (1991): 773–797.

12 Kenneth Plummer, *Telling Sexual Stories: Power, Change, and Social Worlds* (London: Routledge, 1994); Boyd, 'Who Is the Subject?'.

13 This is something we have done carefully, following the protocols for use set out by the interviewees, project coordinators and archivists, including directions on the use or otherwise of real names.

Suggestions for further reading

These books and websites provide rich excursions into – and analysis of – the queer past of different parts of the UK:

Justin Bengry, Matt Cook and Alison Oram, eds., *Locating Queer Histories: Places and Traces across the UK* (London: Bloomsbury, forthcoming).

Brighton Ourstory, *Daring Hearts: Lesbian and Gay Lives in 50s and 60s Brighton* (1992; Brighton: QueenSpark e-book edition, 2015).

Kath Browne and Leela Bakshi, *Ordinary in Brighton: LGBT Activisms and the City* (London: Routledge, 2016).

Marian Duggan, *Queering Conflict: Examining Lesbian and Gay Experiences of Homophobia in Northern Ireland* (London: Routledge, 2016).

Mike Homfray, *Provincial Queens: The Gay and Lesbian Community in the North-West of England* (Oxford: Peter Lang, 2007).

Robert Howes, *Gay West: Civil Society, Community and LGBT History in Bristol and Bath 1970 to 2010* (Bristol: SilverWood, 2011).

Maria Jastrzebska and Anthony Luvera, eds, *Queer in Brighton* (Brighton: New Writing South, 2015).

Daryl Leeworthy, *A Little Gay History of Wales* (Cardiff: University of Wales Press, 2019).

Jeff Meek, *Queer Voices in Post-war Scotland: Male Homosexuality, Religion and Society* (Basingstoke: Palgrave Macmillan, 2015).

Pride of Place: https://historicengland.org.uk/research/inclusive-heritage/lgbtq-heritage-project/.

Queer Beyond London: http://queerbeyondlondon.com.

Queer Heritage South: www.queerheritagesouth.co.uk/s/queer-heritage-south/page/home.

Queer Noise: www.mdmarchive.co.uk/exhibition/id/77/QUEER_NOISE.html.

Sasha Roseneil, *Common Women, Uncommon Practices: The Queer Feminisms of Greenham* (London: Cassell, 2000).

E-J Scott, ed., *Brighton Trans*formed* (Brighton: QueenSpark, 2014).

Helen Smith, *Masculinity, Class and Same-sex Desire in Industrial England, 1895–1957* (London: Palgrave Macmillan, 2015).

West Yorkshire Queer Stories: https://wyqs.co.uk.

Wider perspectives on modern LGBTQ British history:

Sebastian Buckle, *The Way Out: A History of Homosexuality in Modern Britain* (London: I.B. Tauris, 2015).

Matt Cook, ed., *A Gay History of Britain: Love and Sex between Men since the Middle Ages* (Oxford: Greenwood, 2007).

Paul Flynn, *Good as You* (London: Ebury Press, 2017).

Patrick Higgins, *Heterosexual Dictatorship: Male Homosexuality in Postwar Britain* (London: Fourth Estate, 1996).

Rebecca Jennings, *A Lesbian History of Britain since 1600: Love and Sex between Women since 1500* (Oxford: Greenwood, 2007).

Rebecca Jennings, *Tomboys and Bachelor Girls: A Lesbian History of Postwar Britain, 1945–1971* (Manchester: Manchester University Press, 2007).

Alison Oram, *Her Husband Was a Woman! Women's Gender-Crossing in Modern British Popular Culture* (London: Routledge, 2007).

Alison Oram and Annmarie Turnbull, *The Lesbian History Sourcebook: Love and Sex Between Women in Britain from 1780–1970* (London: Routledge, 2001).

Jeffrey Weeks, *Coming Out: Homosexual Politics in Britain from the Nineteenth Century to the Present* (London: Quartet, 1977; 2016).

Jeffrey Weeks, *Between Worlds: A Queer Boy from the Valleys* (Cardigan: Parthian, 2021).

Beyond the UK, we'd recommend these books for a queer take on places beyond the iconic LGBTQ hubs:

Chris Brickell, *Mates and Lovers: A History of Gay New Zealand* (Auckland: Godwit, 2008).

Japonica Brown-Saracino, *How Places Make Us: Novel LBQ Identities in Four Small Cities* (Chicago: University of Chicago Press, 2017).

Matt Cook and Jennifer Evans, eds, *Queer Cities, Queer Cultures: Europe since 1945* (London: Bloomsbury, 2013).

David Higgs, ed., *Queer Sites: Gay Urban Histories since 1600* (London: Routledge, 1999).

John Howard, *Men Like That: A Southern Queer History* (Chicago: University of Chicago Press, 1999).

E. Patrick Johnson, *Sweet Tea: Black Gay Men of the South* (Chapel Hill: University of North Carolina Press, 2008).

Elizabeth Kennedy and Madeline Davies, *Boots of Leather, Slippers of Gold: The History of a Lesbian Community* (New York: Routledge, 1993).

Valerie J. Korinek, *Prairie Fairies: A History of Queer Communities and People in Western Canada, 1930–1985* (Toronto: University of Toronto Press, 2018).

Marc Stein, *City of Sisterly and Brotherly Love: Lesbian and Gay Philadelphia, 1945–1972* (Philadelphia: Temple University Press, 2004).

More on those iconic queer hubs:

Peter Ackroyd, *Queer City: Gay London from the Romans to the Present Day* (London: Chatto and Windus, 2017).

Robert Beachy, *Gay Berlin: Birthplace of a Modern Identity* (London: Penguin Random House, 2015).

Suggestions for further reading

Nan Alamilla Boyd, *Wide-Open Town: A History of Queer San Francisco to 1965* (Berkeley: University of California Press, 2003).

George Chauncey, *Gay New York: Gender, Urban Culture, and the Making of the Gay Male World, 1890–1940* (New York: Basic Books, 2019).

Matt Houlbrook, *Queer London: Perils and Pleasures in the Sexual Metropolis, 1918–1957* (Chicago: University of Chicago Press, 2005).

Rebecca Jennings, *Unnamed Desires: A Sydney Lesbian History* (Clayton: Monash University Publishing, 2015).

Jeremy Atherton Lin, *Gay Bar: Why We Went Out* (London: Granta, 2021).

Gary Wotherspoon, *Gay Sydney: A History* (Sydney: New South, 2016).

Index

Index

Index

Index

Index

Index